Miami

HIDDEN® Miami

Including Miami Beach, South Beach, Little Havana and Fort Lauderdale

Richard Harris

FIRST EDITION

Ulysses Press®
BERKELEY, CALIFORNIA

Copyright © 2005 Ulysses Press and its licensors. All rights reserved, including the right to reproduce this book or portions thereof in any form whatsoever, except for use by a reviewer in connection with a review.

Published by:
ULYSSES PRESS
P.O. Box 3440
Berkeley, CA 94703
www.ulyssespress.com

ISSN 1551-4846
ISBN 1-56975-433-0

Printed in Canada by Transcontinental Printing

10 9 8 7 6 5 4 3 2 1

MANAGING EDITOR: Claire Chun
PROJECT DIRECTOR: Lynette Ubois
COPY EDITOR: Lily Chou
EDITORIAL ASSOCIATES: Jay Chung, Leona Benten, Laura Brancella
TYPESETTER: Lisa Kester
CARTOGRAPHY: Pease Press
HIDDEN BOOKS DESIGN: Sarah Levin
INDEXER: Sayre Van Young
COVER PHOTOGRAPHY: Gettyimages.com

Distributed in the United States by Publishers Group West and in Canada by Raincoast Books

HIDDEN is a federally registered trademark of BookPack, Inc.

Ulysses Press is a federally registered trademark of BookPack, Inc.

The publisher has made every effort to ensure the accuracy of information contained in *Hidden Miami*, but can accept no liability for any loss, injury or inconvenience sustained by any traveler as a result of information or advice contained in this guide.

Write to us!

If in your travels you discover a spot that captures the spirit of Miami, or if you live in the region and have a favorite place to share, or if you just feel like expressing your views, write to us and we'll pass your note along to the author.

We can't guarantee that the author will add your personal find to the next edition, but if the writer does use the suggestion, we'll acknowledge you in the credits and send you a free copy of the new edition.

ULYSSES PRESS
P.O. Box 3440
Berkeley, CA 94703
E-mail: readermail@ulyssespress.com

What's Hidden?

At different points throughout this book, you'll find special listings marked with a hidden symbol:

◄ *HIDDEN*

This means that you have come upon a place off the beaten tourist track, a spot that will carry you a step closer to the local people and natural environment of Miami.

The goal of this guide is to lead you beyond the realm of everyday tourist facilities. While we include traditional sightseeing listings and popular attractions, we also offer alternative sights and adventure activities. Instead of filling this guide with reviews of standard hotels and chain restaurants, we concentrate on one-of-a-kind places and locally owned establishments.

Our authors seek out locales that are popular with residents but usually overlooked by visitors. Some are more hidden than others (and are marked accordingly), but all the listings in this book are intended to help you discover the true nature of Miami and put you on the path of adventure.

Contents

1 MIAMI & BEYOND — 1
Where to Go — 7
When to Go — 8
Seasons — 8
Calendar of Events — 9
Before You Go — 11
Visitors Centers — 11
Packing — 12
Lodging — 12
Dining — 13
Traveling with Children — 14
Women Traveling Alone — 15
Gay & Lesbian Travelers — 15
Senior Travelers — 16
Disabled Travelers — 17
Foreign Travelers — 17
Transportation — 19

2 THE SOUTH FLORIDA LANDSCAPE & OUTDOOR ADVENTURES — 22
Flora — 23
Fauna — 25
Natural Habitats — 26
Outdoor Adventures — 26

3 HISTORY AND CULTURE — 34
History — 34
People — 39

4 MIAMI BEACH — 47
South Beach — 49
South Beach Gay Scene — 67
Central and North Beaches — 71

5 DOWNTOWN MIAMI — **78**
Sights — 79
Lodging — 82
Dining — 84
Shopping — 86
Nightlife — 86

6 LITTLE HAVANA & OTHER ETHNIC NEIGHBORHOODS — **89**
Little Havana — 89
Other Ethnic Neighborhoods — 96

7 COCONUT GROVE & CORAL GABLES — **103**
Coconut Grove — 104
Coral Gables — 112

8 KEY BISCAYNE & BISCAYNE NATIONAL PARK — **120**
Key Biscayne — 120
Biscayne National Park — 129

9 SUBURBAN MIAMI-DADE — **132**
Northern Dade County — 132
Southern Dade County — 144

10 FORT LAUDERDALE AREA — **149**
Hollywood and Hallandale — 150
Fort Lauderdale — 155

Index — 170
Lodging Index — 175
Dining Index — 176
About the Author — 180

Maps

Greater Miami	3
Miami Beach	49
South Beach	51
Central & North Beaches	73
Downtown Miami	81
Little Havana and Other Ethnic Neighborhoods	91
Coconut Grove & Coral Gables	105
Coconut Grove	109
Coral Gables	113
Key Biscayne & Biscayne National Park	123
Key Biscayne	125
Biscayne National Park	129
Northern Dade County	135
Southern Dade County	145
South Broward County	151
Fort Lauderdale	157

OUTDOOR ADVENTURE SYMBOLS

The following symbols accompany national, state and regional park listings, as well as beach descriptions throughout the text.

▲	Camping		Waterskiing
	Hiking		Windsurfing
	Biking		Canoeing or Kayaking
	Swimming		Boating
	Snorkeling or Scuba Diving		Boat Ramps
	Surfing		Fishing

ONE

Miami & Beyond

It happens every year. Biting cold grips most of the United States. Glare ice turns the streets treacherous. A gray-white sky conceals the sun. Your breath hangs in the air in condensation clouds. Icicles hang frozen in mid-drip. And more each day, your imagination toys with the suspicion that somewhere in our great land there is a magical place where winter never comes.

Yes, such places do exist, and most of them are in Florida. That means sun-warmed, busy beaches and all that comes with them—rooms with an ocean view, sun worshippers in skimpy bathing suits, an endless spring-break attitude that will have you whistling "Margaritaville" long after your holiday has become history.

But after a couple days of testing your high-performance sunscreen beside the surf at one of Florida's lesser sunbathing meccas like Daytona Beach or St. Petersburg Beach, you may naturally begin to ask yourself, is that all there is? The answer is, absolutely. Most beach resort towns are pretty much alike, with cookie-cutter hotels and condominiums, national chain pizzerias, block after block of T-shirt and sunglasses shops, and a plethora of miniature golf courses.

Not so Miami. Here, the beach comes with a genuine world-class city attached. Even the name Miami conjures up a variety of visions—delicate orchids, waving palms, tropical waters, white sands and, especially for winter-dodgers, welcome and dependable warmth. A century of dynamic public relations has also kept Miami in the public eye, from the heralding of the first railroads that carried vacationers deep into tropical paradises to present-day pop culture icons—TV shows, fashion models, designers like Donatella Versace and mystery writers like Carl Hiassen, James W. Hall and Elmore Leonard, not to mention Pulitzer Prize–winning humorist Dave Barry.

In Miami, within walking distance of the beach, you'll find dozens of sidewalk cafés where you can enjoy trendy cuisine fusing elements from every corner of the globe while you watch a nonstop parade of fellow vacationers—also from around the globe. You can shop at smart boutiques featuring the latest fashion statements by many of the world's top designers, or browse through dozens of art galleries representing contemporary artists from throughout the Americas. You can dress to the hilt after dark and stand in line, hoping for admission to an ultra-chic club. And that's not all.

While Miami Beach is the city's unrivaled touristic epicenter, Miami has far more to offer. Ride the monorail around downtown, hopping off now and then to explore the big department stores and labyrinths of little shops. Head a little farther inland to cruise up Little Havana's Calle Ocho, where parks and monuments still ring with echoes of the "Old Country"—Cuba, so near the tip of south Florida and yet so far. Or stop in Little Haiti to visit a colorful public market patterned after the one in Port-Au-Prince. You can explore elegant mansions and gardens, see trained parrots and monkeys cavort, and watch movies or magazine fashion features being shot on location, all in the same day. You can visit one of the country's best zoos, discover wild alligators and rare storks in the vast Everglades, or go scuba diving on the living coral reef of Biscayne Bay, and be back to the city in time for dinner. Adventure and excitement await around every corner. And the beauty of it is, you don't even need a passport—just this book.

Intertwined in this 2000-square-mile megalopolis are chic bayside villages, exclusive islands, grand Mediterranean areas and an array of skyscrapers. Across the pancake-flat terrain also lies a maze of bewitching waterways, traffic-choked highways and sprawling residential regions. A close inspection will even reveal a bit of the mangrove wilderness that served as the birthing place of this great resort center.

But as much as its heavenly winter climate and its spectacular sea-and-sand setting, Miami's unique appeal lies in its people. The city seems to transform itself almost annually, so if you last visited five years ago, you'll hardly recognize the place. But as you explore, you'll still find vestiges of its roller-coaster past. Street names recall the era, a century ago, when Mr. Flagler arrived with his railroad, carrying the first vacationers from the chilly north, and when Mr. Collins decided to turn his farm into Miami's first beach resort.

Grandiose old replicas of Italian castles and Arabian Nights palaces evoke the Roaring Twenties, when developers riding the real estate boom indulged in fantasy architecture. Along Miami Beach stand former apartment buildings where in years past elderly retirees from New York shuffled down dingy hallways, now lavishly refurbished as chic little hotels for the trendy set. Names of old-time celebrities like Jackie Gleason and Arthur Godfrey grace buildings and street corners, reminders of the mid-1950s when Miami was touted on television as the ultimate beach resort. Hideaway art studios and raucous public events like Coconut Grove's wacky King Mango Strut hark back to the time when some of Miami's most desirable neighborhoods stood half-abandoned and offered a haven for painters, craftspeople, performing artists and other bohemians who laid the groundwork for today's burgeoning arts and culture scene.

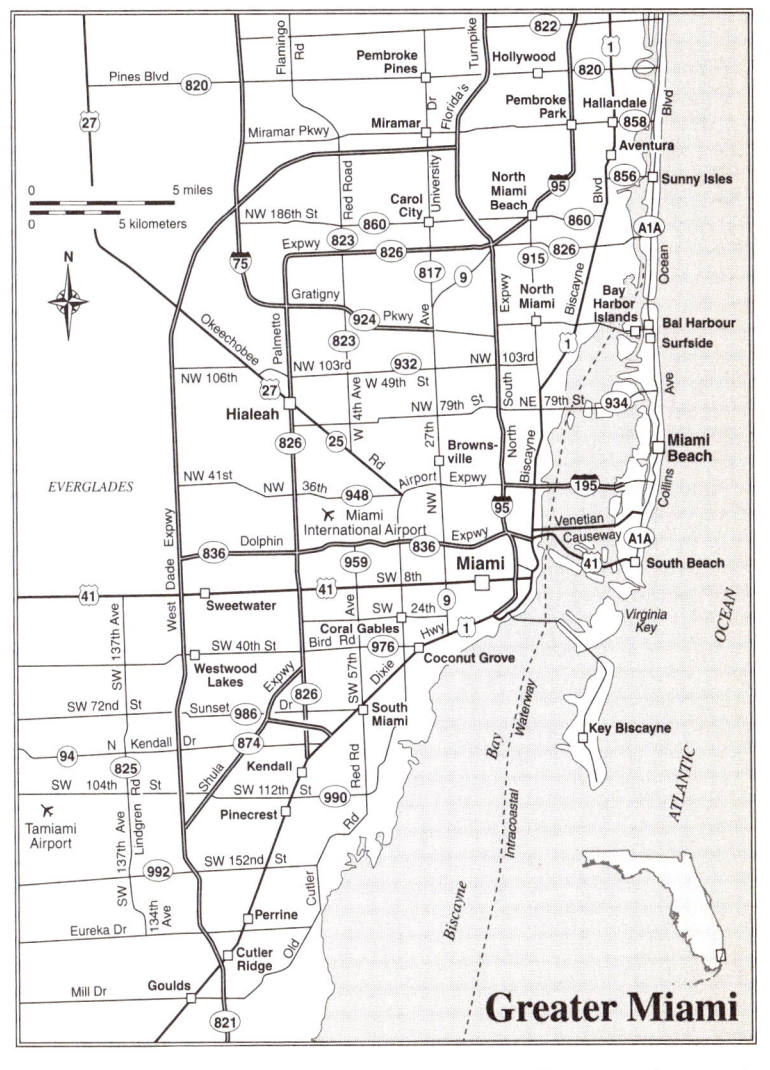

Text continued on page 6.

Three-day Weekend

Miami's Culture and History

Check into one of South Beach's refurbished deco hotels (page 56); then call for reservations to board the *Heritage of Miami* (page 80). Noticeably missing from this itinerary is the Miami Seaquarium (page 121)—if you decide to go, plan to spend the day and include a visit to Key Biscayne (page 120).

Day 1
- After breakfast, head for the **Art Deco Welcome Center** (page 52) in South Beach, which opens at 10:30 a.m. If it's Saturday, join the guided tour; otherwise, rent an Art Deco District Walking Tour tape and headset. Plan on at least two hours of walking.

- Lunch just a few blocks south at the **News Café** (page 62), located on Ocean Drive at 8th Street.

- Continue walking to 10th Street, turn, and head to Washington Avenue. Near the corner, the **Wolfsonian** (page 53) is a fabulous repository for decorative and propaganda arts. Spend about an hour here.

- Resign the rest of your afternoon to browsing the trendy shops at **Lincoln Road Mall**, the 12-block pedestrian shopping mecca. Be sure to visit the **Art Center South Florida** (page 63). For a quarter per ride, the Electrowave will shuttle you the nine or so blocks from Washington Avenue to the mall, with designated stops along the way.

- Dine at Miami's seafood institution, **Joe's Stone Crab** (page 58).

- Still have energy? There may be time to catch the New World Symphony at the **Colony Theater** (page 65) or tonight's headliner at the **Jackie Gleason Theater of the Performing Arts** (page 65).

Day 2
- Indulge in a deli breakfast at **Wolfie Cohen's Rascal House Restaurant** (page 140), then walk three blocks north on Collins Avenue to 23rd Street for a beach stroll along the two-mile boardwalk.

- Return to your car and take Collins Avenue north to the **Fontainebleau Hilton** (page 74), and meander through this palatial 1950s hotel. While you're in the area, drive along **Indian Creek Drive** (page 72) for a view of the luxury houseboats and estates.

- Seeing Miami from the water is essential. Head to the Bayside Marketplace for a two-hour cruise aboard the tall ship *Heritage of Miami* (page 80).

- Head back to Miami Beach and treat yourself to dinner at **The Forge** (page 75).

Day 3
- Begin the day at the **Historical Museum of Southern Florida** (page 79), which offers a comprehensive, highly entertaining history of the cultures, folklife and archaeology of South Florida and the Caribbean.

- Head east to Coconut Grove for a tour of **Vizcaya Museum and Gardens** (page 106), an extravagantly adorned Italian Renaissance–style villa surrounded by ten acres of formal gardens.

- Dine tonight in Little Havana at **La Carreta** (page 93).

- Prefer the blues to flamenco? Then finish the night at **Tobacco Road** (page 86).

As in no other American city, Miami is dominated by Latin politics. Many key government leaders are Latino, vying for their piece of the political pie. Local elections often center around national and foreign issues dealing with Latin America rather than what's going on in Miami. Cuban Americans have had a huge political impact not only on Miami but also on the whole country. In this sharply divided state, rallying the support of Miami's traditionally Republican Cuban exiles has often been viewed as a secret to political success.

Today, Central and South Americans have also established new lives here. Together with the Cubans, they make up over half of Miami-Dade County's 2.4 million residents. Spanish billboards dot the metropolis, and sleek Latin financial institutions line the streets of downtown. Throughout the area, Spanish is spoken just as much as English.

Like virtually every sprawling urban area, Miami is not without big city problems. Healthy crime statistics, racial strife and drug smuggling have not boded well for Miami's vacation image. The city has unique issues as well, like Hurricane Andrew, which struck the coast 25 miles southwest of Miami in August 1992. Packing winds that gusted through Coral Gables at 164 miles per hour, the storm left billions of dollars worth of damage.

Despite such challenges, Miami remains a multifaceted city determined to retain its hold as a vacation center while evolving as a Latin American capital. For some, it is a glorious place in the sun, a sphere of heedless days and tropical nights. For others, it signifies a pulsing international center poised on the southeastern tip of the continent.

The millions of travelers who come here each year have found much to write home about in the city's sophisticated art, architecture and entertainment, and lovely beaches and parks, as well as in the multicultural communities that surround Miami in greater Miami-Dade County.

Within this varied county lie 27 towns, all basking in a continuously breezy, subtropical climate. While the average temperature hovers splendidly between 70° and 80° Fahrenheit, visitors can expect a few dog-day afternoons when the thermometer climbs to 90° in the summer.

Even in the face of rapid development and remarkable tourism, Miami still possesses many hidden treasures. If you leave the massive freeways, look beyond the billboards and meander down the city side streets, you will find them.

This book is designed to help you explore this great city. It will take you to countless popular spots and offer advice on how best to enjoy them. It will also lead you into many off-the-beaten-path locales, the places one learns about by talking with folks at the local café or with someone who has lived in the area all his life. It will acquaint you with the city's history and its residents. It will recommend sights that should not be missed. It will suggest places to eat, to lodge, to shop and to play, with consideration for varying interests, budgets and tastes.

What you choose to see and do is up to you. The old cliché that "there is something for everyone" pretty well rings true in Miami. It is proven by the numbers of retired people who return annually or settle down here, by the families who pour in each summer as soon as school is out, by the sportsfolk and sports fans, as well as by the fanciers of the fast lane. For sun worshippers, there are few places more satisfying than the "Gateway to the Americas."

There is a saying that promises, "Once you get Miami sand in your shoes, you will always return." Many visitors will swear it's true, and so will thousands of permanent residents who have wended their ways here from all over the country and the world and hope to stay forever. May it prove true for you, too.

Where to Go

The touristic center of Miami-Dade County is **Miami Beach**, a glittering chain of oceanside development that's now enjoying rejuvenation. Still a haven for both the elderly and millions of tourists each year, the area is being renovated by new Latin American settlers who are restoring dilapidated condominiums. Along the southern tip, South Beach is emerging as Miami's shining star, where airy pastel enclaves with streamlined designs draw Europeans, artisans, musicians and actors.

The nucleus of Miami-Dade County is stunning **downtown Miami**. At night, its skyscrapers form a brilliant skein with glowing bands of colored light twinkling against Biscayne Bay and winking at the Southern Cross so lucid in the sky. Nearby, ships ebb and flow through one of the nation's busiest ports.

Nestled on the southwest side of downtown is **Little Havana**, Miami's Cuban core, which centers around a bustling street flanked by Latin diners, small motels and glitzy nightclubs. On the opposite side of downtown, other neighborhoods such as **Little Haiti**, the **Design District** and **Overton's** burgeoning club scene invite the adventurous sightseer.

HURRICANE ALERT

No other state has suffered from as many hurricanes as Florida, but though they can be devastating, hurricanes need not keep one away during the fall. Usually developing in September, hurricanes have also been known to occur much later. (Ironically, the worst storm in decades, Hurricane Andrew, which struck here in 1992, occurred in August.) Unlike many other weather phenomena, they come with plenty of warning, allowing visitors either to batten down or depart for inland locations.

Coconut Grove is a former hippie harbor that turned trendy in the '80s. Swank shops and galleries, chic discos and eateries dot the bustling streets here, shrouded in towering oak trees. Nearby **Coral Gables**, touted as the "Miami Riviera," is the area's Mediterranean mecca. Pristine country-club homes mingle with Moorish castles and rows of posh shops. Through the years, these preplanned surroundings have represented the world of Miami's high society.

Southerly **Virginia Key** and **Key Biscayne** are heady little islands smothered in pine and palm trees and blessed with ribbons of billowy sand and demure waters. Movie stars and presidents have long taken refuge among these shores. Farther down the coast, **Biscayne National Park** offers visitors a look at the mangrove-shrouded natural shoreline of Biscayne Bay and the underwater wonders of the only living coral reef in U.S. waters.

Across **Dade County**'s southern reaches, sprawling housing developments—desperate for more space—creep through farmlands and back up to the Everglades. On the flip side, northern Dade has already grown beyond its means, a vast parcel of suburbia bursting to Fort Lauderdale, with a handful of hidden attractions for those who care to look.

You'll hardly know you've left Miami as you continue north through Hollywood, with its greyhound racetrack and condo-lined beaches, to **Fort Lauderdale**. This booming city anchors the south end of Florida's "Gold Coast," a strand of gorgeous beaches and extreme real estate development that stretches all the way to Palm Beach. Unlike Miami-Dade, the Gold Coast is peopled mainly by retirees and snowbirds from the northeastern United States. While Fort Lauderdale has a handful of tourist attractions, not to mention miles and miles of boat canals and marinas, the real reason to go there is to window shop along trendy Las Olas Boulevard.

When to Go

SEASONS

It's said that a daily newspaper, vowing to give away free editions on days when the sun refused to shine, had to keep its promise no more than four times in any one year. No wonder Florida is called the Sunshine State. The weather stays balmy nearly all year, boasting a pleasant semitropical atmosphere. While South Florida can also get both colder and hotter from time to time than one might expect, the region justifiably claims year-round weather nearly as perfect as can be found in the continental United States, especially for lovers of warmth and sun.

Generally the "shoulder seasons," spring and fall, bring the most pleasant days and nights. In Miami, summers tend to be wet, hot and humid. Winters are drier, mild and sunny with moderate readings.

In general, South Florida's winter high temperatures average in the upper 70s, with lows dropping only into the 50s. Summer temperatures are far more uniform; average highs hover around 90° with lows seldom falling below 70°. While summer can bring hot afternoons, offshore breezes keep life comfortable near the coast.

CALENDAR OF EVENTS

If life is a cabaret, then Miami is a fiesta. There are annual celebrations of just about everything from pirates to possum. Check with Miami's visitors centers and chambers of commerce (listed in the "Before You Go" section) to see what will be going on when you are in the area. Below is a sampling of some of the biggest events.

JANUARY

The **Orange Bowl Parade** and one of the largest post-season football games, the **FedEx Orange Bowl Classic**, kick off the New Year. Coconut Grove responds with satirical floats in its rambunctious parade, the **King Mango Strut**. **Three Kings Day**, the traditional end of the Christmas season in Latin America, is an occasion for celebration in Little Havana. The **Art Deco Weekend** takes place in South Beach. Good times continue with the **Taste of the Grove Food & Music Festival** in Coconut Grove.

Fort Lauderdale's **Greek Festival** features Greek delicacies, traditional dancers and live music with a Hellenic beat.

FEBRUARY

Over 300 artists and more than a million visitors celebrate the annual **Washington Mutual Coconut Grove Arts Festival**. The **Miami International Boat Show** at Miami Beach displays craft from just about every major manufacturer and offers free sailing clinics. The prestigious **Miami Film Festival** focuses on Latin American and Spanish-language films. Orientalia presents local and internationally known belly dancers outdoors on Miami Beach's **Lincoln Road Mall**. Hollywood Beach celebrates **Mardi Gras** with a downtown parade and live music on the boardwalk.

In the Fort Lauderdale area, the **Seminole Tribal Festival** showcases pow-wow dancing and alligator-wrestling shows.

MARCH A two-day Latino celebration, **Carnaval Miami International** culminates with a dynamic block party known as **Calle Ocho Festival**. Key Biscayne's **Lipton International Players Championship** features top international tennis players. Race cars whiz through the Homestead Motor Sports Complex during the first weekend in March at the **Marlboro Grand Prix of Miami**.

The ornate mansion Vizcaya is the scene of the **Italian Renaissance Festival**. You can browse the arts-and-crafts booths along Las Olas Boulevard in Fort Lauderdale during the **Annual Art Festival**.

APRIL Miami Beach hosts the **Little Acorns International Kite Festival**. **HispanicFest** in downtown Hollywood presents internationally renowned entertainment, as well as copious amounts of Latin food.

MAY In Coconut Grove, **Commodore Block Party** transforms Commodore Plaza into a tropical version of Paris' Latin Quarter, with dance, music, art and food. In Little Haiti, the **Compas Festival** highlights Haitian music, culture and cuisine.

JUNE **Gay Pride Week** features live entertainment, dancing, booths and a Sunday parade. On alternating years the event takes place in Fort Lauderdale. Costumed junkanoo teams and food, music, arts and crafts of The Bahamas make the **Coconut Grove Goombay Festival** one of the largest black culture celebrations in the U.S. At Hollywood's **Red, White & Bluegrass Festival**, traditional and contemporary bluegrass music is served up with savory barbecue, handmade arts and crafts, and old-time games.

JULY Miami Beach celebrates the **Fourth of July** with parades, fireworks from three ships on Biscayne Bay and other festivities.

AUGUST Jamaican food, art and live music by internationally acclaimed artists and local bands make up the **Miami Reggae Festival**. Enjoy classic summer's-end fun with a clambake and tons of fresh seafood at the **Hollywood Beach Clambake**, which also features live music, arts and crafts and a treasure hunt.

SEPTEMBER — Top competitors come from around the world to strut their stuff at the **Dance Sport Championships** in Hollywood.

OCTOBER — Music such as calypso, soca and reggae highlights the **West Indian American Day Carnaval Extravaganza**. Latin residents celebrate during Miami's **Hispanic Heritage Festival** with multiple events and activities throughout the month. The waters of Biscayne Bay are filled with sails during the **Columbus Day Regatta**. The **Fort Lauderdale International Film Festival** showcases independent cinema from around the world.

NOVEMBER — Adult and children's choirs, jazz trios, the Greater Miami Symphonic Band and over 30,000 Christmas-colored bulbs combine to create the **Miami Lakes Festival of Lights**. The **Miami Book Fair International** is one of the major regional book events in the United States. **White Party Week** consists of many coordinated parties and events to raise awareness and funds for HIV research. Fort Lauderdale's Bubier Park hosts the **Sound Advice Blues Festival**, featuring both national and local blues bands. The bustling **Broward County Fair** has rides, games, food and live music.

DECEMBER — Candlelight tours, parades and Santa festivals highlight many communities throughout December. In Miami Beach, the **Junior Orange Bowl International Championships** draws hundreds of under-18 players from around the world to compete in a variety of events such as golf, tennis and swimming. The **Bayside Boat Parade** makes for an impressive display of lighted yachts on the Inland Waterway. **Santa's Enchanted Forest** in Coral Gables is one of the most impressive community Christmas lighting displays anywhere. The Hollywood Beach **Candy Cane Holiday Parade** celebrates the season with bands, clowns and floats.

Before You Go

VISITORS CENTERS

The **Greater Miami & The Beaches Convention & Visitors' Bureau** offers a complimentary vacation planner. ~ 701 Brickell Avenue; 305-539-3000, 800-933-8448; www.miamiandbeaches.com.

Tourist information is also available from the **Miami Beach Chamber of Commerce**. ~ 1920 Meridian Avenue; 305-672-1270; www.miamibeachchamber.com. For walking tours and other information on South Beach's art deco buildings, contact the Miami Design Preservation League's **Art Deco Welcome Center**. ~ 1001 Ocean Drive; 305-672-2014; www.mdpl.org.

For information on Coconut Grove, there's the **Coconut Grove Chamber of Commerce**. ~ 2820 McFarlane Road; 305-444-7270; www.coconutgrove.com. And in Coral Gables is the **Coral Gables Chamber of Commerce**. ~ 2333 Ponce de León Boulevard; 305-446-1657; www.gableschamber.com.

PACKING

Unless you plan to spend your Miami trip dining in ultra-deluxe restaurants, you'll need much less in your suitcase than you might think. For most trips, all you'll have to pack are some shorts, lightweight shirts or tops, cool slacks, a couple of bathing suits and cover-ups, and something *very casual* for most special events that might call for dressing up. If you plan on seriously sampling South Beach nightlife, go for high-fashion casual, but leave that tux or evening gown at home.

The rest of your luggage space can be devoted to light "beach reading" and a few essentials that should not be forgotten (unless you prefer to shop on arrival). These include good sunscreens (preferably not oils), high-quality sunglasses and some insect repellent, even in winter. Take along an umbrella or light raincoat for the sudden showers that can pop out of nowhere. Even in Miami, a sweater can be welcome on occasional winter days.

Good soft, comfortable, lightweight shoes for sightseeing are a must. Despite its tropical gentleness, Miami terrain doesn't treat bare feet well except along the shore or beside a pool. Sturdy sandals will do well. If you plan to do any hiking in the wetlands (and wetlands can show up where you least expect them), wear canvas shoes that you don't mind wading in.

Serious scuba divers will probably want to bring their own gear, but it's certainly not essential. Underwater equipment of all sorts is available for rent wherever diving is popular. Many places also rent beach toys. Fishing gear is also often available for rent.

If you find you can't seem to walk a beach without picking up shells, take a plastic bag for hauling treasures. A camera is good, too. Binoculars enhance both birdwatching and beach-watching. And don't, for heaven's sake, forget your copy of *Hidden Miami*.

LODGING

Lodgings in Miami run the gamut from little mom-and-pop motels to glistening highrise condominiums in which every room faces the sea. Large hotels with names you'd know anywhere appear downtown, around the airport and on the South Beach waterfront. Poshest of all are the upscale resorts. Here one can drop in almost from the sky and never have to leave the grounds—though you may miss the authentic Miami. Other lodgings offer more personality, such as historic inns or elegant little European-style hotels where you can eat breakfast with the handful of other guests.

Whatever your preference and budget, with the help of this book you can probably find something to suit your taste. Remember, rooms are scarce and prices rise in the high season, which is generally winter to the south. Off-season rates are often drastically reduced in many places, allowing for a week's, or even a month's, stay to be a real bargain. Whatever you do, plan ahead and make reservations, especially in the prime tourist seasons.

> Be warned that "waterfront" lodging can mean bay, lake, inlet or even a slough in some cases.

Accommodations in this book are organized by neighborhood and classified according to price. Rates referred to are high-season rates, so if you are looking for low-season bargains, it's good to inquire. *Budget* lodgings generally are less than $80 per night for two people and are satisfactory and clean but modest. *Moderate*-priced lodgings run from $80 to $120; what they have to offer in the way of luxury will depend on their location, but they tend to offer larger rooms and more attractive surroundings. At a *deluxe* hotel or resort, you can expect to spend between $120 and $200 for a double; you'll likely find spacious rooms, a fashionable lobby, a restaurant and often a group of shops. *Ultra-deluxe* facilities, priced above $200, are a region's finest, offering all the amenities of a deluxe hotel plus plenty of extras.

If you crave a room facing the surf, ask specifically. If you are trying to save money, lodgings a block or so from the beach often offer lower rates than those within sight of the waves and, because Florida beaches are public, are often worth the short stroll.

DINING

Eating places in Miami seem to be as numerous as the fish in the sea, and fish is what you will find everywhere. You can almost always count on it being fresh and well prepared. In the downtown and Little Havana areas, you'll find not only the best Cuban food in the free world but also hole-in-the-wall restaurants that serve *pupusas* and other specialties from Nicaragua and El Salvador.

Within a particular chapter, restaurants are categorized geographically, with each restaurant entry describing the establishment according to price. Dinner entrées at *budget* restaurants usually cost $10 or less. The ambience is informal, service typically speedy and the crowd often a local one. *Moderately* priced restaurants range between $10 and $20 at dinner; surroundings are casual but pleasant, the menu offers more variety and the pace is usually slower. *Deluxe* establishments tab their entrées from $20 to $30; cuisines may be simple or sophisticated, depending on the location, but the decor is plusher and the service more personalized. *Ultradeluxe* dining rooms, where entrées begin at $30, are often the gourmet places; here cooking has become a fine art and the service should be impeccable.

> South Beach is virtually lined with chic sidewalk cafés serving Indian tandoori, Japanese sushi, Argentinean pastries or just about anything else that strikes your fancy.

Some restaurants change hands often and are occasionally closed in low seasons. Efforts have been made in this book to include places with established reputations for good eating. Breakfast and lunch menus vary less in price from restaurant to restaurant than evening dinners.

TRAVELING WITH CHILDREN

With its first-rate zoo, its monkey and parrot jungles and the nearby Everglades, Miami can be a great destination for families traveling with children. A few guidelines will help make travel with children a pleasure.

Book reservations in advance, making sure that the places you stay accept children. If you need a crib or extra cot, arrange for it ahead of time. A travel agent can be of help here, as well as with most other travel plans.

If you are traveling by air, try to reserve bulkhead seats, where there is lots of room. Take along extras you may need, such as diapers, changes of clothing, snacks, toys or small games. When traveling by car, take along the extras, too. Make sure you have plenty of water and juices to drink; dehydration can be a subtle problem, especially in the tropics.

A first-aid kit is a must for any trip. Along with adhesive bandages, antiseptic cream and something to stop itching, include any medicines your pediatrician might recommend to treat allergies, colds, diarrhea or any chronic problems your child may have.

If you plan to spend much time at the beach, take extra care the first few days. Children's skin is usually more tender than adult skin, and severe sunburn can happen before you realize it. A hat is a good idea, along with a reliable sunblock. And be sure to keep a constant eye on children who are near the water.

For parents' night out, many hotels provide a dependable list of babysitters. In some areas you may find drop-in child care centers; look in the Yellow Pages for these, and make sure you choose ones that are licensed.

Many towns, parks and attractions offer special activities designed just for children. Consult local newspapers and/or call the numbers in this guide to see what's happening where you're going.

WOMEN TRAVELING ALONE

Traveling solo grants an independence and freedom different from that of traveling with a partner, but single travelers are more vulnerable to crime and must take additional precautions.

It's unwise to hitchhike and probably best to avoid inexpensive accommodations on the outskirts of town; the money saved does not outweigh the risk. Bed and breakfasts, youth hostels and YWCAs are generally your safest bet for lodging, and they also foster an environment ideal for bonding with fellow travelers.

Keep all valuables well-hidden and clutch cameras and purses tightly. Avoid late-night treks or strolls through undesirable parts of town, but if you find yourself in this situation, continue walking with a confident air until you reach a safe haven. A fierce scowl never hurts.

These hints should by no means deter you from seeking out adventure. Wherever you go, stay alert, use your common sense and trust your instincts. If you are hassled or threatened in any way, never be afraid to yell for assistance. It's also a good idea to have change for a phone call and a number to call in case of emergency.

For more helpful hints, get a copy of *Safety and Security for Women Who Travel* (Travelers' Tales).

Mainly run for the benefit of students and others in the campus community, the **University of Miami Women's Health Center** can provide referrals and information. ~ 1306 Stanord Drive; Coral Gables; 305-284-430. In case of emergency, there's the **Miami Rape Treatment Center.** ~ 1611 Northwest 12th Avenue; 305-585-7273.

GAY & LESBIAN TRAVELERS

The prime gay destination is no doubt Miami's South Beach, located on a barrier island off Florida's east coast. In fact, the gay community's involvement was crucial in restoring South Beach's classic art deco architecture. Here you'll find a grand selection of accommodations, eateries, shops and nightclubs catering to gay and lesbian travelers. (See "South Beach Gay Scene" in Chapter Four.) Fort Lauderdale's long-established, low-key gay scene focuses around gay-friendly beaches and a number of lively bars.

Numerous resource centers and publications are ready to help gay and lesbian travelers tap into the local happenings. *Hotspots* covers nightlife and entertainment in South Beach and Fort Lauderdale. ~ 954-928-1862; www.hotspotsmagazine.com. For information about South Florida online, there's **Florida Outlooks**. ~ www.floridaoutlooks.com.

> Over 40 million tourists come to Miami each year, attracted as always by the warm winter climate and the beaches.

Miami-Dade Gay & Lesbian Chamber of Commerce is an excellent resource for gays and lesbians. ~ 4500 Biscayne Boulevard, Miami Beach; 305-534-3336.

TWN (*The Weekly News*) focuses on the South Florida scene (including Miami and Fort Lauderdale). In it you'll find news and features pertaining to the gay community. Can't think of anything to do? They also have a comprehensive events listing. ~ 901 Northeast 79th Street, Miami; 305-757-6333; twnonline.org.

The Express is Florida's leading gay and lesbian community newspaper. Covering the entire state, they also list upcoming events. ~ 1595 Northeast 26th Street, Wilton Manors; 954-568-1880; www.expressgaynews.com.

Fort Lauderdale also has some handy resources. Stop by their **Gay/Lesbian Community Center** to pick up brochures and flyers, as well as to see what events and recreational activities they have planned. Closed Sunday. ~ 1717 North Andrews Avenue, Fort Lauderdale; 954-463-9005; www.glccftl.org.

SENIOR TRAVELERS

As millions have discovered, South Florida is an ideal place for older vacationers, many of whom turn into part-time or full-time residents. The climate is mild, the terrain level, and many destinations offer significant discounts for seniors. Off-season rates make most areas exceedingly attractive for travelers on limited incomes. Florida residents over 65 can benefit from reduced rates at most state parks, and the Golden Age Passport, which must be applied for in person, allows discount admission to national parks and monuments for anyone 62 or older.

The **American Association of Retired Persons** (AARP) offers membership to anyone over 50. AARP's benefits include travel discounts. ~ 601 E Street NW, Washington, DC 20049; 800-424-3410; www.aarp.org, e-mail member@aarp.org.

Be extra careful about health matters. In addition to the medications you ordinarily use, it's a good idea to bring along the prescriptions for obtaining more. Consider carrying a medical record with you—including your medical history and current medical status, and your doctor's name, telephone number and address. Make sure your insurance covers you while away from home.

DISABLED TRAVELERS

Miami is striving to make more and more destinations fully accessible to travelers with disabilities. For information on the local scene, contact the **Center for Independent Living of South Florida**. ~ 6660 Biscayne Boulevard; 305-751-8025; www.soflacil.org.

There are numerous organizations providing helpful information for disabled travelers. Among them are: **Society for Accessible Travel & Hospitality** at 347 5th Avenue, Suite 610, New York, NY 10016, 212-447-7284, www.sath.org; the **Moss-Rehab Resource Net**, Corman Building, 1200 West Tabor Road, Philadelphia, PA 19141, 215-456-9600, www.mossresourcenet.org; and **Flying Wheels Travel** (which specializes in trip packages for the disabled) at P.O. Box 382, Owatonna, MN 55060, 507-451-5005, e-mail thq@ll.net. For general traveling advice, contact **Travelin' Talk**, a networking organization. ~ P.O. Box 1796, Wheatridge, CO 80034; 303-232-2979; www.travelintalk.net. The **Access-Able Travel Source** provides traveling information on the web: www.access-able.com.

FOREIGN TRAVELERS

Passports and Visas Most foreign visitors need a passport and tourist visa to enter the United States. Contact your nearest United States Embassy or Consulate well in advance to obtain a visa and to check on any other entry requirements.

Customs Requirements Foreign travelers are allowed to carry in the following: 200 cigarettes (1 carton), 50 cigars, or 2 kilograms (4.4 pounds) of smoking tobacco; one liter of alcohol for personal use only (you must be 21 years of age to bring in alcohol); and US$100 worth of duty-free gifts that can include an additional quantity of 100 cigars. You may bring in any amount of currency, but must fill out a form if you bring in over US$10,000.

Carry any prescription drugs in clearly marked containers. (You may have to produce a written prescription or doctor's statement for the custom's officer.) Meat or meat products, seeds, plants, fruits and narcotics are not allowed to be brought into the United States. Contact the **United States Customs Service** for further information. ~ 1300 Pennsylvania Avenue NW, Washington, DC 20229; 202-297-1770; www.customs.treas.gov.

Driving If you plan to rent a car, an international driver's license should be obtained before arriving in the United States. Some car rental agencies require both a foreign license and an international driver's license. Many also require a lessee to be at least 25 years of age; all require a major credit card. Seat belts are mandatory for the driver and all passengers. Children under the age of six or under 60 pounds should be in the back seat in approved child-safety restraints.

Currency United States money is based on the dollar. Bills come in denominations of $1, $2, $5, $10, $20, $50 and $100. Every dollar is composed of 100 cents. Coins are the penny (1 cent), nickel (5 cents), dime (10 cents) and quarter (25 cents). Half-dollar and dollar coins are rarely used. You may not use foreign currency to purchase goods and services in the United States. Consider buying traveler's checks in dollar amounts. You may also use credit cards affiliated with an American company such as Interbank, Barclay Card or American Express.

Electricity and Electronics Electric outlets use currents of 110 volts, 60 cycles. To operate appliances made for other electrical systems, you need a transformer or other adapter. Travelers who use laptop computers for telecommunication should be aware that modem configurations for U.S. telephone systems may be different from their European counterparts. Similarly, the U.S. format for videotapes is different from that in Europe; National Park Service visitors centers and other stores that sell souvenir videos often have them available in European format on request.

Weights and Measures The United States uses the English system of weights and measures. American units and their metric equivalents are: 1 inch = 2.5 centimeters; 1 foot (12 inches) = 0.3 meter; 1 yard (3 feet) = 0.9 meter; 1 mile (5280 feet) = 1.6 kilometers; 1 ounce = 28 grams; 1 pound (16 ounces) = 0.45 kilogram; 1 quart (liquid) = 0.9 liter.

Transportation

CAR

If you arrive in Miami by car, you'll find the area laid out in a somewhat orderly fashion, with major highways and thoroughfares easily navigated.

From the north, **Route 95** runs due south through Fort Lauderdale and Miami to join **Route 1**, which continues through Coconut Grove, Coral Gables and south Dade County. **Florida's Turnpike** and **Route 826**, better known as the Palmetto Expressway, head south along the western corridor.

Route 41, also called the Tamiami Trail, will bring you in from Florida's West Coast, and **Route 27** cuts in from Central Florida.

Your main east–west connections through Miami are **Route 836** and **Route 112/195**, which transport you to scenic causeways leading to Miami Beach. **Route A1A** runs north and south along the ocean throughout Miami Beach and up through the Fort Lauderdale area.

AIR

Lying eight miles west of downtown, **Miami International Airport** (Wilcox Field) is served by many domestic/international carriers, including American Airlines, Continental Airlines, Delta Airlines, Northwest Airlines, United Airlines and US Airways. There are even more international carriers, including Aerolineas Argentinas, Aero Mexico, Air Canada, Air France, Air Jamaica, Avianca, British Airways, BWIA, Cayman Airways, El-Al, Iberia, LAB, Lan Chile, LASCA, Lufthansa, Mexicana, Varig and Virgin Atlantic. ~ 305-876-7000; www.miami-airport.com.

Taxis, limousines and buses wait to take passengers to points all over Dade County.

The **Fort Lauderdale–Hollywood International Airport** (about an hour's drive from Miami) has regularly scheduled service by Air Canada, American Airlines, Continental Airlines, Delta

---

ON THE MOVE

The quickest way to get around Miami is by **Metrorail**, a futuristic train that glides 21 miles along an elevated track between north and south Miami. Downtown, the **Metromover** monorail makes a two-mile radius around the city's perimeter, stopping at major centers and attractions.

Airlines, jetBlue, Northwest Airlines, Southwest Airlines, United Airlines and US Airways. ~ www.fort-lauderdale-fl1.com.

In Fort Lauderdale, take **Broward County Transit** Route 1 for bus service between the airport and its main terminal at Northwest 1st Avenue and Broward Boulevard. ~ 954-357-8400.

BUS

Greyhound Bus Lines (800-231-2222; www.greyhound.com) brings passengers from all over the country to the Miami area. The main Miami terminal is at 4111 Northwest 27th Street, 305-871-1810; in North Miami Beach at 16000 Northeast 7th Avenue, 305-688-7277; in Homestead at 5 Northeast 3rd Road, 305-247-2040; in Hollywood at 1707 Tyler Street, 954-922-8228; and in Fort Lauderdale at 515 Northeast 3rd Street, 954-764-6551.

If you would like service in Spanish, **Astro Tours** offers shuttles three days a week between Miami and New York. ~ 2909 Northwest 7th Street; 305-643-6423.

Omnibus La Cubana has daily service between Miami and Virginia, New York, New Jersey and Philadelphia. ~ 1101 Northwest 22nd Avenue; 305-541-1700.

TRAIN

Amtrak will bring you into Miami from the northeastern states on its "Silver Service/Palmetto" route. ~ Miami Station, 8303 Northwest 37th Avenue; 800-872-7245; www.amtrak.com.

CAR RENTALS

It's wise to have a car in Miami, even though downtown parking is scarce and expensive.

Several major agencies operate in the Miami airport terminal, including **Avis Rent A Car** (800-331-1212), **Dollar Rent A Car** (800-800-4000), **Enterprise Rent A Car** (800-325-8007), **Hertz Rent A Car** (800-654-3131) and **National Car Rental** (800-227-7368).

Companies with free airport pickup in Miami are **Alamo Rent A Car** (800-327-9633), **Global Rent A Car** (866-635-3060), **Budget Rent A Car** (800-527-0700) and **Thrifty Car Rental** (305-871-5050).

Among the major firms located in or near the terminal at Fort Lauderdale–Hollywood International Airport are: **Alamo Rent A Car** (800-327-9633), **Avis Rent A Car** (800-831-2847), **Budget**

Rent A Car (800-527-0700), **Dollar Rent A Car** (800-800-4000) and **Hertz Rent A Car** (800-654-3131).

Although public transportation in Miami is lethargic, you can still get around. The **Miami Dade Transit** has about 100 Metrobus routes covering roughly 2000 square miles.

PUBLIC TRANSIT

For transit maps and a list of schedules, send for the "First Time Rider's Kit," available from the Miami Dade Transit. ~ 6601 Northwest 72nd Avenue in Lehman Center; 305-884-7567.

Tri-Rail is a commuter rail system operating throughout the Greater Miami area, with service between Miami International Airport and Fort Lauderdale (and many points in between), as well as free shuttle bus service at all major airports and many nearby areas. ~ 800-874-7245; www.tri-rail.com.

Bus service throughout Broward County is provided by **Broward County Transit**. Public libraries, chamber of commerce offices and many beachfront hotels and motels sell weekly Transpasses, which entitle the buyer to unlimited use of the bus system for seven days. ~ 954-357-8400; www.broward.org/bct.

Many cab companies serve Miami International Airport, including the ubiquitous **Yellow Cab** (305-444-4444).

TAXIS

Service at the Fort Lauderdale airport is available from **Friendly Checker** (954-923-2302) and **Yellow Cab** (954-565-5400).

TWO

The South Florida Landscape & Outdoor Adventures

The landscape in and around Miami is characterized by a collision between the forces of raw nature and the influx of hundreds of thousands of people. Sandwiched between a hurricane-prone coastline and an interior infested by alligators and snakes, Miami may be a paradise for snowbirds and retirees, yet wilderness is never far away and often creeps into suburban backyards.

People living in the Miami area in the 1920s, including thousands who had bought real estate without realizing that it was underwater for half the year, were forced to endure swarms of mosquitoes whenever wind blew them in from the Everglades in summer. Couple this with the dreadful, damp heat of Miami in August—a time when even today many South Floridians take vacations to more temperate climes—and it becomes obvious why South Florida remained one of the last uncivilized stretches of the U.S. East Coast well into the 20th century.

All that changed with an invention that had first been conceived by Apalachicola, Florida, resident Dr. John Gorrie in the 1850s but was not successfully implemented until the 1940s: air conditioning. With the ability to control the indoor climate independently of the natural environment, the stage was set for a running battle between land developers and conservationists that has been escalating for half a century and continues today.

GEOLOGY Compared to most land masses, Florida is a mere child, having emerged from the sea as recently as 20 to 30 million years ago. For eons its bedrock lay beneath the warm ocean waters, slowly collecting sediment and forming limestone deposits that would one day break the surface and become a new land. Washed by waves, worn by wind and rain, the mass alternately enlarged and shrank as Ice Age glaciers formed and reformed, intermittently raising and lowering the level of the sea. Following the Ice Age, centuries of heavy rain filled limestone scars and caves created by the changing seas. Springs appeared—hints of the giant aquifers that were aborning underground.

The constant wearing by warm sea waves, wind and rain has resulted in a land that often seems as level as a banquet table. But the limestone that serves as anchor—much of it covered with sand, some with red clay or soils rich enough to nourish superb vegetables and fruits—offers up a variety of treasures beneath its ever-eroding, brittle crust.

Like a watery fringe, the Atlantic coastal plain bounds South Florida, extending inland as far as 60 miles in some places. Mostly level and low, they are often wooded and dense; offshore they take the form of sand bars, coral reefs, lagoons and islands. The Everglades is a giant "river of grass" flowing from Lake Okeechobee and its neighboring Big Cypress Swamp.

Flora and Fauna

FLORA

Lying on the edge of the tropic latitudes, the Miami area boasts a "best of both worlds" plant life. So conducive is Miami's climate to all kinds of flora that the city's showplace gardens blossom with an amazing array of flowers year-round. Driving around some of the city's more exclusive neighborhoods or visiting public gardens such as Vizcaya or the Fairchild Tropical Botanic Garden in midwinter, you'll find amazing splashes of color from Christmas flowers (a relative of the poinsettia that grows as ten-foot-tall shrubs covered with blooms), the bright yellow blossoms of the golden shower tree and the sublime blue petals of the Cape plumbago, as well as more familiar tropical varieties such as Tahitian gardenias, royal poincianas, chenille, morning glories and trumpet flowers.

An unusual series of four hurricanes, each on the heels of the last, ripped across South Florida in August and September of 2004. Although Miami was spared the brunt of all four storms, vegetation in surrounding areas, from the mangrove coastline of Biscayne National Park to the farmlands adjoining the Everglades, was stripped. The loss of crops caused shortages of tomatoes and other vegetables nationwide. But with extraordinary resilience, South Florida's plant life is rapidly returning to its normal lush condition.

Nor are hurricanes the only threat to coastal flora. Two palm tree diseases, lethal yellowing and ganoderma, have periodically decimated the Miami area's coconut palms, prompting a worldwide search by landscapers for palm trees that are resistant to these plagues. Among the palms you're likely to see in the Miami area today are Bismarck palms from Madagascar, Sargent's cherry palms from the Yucatán and tall, slender Veitchia palms from the South Sea Islands, the latter identifiable by their bright red coconut-like fruit. In addition, the majestic sabal palm, Florida's state tree, is widely distributed in the region, flourishing in many types of soil.

Caribbean trees, abundant in subtropical South Florida, include mahogany, gumbo-limbo and many other species of palm, including the handsome royal palm. Cabbage palmetto can be found in coastal regions. Because lumbering was one of the state's earliest industries, few virgin stands remain.

Most of the wilderness in the South Florida interior consists of everglades, wetlands covered with tall, sharp sawgrass that are inundated during the summer months with a thin layer of water that flows from Lake Okeechobee to the ocean—an endangered environment since much of the water that previously covered the 'glades is now diverted to the city by canals.

Throughout the Everglades, native orchids and air plants provide an exotic beauty. Oleander, hibiscus, poinsettia, gardenia, jasmine, trumpet vine and morning-glory thrive almost everywhere. For brilliant floral displays, nothing can match a blooming royal poinciana or a colorful shower of bougainvillea, common where temperatures do not dip too low.

Within this sea of grass are pine islands, as well as island-like hardwood hammocks, or forests, where the big trees reside. They are quite varied and may be found in many differing forms.

RIVER OF GRASS

The Everglades, which take up the southern one-third of the Florida Peninsula, are unique. No other place on earth has the same vegetation or ecology. For centuries, this squishy prairie of inedible grass posed a seemingly insurmountable barrier to settlement by Spanish and English colonists. Military expeditions to round up the Seminole Indians were forced to turn back as their horses foundered knee-deep in mud. Farmers along the northern extent of the 'glades often repeated a tall tale about how their cows would wander off into the grassy wetlands, only to be found the next day drained of blood by hellish swarms of mosquitoes.

Tropical hammocks of southern Florida are perhaps the most intriguing, for here northern and Caribbean trees grow together—live oaks side by side with gumbo-limbo, mahogany and poisonwood. To the north of the Everglades, Big Cypress Swamp is also underwater part of the year; its shadowy depths host hundreds of species of wild orchids and bromeliads.

FAUNA

Early Florida explorers reported amazing numbers of animals everywhere they went. Even veteran travelers living today can recall the abundance of birds soaring above the Everglades' Tamiami Trail when it was still a new roadway. Today, 90 percent of Everglades birds are gone, and ever-increasing civilization has reduced the mammal and reptile population considerably. However, in the protected areas where natural habitats remain, native wildlife still thrives and South Florida continues to be a zoological wonderland.

There are numerous land mammals still found in the wild areas of South Florida within an hour's drive of metropolitan Miami, including the black bear, gray fox, puma and wild cat. The Florida panther is among the rarest. Deer are common in many regions and are even likely to invade lawns and gardens in some of Miami's inland suburbs. Also abundant are squirrels, rabbits, raccoons and opossums; less prolific are otters and minks, long trapped for their pelts. Armadillos poke around noisily for insects; feral hogs can be encountered in some wild, wooded areas.

Once common in Florida but long a victim of civilization, the gentle manatee, or sea cow, is dwindling in numbers despite efforts to save it. These bulky, homely animals may be observed in several protected areas. They often feed trustingly at the water's surface close to boaters and fishermen, where they can become victims of motor blades and abandoned tackle. Manatees can still be found in the grassy shallows of Biscayne Bay.

Alligators live in lakes, rivers and marshy areas throughout the state. Long protected by law, they can be seen in various parks as well as in the wild and, for safety, should be respected. Urban legends of large alligators wandering into Miami suburbs to bask on residential lawns and in swimming pools are true. The gator's cousin, the American crocodile, is endangered and rare.

A variety of snakes thrive in Florida; the venomous ones include rattlesnake, coral snake, cottonmouth moccasin and copperhead, though they are rarely encountered in urban areas. Frogs, lizards and turtles, including loggerhead sea turtles, can often be seen.

Birdwatchers have listed over 400 species and subspecies of birds throughout the state. Endangered species such as woodstorks are drastically reduced in number, but are still present in the Everglades. Everglades and Biscayne national parks are also home to approximately 70 mated pairs of bald eagles.

Coastal regions abound in shore birds such as the brown pelican, varieties of gull, sandpipers and terns. Ducks, geese and many other migratory birds make their winter homes in Florida. Natural rookeries, protected sanctuaries and a thriving Audubon Society contribute to the maintenance of the rich bird life in the state.

One of Florida's most popular mammals resides in the sea. The sleek bottle-nosed dolphin, popular with humans because of its high intelligence and playfulness displayed in captivity, can also present an enchanting spectacle as it sports alongside a beach or among boaters in Biscayne Bay.

NATURAL HABITATS

Human beings have altered so much of South Florida that it's almost possible to believe condominiums and sprawling resort complexes have replaced whatever natural environs once existed. Fortunately, this is not entirely so. A broad variety of habitats still exists, many of them protected in parks and preserves including Everglades and Biscayne national parks as well as Bill Baggs Cape Florida State Park on Key Biscayne.

Outdoor Adventures

The Miami area is an outdoor enthusiast's heaven. Those of you who love the water will find plenty to do. From sailing to diving, let the beauty of Miami's waters guide your sensibilities.

SPORT-FISHING

You can wrangle with a sailfish, marlin or even a barracuda when fishing the Gulf Stream current, three miles out of Miami Beach. All outfits provide bait, tackle, coolers and ice, but be prepared to bring your own food and drink. Day trips usually last four hours.

Thomas Flyer catches its own live bait before heading out for tuna, grouper, amberjack and sailfish. ~ Bayside Marina, Miami; 305-374-4133.

If you're not afraid to bite off more than you can chew, call **The Shark** for half-day and full-day fishing excursions. ~ 10800 Collins Avenue, Sunny Isles; 305-949-2948. Or get out your aquatic aggressions aboard **Therapy IV** to catch kingfish, bonita, mahimahi and dorado. ~ 10800 Collins Avenue, Sunny Isles; 305-945-1578.

Expect winter catches of grouper, snapper and tuna with the **Carie Ann**. ~ Crandon Park Marina, Key Biscayne; 305-361-0117. Be sure to bring your scaling knife aboard **The Cutting Edge** for dolphin hunting (not the bottle-nose mammal, but the fish). The Cutting Edge provides mostly game fishing, but will fish for shark trophies. They also offer kite fishing, a sport that suspends the bait from flying kites. ~ 4000 Crandon Boulevard, Key Biscayne; 305-361-9740.

Flamingo Fishing offers four-hour trips, three times a day, and provides the tackle, fishing license and parking fee. You can expect to reel in bonita, kingfish, grouper and nearly 20 different kinds of snapper. ~ Bahia Mar Yacht Basin, 801 Seabreeze Boulevard, Fort Lauderdale; 954-462-9194; www.flamingofishing.com.

BOATING

The Intracoastal Waterway, which extends the length of the coast, can be explored via sailboat or motorboat. Fort Lauderdale, dubbed "The Venice of America" for its extensive canal system, is a boater's paradise.

You can rent motorboats via the **15th Street Boat Company**. Prior experience is required. ~ 1900 Southeast 15th Street, Lauderdale Marina, Fort Lauderdale; 954-765-1334; www.whalerrent.com.

URBAN WILDLIFE

Some wild animals native to the Everglades have adapted surprisingly well to city life. In the busiest commercial and residential areas of Miami Beach, visitors are often shocked to encounter opossums, which are readily mistaken for giant rats. Escaped and abandoned pets also thrive in the subtropical climate of urban Miami. While wild and stray dogs are kept well under control by the city, cats are harder to catch, and Miami Beach and other parts of the city have phenomenal numbers of wild cats ranging from dangerous feral felines to former house cats who prefer to stay in their old neighborhoods, mooching food and affection from neighbors, when their owners move away. Imported birds are also often seen, from the green parrots that congregate in the palm trees along South Beach's busy Ocean Drive to the free-flying colony of hundreds of Cuban flamingos that has its nesting grounds in the infield of the old Hialeah Racetrack in North Miami.

The ubiquitous **Club Nautico** rents powerboats. ~ Pier 66, Fort Lauderdale; 954-523-0033; www.boatrent.com.

DIVING

You'll find plenty of diving possibilities in the area, especially around nearby coral reefs and old shipwrecks.

For equipment rentals and purchases, contact **Aquanauts**. They also provide certification classes for all levels and are a good resource for maps and diving suggestions. ~ 140 Southwest 57th Avenue, Miami; 305-545-9000. **South Beach Dive and Surf Centers** sell and rent all equipment. Trips to Miami and Key Largo waters last a half or full day. If you're not certified, they have a three-day certification course. ~ 850 Washington Avenue, Miami Beach; 305-531-6110. **Mermaid Dive Center** offers dives from West Palm Beach all the way to the Bahamas. Boats provide full equipment rentals. ~ 16604 Northeast 2nd Avenue, North Miami Beach; 305-940-0926.

Venture through mazes of ship and plane wrecks, including a 727 jet, with **Diver's Paradise**. Licensed, insured instructors can lead you around a choice of 30 wrecks or teach you the diving fundamentals in a three-day course. Half-day, full-day and night dives available. ~ 4000 Crandon Boulevard, Key Biscayne; 305-361-3483; www.miamiscubacharters.com.

Divers Unlimited has a Friday-night dive that leads you through 130-foot wrecks and into shallower reefs to look at marine life. In the reefs, expect hard corals and tropical fish typical of the Caribbean: angelfish, grunts, hogfish and soldiers. Other dives are offered Tuesday through Sunday. ~ 10191 Pines Boulevard, Hollywood; 954-430-3483; www.diversunlimited.com.

One of the most highly respected dive shops is **Pro Dive**, which offers daily reef and wreck dives as well as basic, open-water and advanced certification classes. ~ Located next to the Radisson Bahia Mar Beach Resort, 515 Seabreeze Boulevard, Fort Lauderdale; 954-776-3483; www.prodiveusa.com.

WIND-SURFING

It's windsurfer heaven around Key Biscayne, so grab a board from **Sailboards Miami**. Rent everything you need from wetsuits to harnesses or take a class, offered daily. Kayaks are available as well. ~ Rickenbacker Causeway; 305-361-7245. In North Miami Beach, look for jetski rentals in front of the **Newport Beachside Resort**. ~ 16701 Collins Avenue; 305-949-1300.

Surfers and windsurfers will find an endless summer on the Fort Lauderdale waters. Everything from surfboards to wakeboards, boogieboards and skin boards, as well as apparel and accessories, can be rented from **BC Surf & Sport**. ~ 1495 North Federal Highway, Fort Lauderdale; 954-564-0202; www.bcsurf.com.

SAILING

Let the wind guide you around Miami's scenic waters. For sailboat, catamaran and powerboat rentals and charters, check out **Florida Yacht Charters and Sales**. ~ 390 Alton Road, Miami Beach; 305-532-8600. Also along Miami Beach, look for the sailboat vendors at **46th Street Beach**. ~ Collins Avenue and 46th Street. In North Miami, **Gold Coast VIP Services/Yacht Charters** offers a range of rentals, from two-person yachts to dine and cruise mega-yachts for parties of 500. They also provide overnight "honeymoon" yachts, sailboats, speedboats and trawling powerboats for sportfishing tours. ~ 1302 Northwest 188th Terrace; 305-653-0591. In Southern Dade County, try **Castle Harbor Sailing and Powerboat School**. Smaller boats are rented by the day or half-day for U.S. certified sailors. Larger boats can be chartered for overnight or longer excursions. Sailing and powerboat instruction is also available. ~ Matheson Hammock Marina; 305-665-4994.

> At least 344 species of trees, about 80 percent of those native to the United States, grow here.

WATER-SKIING

Instruction is available at **McGinnis Water Ski**. They supply the boat, equipment, driver and, of course, the waterski coach. Classes offered for all levels. Closed Sunday. ~ 2421 Southwest 46th Avenue, Fort Lauderdale; 954-321-0221; www.mcski.com.

PARA-SAILING

On a clear day, one of the loveliest sights in Fort Lauderdale is parasailors soaring above the ocean. **Aloha Water Sports** offers parasailing and rents waverunners, catamarans, boogieboards and mats. ~ Located on the beach in front of the Marriott Harbor Beach Hotel, 3030 Holiday Drive, Fort Lauderdale; 954-462-7245.

JOGGING

Scenic jogging trails abound in the Miami area, including ones at **Haulover Beach Park**. ~ 10800 Collins Avenue, Sunny Isles; 305-944-3040. In Key Biscayne, try **Crandon Park Beach**. ~ 4000 Crandon Boulevard, Key Biscayne; 305-361-5421. Another is **Matheson Hammock County Park**. ~ 9610 Old Cutler Road, South

Dade County; 305-665-5475. In South Dade County, be sure to check out **Larry and Penny Thompson Park**. ~ 12451 Southwest 184th Street, South Dade County; 305-232-1049. In North Miami, try **Greynolds Park**. ~ 17530 West Dixie Highway, North Miami; 305-945-3425.

INLINE SKATING

Florida's flat terrain and abundance of bike paths make inline skating very popular.

In South Beach, **Fritz's Skate, Bike and Surf Shop** rents skates and other gear by the hour, day or week. ~ 730 Lincoln Road; 877-699-5252.

BC Surf & Sport has the best selection of inline skates in Fort Lauderdale. They are well stocked with every size, including children's. ~ 1495 North Federal Highway, Fort Lauderdale; 954-564-0202; www.bcsurf.com.

GOLF

You can tee up at numerous public golf courses, most of which offer club and cart rentals. **Miami Beach Golf Club** is a challenging semiprivate 18-hole course. ~ 2301 Alton Road, Miami Beach; 305-532-3350. **Haulover Beach Golf Course** is a public, par-3, nine-hole course. Pull carts are available. ~ 10800 Collins Avenue, Miami; 305-940-6719. **Fontainebleau Golf Course** is another championship course, designed by Mark Mahannah. The two 18-hole greens are seldomly crowded and are filled with lots of challenging sand and water obstacles. ~ 9603 Fontainebleau Boulevard, Miami; 305-221-5181. **Country Club of Miami** hosts a year-round series of championship matches and features two 18-hole, par-70 and par-72 championship courses. The greens, designed by Robert Trent Jones, are extremely popular and difficult to master. There are also chipping and putting areas. ~ 6801 Northwest 186th Street, North Miami; 305-829-8456. **Greynolds Park** has a well-kept par-36, nine-hole intermediate course that is popular with older folks. There are bunkers on all holes. ~ 17530 West Dixie Highway, North Miami; 305-949-1741. **Crandon Golf Course** is the host of the Royal Caribbean Senior PGA tournament. The par-72, 18-hole course offers gorgeous views of Biscayne Bay and downtown Miami. ~ 6700 Crandon Boulevard, Key Biscayne; 305-361-9129. In South Dade County, consider the 18-hole **Palmetto Golf Course**. ~ 9300 Southwest 152nd Street; 305-235-1069.

Water Safety

Few places match Florida for the variety of water sports available. Swimming, scuba diving, snorkeling or just basking on a float are options wherever you can get to the shore. Surfing is popular when the wind is up. Drownings do occur now and then, but they can be avoided as long as you respect the power of the water, heed appropriate warnings and use good sense.

Wherever you swim, never do it alone. If the surf is high, keep your face toward the incoming waves. If you go surfing, learn the proper techniques and dangers from an expert before you start out. Respect signs warning of dangerous currents and undertows. If you get caught in a rip current or any tow that makes you feel out of control, don't try to swim against it. Head across it, paralleling the shore. Exercise caution in the use of floats, inner tubes or rafts: unexpected currents can quickly carry you out to sea.

Jellyfish stings are commonly treated with papain-type meat tenderizers. If you go scalloping, swim in or wade around in murky waters where shellfish dwell, wear canvas shoes to protect your feet.

Remember, you are a guest in the sea. All rights belong to the creatures who dwell there, including sharks. Though they are rarely seen and seldom attack, they should be respected. A wise swimmer who spots a fin simply heads unobtrusively for shore. On the other hand, if dolphins are cavorting in your area, don't worry; they may put on quite a show.

Life jackets are a must if you want your boating trip to end happily. This goes for canoes as well as larger and faster craft. And never, never take your eyes off a child who is near the water, no matter how calm conditions may appear. With so much wonderful shoreline available in Miami, the best protection is to know how to swim, and to use your good sense.

Robert Trent Jones designed the 18-hole executive course at the **American Golfers Club**. ~ 3850 North Federal Highway, Fort Lauderdale; 954-564-8760. **Bonaventure Country Club** has two challenging 18-hole courses. The club also features a practice range, putting greens and a well-stocked pro shop. Tee times can be arranged up to 21 days in advance. ~ 200 Bonaventure Boulevard, Fort Lauderdale; 954-389-2100; www.golfbonaventure.com.

TENNIS

Tennis is the rage around Miami, so not surprisingly there are many top spots for racquet addicts. Most courts are lit and offer racquets for rent and balls for sale. **Flamingo Park Tennis Center** has 19 courts, most of which are lit. A ball machine is available for rent during non-peak hours. Fee. ~ Corner of 11th Street and Jefferson Avenue, Miami; 305-673-7761. **Haulover Beach Park** has six clay courts. Fee. ~ 10800 Collins Avenue, Sunny Isles; 305-940-6719. Bring your own racquet to the seven outdoor courts at **Morningside Park**. Fee. ~ 750 Northeast 55th Terrace, Miami; 305-754-1242. **Moore Park** has 13 outdoor courts but no rentals. Fee. ~ 765 Northwest 36th Street, Miami; 305-635-7459. In Coral Gables, you'll find 13 outdoor courts with rentals at **Salvadore Park Tennis Center**. Fee. ~ 1120 Andalusia Avenue, Coral Gables; 305-460-5333.

In Hollywood, **West Lake Park** has four courts. Fee. ~ 751 Sheridan Street, Hollywood; 954-926-2410. Six lit courts and instruction are available at **George English Tennis Center**. Balls and racquets can be rented. Fee. ~ 1101 Bayview Drive, Fort Lauderdale; 954-396-3620. **Holiday Park** has 18 clay and three hard courts. Fee. ~ 701 Northeast 12th Avenue, Fort Lauderdale; 954-828-5346.

BIKING

Traveling via bike offers a different perspective of the area, but be sure to steer clear of congested downtown. The best bicycle trails are found throughout the suburbs, parks and beaches.

Along **South Miami Beach**, bicyclists take advantage of a wide sidewalk that stretches for more than 20 blocks in South Beach. Farther north, **Haulover Beach** has a 1.5-mile trail along the billowy sand dunes. There are few designated bike paths or lanes on Central Miami Beach, making cycling a little tricky along the crowded, busy streets.

If island cycling is your bag, you'll love Key Biscayne, where you can cruise through eight miles of shady pines, past sumptuous homes and hidden beach coves. Down in **Matheson Hammock County Park**, a 1.5-mile trail meanders through dense mangroves and along the beaches.

The best places to ride in the Fort Lauderdale area are along the wide paved roads on the west side of the city, such as **Nob Hill Road** north of Broward Boulevard, or along **Atlantic Boulevard**, which parallels Route A1A on the east side of the city.

Every Sunday at 8 a.m. groups leave from **Big Wheel** and ride a westerly 35-mile loop. There are three levels of difficulty, depending on experience. Technically, rentals are not available, but they will "sell" you a used bike and then "buy" it back after the ride. ~ 7029 Taft Street, Hollywood; 954-966-5545, fax 954-985-0699.

The smooth road inside **John U. Lloyd State Beach Recreation Area** is a good cycling route (four miles roundtrip). In this area, a 40-mile group ride is organized by **Mike's Cyclery**. Closed Sunday. ~ 5429 North Federal Highway, Fort Lauderdale; 954-493-5277.

Bike Rentals To rent a mountain bike or beach cruiser in the Miami area, you can try **Miami Beach Bicycle Center**. A bike (lock, helmet and map of the art deco district included) can be rented by the hour or by the day. ~ 601 5th Street; 305-531-4161. **Key Biscayne Mangrove Bicycle** rents all types of bikes: 21-speed, cruisers and kids' bikes (with or without training wheels). This full-service shop provides customers with a free bicycle-trail map. All rentals come with helmets and locks. Baby seats and child tandems also available. ~ 260 Crandon Boulevard; 305-361-5555.

You can rent bicycles in Fort Lauderdale from **Neon Dolphin**, an adventure tour company specializing in fun tours and cruises. ~ 2896 East Sunrise Boulevard, Fort Lauderdale; 954-630-9146; www.neondolphin.com.

AUTHOR FAVORITE

Though I won't test it during rush hour, the bike path along **Old Cutler Road** offers true enjoyment at other times of day. Cutting a swath from Coconut Grove southward to Cutler Ridge, this 14-mile route winds along Biscayne Bay and offers a glimpse into the area's remaining agricultural communities.

THREE

History and Culture

Miami's story is one of overnight success, a place built so fast and loved so soon that it's easy to forget how young it really is. Little more than a fishing village when it was incorporated in 1896, Miami didn't really evolve as a city until its frenetic 1920s land boom.

Likewise, as late as 1910, that silvery thread of barrier islands called Miami Beach was still awash with avocado and mango plantations. Not until the following decade did the ten miles of coastline finally burst with plush hotels and communities that were immediately frequented by celebrities.

The tale's prologue trickles back to 1513—and before . . .

HISTORY **EARLY EXPLORATION** When Spaniard Ponce de León first set foot on this island strand, he encountered perilous coral reefs and mosquito-infested scrublands that made navigation difficult, even for the Calusa and Tequesta Indians who inhabited the shores. In the 1500s, the Tequesta Indians called the swamplands Mayaime, or "fresh water," referring to Lake Okeechobee and the shallow rivers that flowed from there to the sea. The passage of time transformed the word into Miami.

Modern archaeologists tell us that human beings have been harvesting the waters, roaming the hills and wading the swamps of Florida for at least 12 centuries. Little remains of the early wanderers but bits and pieces of tools and artifacts, mystifying mounds and occasional piles of refuse deposited by generations of these early partakers of oyster on the half shell. When Europeans arrived in Florida, they encountered a number of resident American Indian tribes. Warlike Calusas resided in the

Everglades. Smaller tribes such as the Tequestas and Ais struggled among the larger groups.

Though Ponce de León is credited with being the first European to set foot in South Florida, during the next two-and-a-half centuries the only others to follow in his footsteps were castaways. As galleons carrying the treasure of Mexico around the tip of Florida and back to the courts of Spain foundered on the treacherous reefs of Biscayne Bay, their crews became marooned on the islands that are now Miami Beach and Key Biscayne. Eventually permanent houses of refuge were built there to provide shelter to those awaiting rescue.

In 1763, following the devastating Seven Years' War, Spain traded Florida to the British for Cuba, abandoning the glorious dreams of eternal youth and gleaming treasure for which Ponce de León had struggled.

England had great plans for Florida. The territory was divided into two sections—East and West Florida—with capitals at St. Augustine and Pensacola. Settlers were promised land grants and other benefits; areas were mapped in detail; tentative peace was made with some of the Creek Indians, who had been gradually moving into the territory and down the peninsula. But the English were able to fulfill few of their hopes in Florida, since they had to turn their attention to the American Revolutionary War. The United States lay claim to Florida during the war, but as a condition of the 1783 Treaty of Paris that ended the revolution, they had to return it—to Spain. In the northern part of Florida, colonizing began in earnest. Spain offered generous land grants both to its own people and to the new Americans. Florida also became an accessible and safe haven for escaping slaves from the new states.

But no matter who owned Florida according to the map, the reality was that its unsettled coastline served mainly as a haven for pirates. After 1808, when Thomas Jefferson prohibited the importation of African slaves, the illegal slave trade became rampant along Florida's Atlantic Coast because it was outside U.S. territory. Finally in 1817, Scottish mercenary Gregor MacGregor seized the slave port at Amalie Island, and after he moved on to greener pastures, his subordinates formed a partnership with Mexican pirate Luís Aury to operate the disreputable port under the flag of Mexico. U.S. soldiers invaded the enclave later the same year, though the question of ownership of Florida would not be settled for another five years.

WAR AND CONFLICTS WITH THE AMERICAN INDIANS Conflict between American Indians and settlers, which had raged through much of Florida's brief history, became more and more serious. By this time, most of the original tribes had been killed or scattered, victims of European exploration, raids and wars, but as time went on, more Creek and other southeastern Indians began filling the void. They became known as "Seminoles," a name derived, most likely, from "siminoli," meaning exiles or wanderers. On a pretext of hunting down runaway slaves, Andrew Jackson led troops into northern Florida in 1817 and attacked American Indian settlements, precipitating the First Seminole War.

Wars with the American Indians and other assorted skirmishes finally encouraged Spain to sell the territory to the United States in 1821. Andrew Jackson became the first territorial governor. The two "Floridas" were united for good. Two men were assigned the task of locating a new capital.

As in the rest of the country, the American Indians struggled to hold onto their homeland. But the settlers found them an "annoyance" and the government decided to have them removed to Indian Territory west of the Mississippi. As president in 1835, Andrew Jackson declared the Second Seminole War, hoping to get rid of the American Indians in short order. But he had not reckoned with the Seminoles' commitment to fight for what was theirs. From their midst rose a powerful leader, Osceola, whose skill and dedication gained respect even from those who fought against him. Only after investing seven years, 1500 lives and $20 million was the government able to declare a victory. At last, under dreadful conditions, most of the surviving Seminoles were removed to Indian Territory.

Several hundred American Indians, however, escaped into the Everglades to spend the rest of the century living a nomadic life in the swamp. They finally resumed official relations with the United States in 1962, 125 years after their self-imposed independence.

BUILDING PARADISE Not until the 1880s would the peninsula to the south begin to reveal its tremendous treasures. At this time, a millionaire with dreams as grand as Ponce de León's made America's subtropical paradise accessible and set in motion a land development boom that, though it has had some tough periods of hesitation, has steamrolled through the 20th century and into the present day.

It all began when Henry Flagler built his railroad down the Atlantic coast, establishing lavish resorts in tropical settings that attracted visitors, speculators—and the thousands of workers that such projects require. Flagler was drawn to the state's southern reaches in 1896 by a fragrant bouquet of orange blossoms, sent by an astute pioneer named Julia Tuttle. When an unusually harsh freeze killed citrus groves as far south as West Palm Beach, where Flagler had created an elite vacation community, Tuttle dispatched the blooms as proof of warmer climes to the south. Previously skeptical of Miami's treasures, Flagler was at last convinced.

> Today, American Indians in Florida number 117,800. The Seminole tribe (numbering about 3000) has six separate reservation lands scattered throughout South Florida.

Flagler's railroad fueled progress in the area, bringing curious northern settlers to a land of warm ocean breezes and sunshine. New Jersey businessman John Collins was one of the first to catch a train southward to inspect a yet unseen coconut plantation he had purchased on Miami's barrier islands. Enchanted by the scene, he planted more fruit trees and began constructing a wooden bridge that would link these windswept isles to the mainland.

By 1913, Collins went broke with only half the bridge built and turned to Carl Fisher, inventor of the auto headlight and owner of the Indianapolis Speedway, for help. A shrewd businessman, Fisher finished the bridge in exchange for a swath of island property, then set about molding his new sandspur into beach-rimmed isles with pretty shopping plazas, golf courses, hotels and waterfront homes.

When the 1920s land boom struck, Miami was primed. "Binder boys" stood on street corners hawking real estate for mere pennies, land that turned thousands of investors into overnight millionaires. Dazzled by this newfound investment, wealthy industrialists built fancy oceanfront estates and began shaping the downtown area. To the south, Staten Islander Ralph Munroe formed a quaint bayside village while pioneer George Merrick carved a Mediterranean-style community out of palmetto fronds.

Waves of "tin can tourists" arrived from the frigid north, setting up tents and other makeshift homes along Miami's shores. "Miami or Bust" read the signs that sprinkled highways across the country. Suddenly, Miami Beach was the dream vacation of every red-blooded American.

But the dream was temporarily dashed in 1926 when a perilous hurricane proved that even paradise can go awry. Nearly 400 people were killed and thousands of buildings destroyed or damaged. Then the Great Depression hit. So did the Mediterranean fruit fly, and both took their toll.

Although Merrick and other land developers who had raked in millions during the boom days were plunged into bankruptcy when real estate prices plummeted, a new wave of financing began to pour into Miami from investors in northern cities. Miami was glamorized in the movies as a land of sea and sunshine, year-round golf courses and one of America's most famous horse racetracks. A new building boom changed the look of southern Miami Beach: art deco architecture began sprouting everywhere. Radiant pastel buildings sporting geometric and streamlined moderne designs—deemed visual metaphors of progress—breathed new life into the area.

> The greater Miami-Dade County area is now home to over 2 million people.

At the same time, Pan American Airlines established its Miami-based air service, which linked Miami to dozens of cities in both the United States and Latin America and began to promote the city as the "Gateway to Latin America" (a moniker that Miami-Dade County has recently trademarked as its exclusive property).

During the next two decades, central Miami Beach was a flurry of activity as more glitzy hotels took their places on the sand and posh neighborhoods sprouted along the waterways. At the same time, cultural change was having a major impact on the area. Previously an exclusive niche for the old-money elite, Miami Beach was beginning to attract many retirees escaping the cold northeastern states or looking for retirement havens.

MODERN TIMES No doubt Miami's image as a land of promise was also partially responsible for drawing a new group of immigrants between 1960 and 1980. Sparked by Fidel Castro's Cuban revolution in 1959, more than half a million Cubans fled to Miami during subsequent years, searching for political sanctuary and a better life. Yet another large exodus occurred in 1980, when about 125,000 Cuban refugees arrived on Miami's shores by boat. Central Americans also began arriving in search of new lives, as did thousands of refugee "boat people" fleeing the political repression and poverty of Haiti. More recently, people from other Latin American countries, notably Argentina, Venezuela and Brazil, have flocked to Miami as well.

Retirees continue to contribute to the senior population, especially in Miami's northern beach suburbs and its neighbors Hollywood and Fort Lauderdale. Thanks to both retirement and immigration, the year 2000 census ranked Florida as the sixth fastest-growing state in the nation. It is not only one of the most populous states, but also one of the most culturally diverse, and no place reflects this diversity as much as the greater Miami metro area, now officially designated Miami-Dade County.

Dreams of gold and eternal youth have been replaced by promises of dollars, pleasant retirements and the good life in a land where the sun almost always shines and snow almost never falls. But there is a nagging cloud on the horizon that may affect Miami's future as forcefully as the explorers and the railroad impacted her past. It is a cloud observed by many who feel South Florida has grown much too fast, that care and caution have been thrown to the winds of profit and growth. In its shadow are predictions of what could happen one day to a land that has developed too quickly, whose consumption of its crystal water has gone unchecked, whose pollution may kill the land that feeds it.

But there are encouraging signs. Recent actions at the capital have resulted in the state's acquiring more wild areas and preserves. Archaeological exploration of Spanish missions, American Indian sites and shipwrecks has kindled interest in forgotten history. Florida heritage is rich. It may well have much to teach about where the real treasures lie.

PEOPLE

Ethnic diversity is a keynote in the neighborhoods scattered across Miami's balmy environs, where the population includes African Americans, Asians, Haitians and Jews, as well as numerous Latino cultures. Other groups have found their niches here, too, including artists, pop stars, gangsters, trendsetters, gays and aristocrats.

Text continued on page 42.

South Florida Cuisine

With salt water on three sides and rivers, lakes and streams abounding in its interior, seafood and freshwater fish top the list of Florida foods. From the ocean and Gulf come fresh pompano, scamp, grouper, shrimp, yellowfin tuna and mullet—and the list goes on and on. Florida lobster, a giant crawfish, gives Maine a run for its money. Alligator tail shows up on Everglades-area menus. Stone crab, available from October to May, is even a humane dish: while you are dining on the claw meat of this accommodating creature, he is busy growing a new claw for the next year.

No matter where you live, you have undoubtedly partaken of Florida citrus fruits and mixed water into a can of Florida concentrated juice. In many areas, in the winter months, you can see oranges, grapefruit, limes and tangelos right alongside the road, both on trees and for sale at inviting roadside stands. Varieties seem endless, with some fruit offering special qualities such as remarkable sweetness or no seeds. A freshly picked, easily peeled tangerine is an entirely different item from its stored-and-transported grocery-store cousin. Late fruits, such as valencia oranges and seedless grapefruit, are available into June and July. Even out of season, you'll find citrus products—marmalades, novelty wines, calamondin and kumquat jellies, and lemon candies. Key lime pie is a traditional dessert from the Keys, made originally from the tiny yellow limes that grow there.

Exotic fruits have joined the list of Florida produce, familiar ones such as mangos, avocados and papayas and lesser-known zapotes, lychees and guavas. Coconuts grow in backyards in southern Florida. Swamp cabbage yields up its heart as the chief delicacy in "hearts of palm" salad. Winter vegetables and fruits thrive in the drained Everglades regions, where you can stop and pick strawberries, peppers, tomatoes or whatever else is left over from the great quantities shipped across the United States.

Ethnic foods have long influenced Florida cuisine. Cuban fare such as *picadillo*, black beans and yellow rice, and fried plantains entered southern Florida when travel from the island neighbor was unrestricted.

The population influx from other parts of Latin America have enhanced local restaurant fare as well. Central American refugees in the 1980s brought the Honduran *baleadas* (bean-and-cheese soft tacos) and Nicaraguan *asada* (spicy marinated beef strips), sold at countless small eateries. More recently, South American restaurants have sprung up, serving treats such as Peruvian ceviche (marinated fish), Uruguayan *chivitos* (steak sandwiches), Venezuelan *arepas* (corn-and-cheese pancakes) and Brazilian *rodizio* (mixed meats grilled over an open fire).

Lately, inventive young chefs have been using local fruits and other tropical ingredients to create a new style of cooking. Seafood, chicken, lamb and beef get tropical treatments, and are often grilled, smoked or blackened. Some call it "tropical fusion" or "nuevo Cubano," while others deem it "new Florida cuisine." Whatever the name, one thing is certain: This brand of cooking is marvelously adventurous. After all, where else can you find Key lime pasta or grilled grouper with mango salsa, plantains and purple potatoes?

JEWISH HERITAGE The Jewish presence in South Florida began in Key West in the 1880s with Hungarian immigrant Joseph Wolfson, who was shipwrecked there and liked it so much that he brought his family and invited friends and business associates to join him.

In the wake of the Miami real estate bust in the late 1920s, most of the new developers buying up distressed properties in South Beach were Jewish investors from Key West. They promoted their property to residents of Jewish neighborhoods in the northeast as a retirement haven. Areas that had previously been the exclusive province of wealthy WASPs who came for "the season" and lived in the north for the rest of the year were transformed overnight.

> In the late 1800s, the Key West Jewish community became the major importers of Cuban cigars to the United States.

With the repeal of Prohibition in 1933, Jewish mobster Meir Lansky turned his eye toward Miami Beach as a promising place to invest millions from past liquor smuggling operations on the Florida coast. Lansky and his associates became prominent figures in South Beach, and Temple Beth Jacob, built in 1936 on Washington Street, was dubbed "the gangster shul" because Lansky worshipped there.

Some long-time locals resented the Jewish intrusion, and as anti-Semitism grew, segregation followed. Signs reading "Gentiles Only" appeared along the dividing line, Lincoln Road. Despite such hostilities, half the Miami Beach population was Jewish by 1947. Miami's first Jewish mayor, Abe Aronowitz, was elected in 1953.

With the Cuban revolution and Fidel Castro's rise to power, most Cuban Jews fled to Miami. They were not welcomed by the local Jewish community. Old-timers resented the sudden transformation of Miami's ethnic makeup, echoing the way that they themselves had experienced discrimination a generation earlier. Today, Cuban Jews have displaced retirees from the north in most of Miami Beach, and Spanish-speaking temples like South Beach's Temple Beth Shmuel have sprung up, along with other Cuban temples such as Miami's Temple Moses, a Sephardic Cuban synagogue whose congregation is mostly of Turkish descent. Traditional Hasidic and other Jewish influences can still be found in Miami Beach, though they are less obvious than in the past.

CUBAN INFLUENCES No other event in Miami's rollercoaster history has affected the city's character as much as the exodus of refugees from Cuba. It began in 1959 when leftist revolutionary Fidel Castro overthrew Cuba's corrupt dictator, Fulgencio Batista, and then declared his alliance with the Soviet Union. Most of the first wave of Cuban *exilados*—they called themselves "exiles" instead of "immigrants" because they planned to return home one day—were upper-class and educated middle-class professionals. The Castro regime was seizing property, homes and businesses from the wealthy in Cuba and, in some cases, even executing them, especially those who had had business dealings with Batista.

The newcomers formed a Cuban government-in-exile in Miami and plotted Castro's overthrow with the help of the Central Intelligence Agency, which sponsored the training of Cuban exile militias in remote areas of South Florida. In 1961, the militia called Brigade 2506 launched an invasion of Cuba at the Bay of Pigs, but promised U.S. air support never materialized, and they were defeated with 114 troops killed and 1189 people captured. Their martyrdom helped keep the dream of a free Cuba alive, though it appeared more distant by the year.

Despite Castro's attempts to keep people from leaving the country, the exodus continued over the next 20 years, then exploded in 1980 with the Mariel Boatlift. It began with Castro's agreeing, one time only, to let Cubans emigrate to the United States on the boats of volunteers from Miami. The agreement backfired on the U.S. when Castro used the boatlift as an excuse to empty Cuba's prisons and mental hospitals. These undesirables made up as much as 20 percent of the 125,000 people who arrived in the boatlift. By the time it was over and the refugee claims had all been processed, Cubans were Miami's largest cultural group and accounted for one-third of the city's total population.

It has been largely to placate the exile community that the United States has continued its near-total trade embargo against Cuba for more than four decades. In the 2000 election year, the Clinton Administration's decision to return eight-year-old refugee Elian González to his father in Cuba because of what many saw as a legal technicality is widely credited with securing George W. Bush's victory in Florida and thus his election as President of the United States.

Although more recent Cuban Americans, including those who came on the Mariel Boatlift, have not supported the exiles' old grudges or the embargo, they have not fit into the political equation until recently because polls showed that relatively few recent Cuban immigrants vote. During the George W. Bush administration, however, tightening the embargo on Cuba has included new restrictions on Cuban Americans' ability to visit or send money to family members in Cuba, and this has resulted in greater political activism. Today, Miami's Cuban community is split on the issue of keeping or ending the embargo.

OTHER LATINO GROUPS While Miami has been hailed as the "Gateway to Latin America" since Franklin D. Roosevelt's time, the waves of newcomers from Cuba have secured its status as the gateway to the United States for Latino people throughout the Americas.

For most, the right to remain in the United States has depended on the Immigration and Naturalization Service's rules about refugees. People who make it to dry land, rather than being intercepted at sea, are allowed to file claims for refugee status. They are required to prove that they did not simply come to the United States for economic opportunities and that their lives would be in danger if they returned to their country of origin. Except for Cubans (who can't be deported without the Cuban government's consent), most claims for refugee status are ultimately denied, but claimants can stay until a hearing is held on their case, usually after many months. During the waiting period, many people simply disappear into the underworld of undocumented workers. If refugee status is granted and a person remains in the United States long enough to obtain permanent residency, he or she may be able to sponsor relatives who also wish to come to the United States.

Whether people of a given nationality are granted refugee status has generally depended on U.S. foreign policy. For instance, during the 1980s guerrilla wars in Central America, many refugees from communist Nicaragua were accepted, while applicants from El Salvador were routinely rejected because the U.S. supported that country's government. Undeterred, legally or illegally, tens of thousands of people fled to Miami to escape the violence in both countries as well as Guatemala and Colombia.

Since the 1990s, the largest influx of Spanish-speaking newcomers to Miami has been from South American countries. Like the first wave of Cubans, these pseudo-refugees have usually been educated and wealthy. They have also tended to be young.

The biggest influx came in 2000 to 2002, when Argentina was in the throes of collapse. Since Argentina was a participant in the U.S. Visa Waiver Program and its citizens could enter the country as tourists without prior approval, thousands of Argentineans wishing to sit out the depression in comfort flew to Miami and simply did not leave when their tourist cards expired. If apprehended by the INS, they found someone among Miami's army of immigration lawyers to keep postponing their deportation hearings. The situation became so critical that in February 2002 Argentina was removed from the Visa Waiver Program, but by that time many Argentineans had bought second homes and businesses in Miami and simply adopted a migratory lifestyle, returning to Argentina every few months and re-entering the U.S. under a new tourist visa. The Argentinean experience has inspired similar waves of Venezuelan and, most recently, Brazilian immigrants.

> Today, non-Cuban Latinos account for about 20 percent of Miami's population (the same as Anglos). The fact that Spanish is spoken more widely than English in Miami-Dade County makes the city doubly attractive to both legal and illegal Latino immigrants.

HAITIAN INFUSION Since 1980, the largest group of immigrants to put down roots in Miami has been the Haitians. They have often been a source of controversy since they began arriving by the thousands in rickety, handmade wooden boats, many dying during the crossing. Haitian refugees have generally not been treated as well as Cubans. Although Haiti has been run by dictators at least as brutal as the one in Cuba, the official attitude has been that Haitians are fleeing from poverty rather than communism and are therefore "economic refugees," not entitled to asylum in the United States.

Yet they arrived in overwhelming numbers. In 1986, Congress passed the Haitian Act, granting amnesty—legal forgiveness and permission to stay in the U.S. indefinitely and apply for citizenship—to all Haitians who had lived here for four years or more or were illegally working in agriculture. The law also let Haitians bring their relatives into the country under certain circumstances. Fifty-thousand Haitians—almost all of them in Miami and rural South Florida, were legalized. Neither the U.S. amnesty nor democratic elections in Haiti did much to quell the flow of Haitian boat people to the shores of Biscayne Bay.

Today, just about everyone in Miami has a strong opinion one way or the other about the fact that if a Cuban boat person wades ashore on Miami Beach, he can stay, but if a Haitian boat person wades ashore on the same beach, he is sent back where he came from. Meanwhile, in the poverty-stricken streets of Little Haiti, they paint the modest shops and bungalows crayon colors, and fuse Caribbean Creole flavor into the area. Signs of "Bienvenue!" (Welcome!) greet visitors.

OTHER RECENT IMMIGRANTS Besides influxes from the Caribbean and Latin America, Miami has been a favorite choice for people from other parts of the world. In the months before Hong Kong was turned over to China, many wealthy Hong Kong businesspeople bought second homes and businesses in Miami just in case they decided to leave their own country for good. Similarly, many Middle Easterners with money invest in a Miami residence as insurance against the possibility of war at home. And Miami has always been a top choice for Europeans moving to the United States or just migrating here for the winter. After the fall of the Soviet Union, Miami attracted a large percentage of the Russian immigrants who chose to exercise their newfound right to move to another country, and today there are neighborhoods in northern Miami-Dade County where you'll only hear Russian spoken.

FOUR

Miami Beach

A history of sudden transitions has brought Miami Beach, the fully urbanized barrier island along Miami's Atlantic coast, to its present trendy state, where a glamourous veneer overshadows a vibrant immigrant Latino community and a noirish underbelly of dark alleys and neon lights. Part resort, part art district, part high-fashion scene, part slum, all exciting, the Beach is like no place else on earth.

Miami Beach residents still refer to the era from the mid-1930s to the late 1950s as "the heyday." And what a time it was! Squint your eyes as you stroll down Ocean Drive and you can almost imagine that you've stumbled into the set for a Busby Berkeley musical, where chic women wearing evening gowns and diamond tiaras peer from the portholes and ribbon windows of the streamlined, moderne-style hotels, awaiting their cues to emerge on the arms of tuxedoed gentlemen. Such was the glamour of Old Miami Beach that Jackie Gleason and Arthur Godfrey proclaimed it to early-day television audiences as "the sun and fun capital of the world."

But times change. A new generation of vacationers shunned Old Miami Beach, seeing the grand old art deco hotels as decaying monuments to bad taste. The heyday was long gone by 1980, when the "freedom flotilla" brought a new wave of Cuban refugees to the Miami area. Many of the immigrants, known as Marielitos because they had arrived via the massive refugee boatlift from Cuba's Mariel Harbor, moved into the crumbling structures of the art deco district, where rents were cheap. Today Cuban expatriates make up three-fourths of Miami Beach's population.

With the Latinization of Miami Beach, people with money from Latin America began flocking to the area on shopping sprees, and economically distressed Lincoln Road converted almost overnight into a mall of shops selling discount appliances, consumer electronics and other "American" goods, many of them imported from Asia. (A few such shops remain today, though you'll find many more in downtown Miami.) But by the late 1980s, economic recessions in many Latin American countries had greatly reduced the shopping stampede.

Cheap rents and an easygoing, supportive atmosphere made Old Miami Beach a haven for artists. For several years, the storefronts along Lincoln Road became live-in studios for painters, musicians, dancers and underground newspaper publishers; open drug dealing spread along Ocean Drive and Collins Boulevard; and homeless people pitched camp along the dwindling beach, which itself was slowly washing out to sea. Meanwhile, the U.S. Army Corps of Engineers laid the groundwork for a tourist revival by dredging sand from the sea floor to restore and widen the beach—making it very wide indeed.

With the enormously popular television series "Miami Vice," director Michael Mann introduced a national audience to a version of Miami Beach that didn't really exist at the time, a world of supersaturated tropical pastels and neon where cops drove sports cars and drug kingpins rubbed shoulders with fashion models under the palm trees at open-air cafés. It became a self-fulfilling prophecy. Investors poured onto the beach, buying up old deco buildings that were now viewed as historic, raising the rents as much as 500 percent to drive the artists out and refurbishing the historic structures into hotels and clubs much posher than they had ever been during the heyday. Celebrities and fashion figures, from Madonna to Gianni and Donatella Versace, laid down roots along Ocean Drive. A lively and highly visible gay community sprang up overnight. Soon, major resort hotel chains were demolishing historic buildings that were too decrepit to save and replacing them with highrise neo-deco towers along the oceanfront.

Today, Miami Beach is divided into two or three districts, depending on who you talk to. Locals have traditionally considered Lincoln Road Mall, the pedestrians-only boulevard between 15th and 17th streets, to be the divide between action-packed South Beach and the more staid North Beach. Officially, South Beach now includes everything north to 23rd Street and is reached from the mainland by the MacArthur and Venetian causeways; Central Miami Beach is between 23rd and 63rd streets, reached by the Julia Tuttle Causeway; and North Beach is from 63rd Street to 87th Terrace, reached by the John F. Kennedy Causeway. (To confuse matters, Miami has another municipality called North Miami Beach farther up the coast adjacent to North Miami, but it has nothing to do with Miami Beach and is on the Inland Waterway, not the ocean.)

South Beach

During the building boom of the late 1920s and early '30s, South Miami Beach became flush with an architectural rage called streamlined moderne. These geometric, art deco buildings popped up on every street corner and were soon the neighborhood's mainstay. Now, 80 square blocks—bordered roughly by the ocean, Lenox Court, 5th Street and 23rd Street—bulge with more than 800 historic buildings, making this the most concentrated historic district in the nation.

These days, South Beach is experiencing a grand revival of the 1930s and '40s. This oceanside necklace of pastel-coated buildings, breezy alfresco cafés and palm tree–studded sidewalks is foremost a traveler's fairy-tale world.

SIGHTS

The deco beauties of South Beach frequently star in television shows and commercials. European modeling firms, also taking advantage of the artsy surroundings, fill up several hotels during the winter months while filming.

The touristic epicenter of South Beach—so congested with traffic, beachgoers and clubgoers that many locals avoid it completely—is **Ocean Drive**, flanked by nonstop neon on one side and the beach on the other. The ten-block stretch between 5th and 15th streets is lined with distinctively tropical deco hotels and cafés. Notice the ornate mansion at 1116 Ocean Drive. A replica of Christopher Columbus' house in Santo Domingo, Hispaniola (now the Dominican Republic), it was a low-rent apartment building known as the Amsterdam Palace before the late fashion designer Gianni Versace bought it in 1992 and converted it into a vacation home. (He was murdered there five years later.)

A favorite of film crews is **Española Way** (between Washington and Drexel avenues). Walk this whimsical way and you will discover a Disneyesque vision of peach Mediterranean buildings, colorful striped canopies, wrought-iron balconies and arched windows—all framed by palm trees and gas lamps. Along the way are marvelous vintage clothing nooks, an alfresco café and galleries where you're apt to find artists at work.

Founded in 1922 by settlers who envisioned a Spanish-themed artists' colony, the area never really took off. Locals will tell you, though, how Desi Arnaz started the rumba craze on this very street. Restoration has lent a magical look to the street.

Just around the corner, eye-catching cameo embellishments adorn the lobby of the **Crobar**. The district's premier theater drew jetsetters to international films when it opened in 1938. As fate would have it, the venue has turned into a popular nightspot. Closed Tuesday and Wednesday. ~ 1445 Washington Avenue; 305-531-8225, fax 305-531-7736; www.crobar.com, e-mail info@crobar.com.

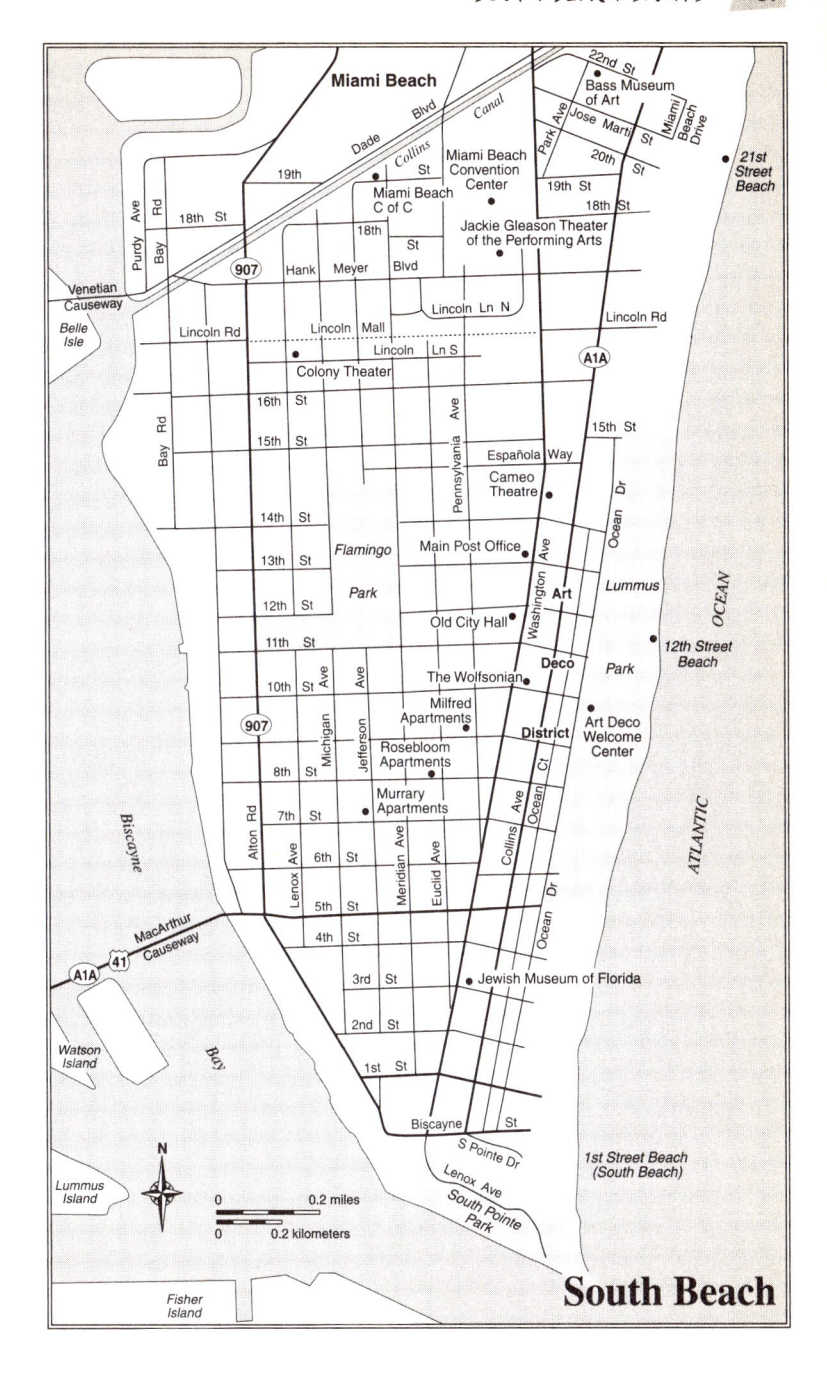

SOUTH BEACH SIGHTS

South Beach

WALKING TOUR
Deco Delights

Art deco defines Miami's architectural ambience. Flourishing from the 1930s through the 1950s, art deco is characterized by elegant sweeping curves and surprising whimsical touches. Today, more than 800 buildings throughout Miami Beach are on the National Register of Historic Places—the first 20th-century buildings to be so honored. To best absorb South Beach's deco heritage, stroll down Ocean Drive between 6th and 23rd streets. Like a decorated candy store, this beachfront roadway brims with sherbet-colored hotels and cafés that snatch continuous ocean breezes.

PARK CENTRAL HOTEL True to deco style, this is a powder-blue-and-white three-building study in geometrics. The 1937 beauty is adorned with fluted eaves, octagonal windows and dramatic vertical columns. For a peek at South Beach life in the '30s, check out the black-and-white photographs in the hotel lobby. ~ 640 Ocean Drive; 305-538-1611; www.theparkcentral.com.

BEACON HOTEL Parapets climb the facade and thin racing stripes slip around the sides of this 1936 building. ~ 720 Ocean Drive; 305-674-8200; www.beacon-hotel.com.

BEACH PATROL STATION The monolithic date and temperature sign at 1001 Ocean Drive still spits out the numbers, as it has since the 1930s. Rooted firmly in the sand next to the station, the sign is a classic. Also check out the funky lifeguard station, a nautical design that sent girls swooning in those days. Located inside the Oceanfront Auditorium, the **Miami Design and Preservation League** and the **Art Deco Welcome Center** can supply maps and information. A one-and-a-half-hour

One of the grandest deco buildings, the 1928 **Main Post Office** is crowned by a marble-and-stained-glass lantern. Light streams inside through the glass, reflecting on rich murals and bronze grillwork that creep up a vast rotunda. ~ 1300 Washington Avenue; 305-672-2447.

Also in the government district, **Old City Hall** asserts its presence with an eight-story neoclassical tower, one of the tallest in these parts. Mediterranean in style, this 1927 building has column-studded corridors that brood with history. ~ 1130 Washington Avenue.

guided walking tour is available Wednesday through Sunday. ~ 1001 Ocean Drive; 305-672-2014, fax 305-672-4319; www.mdlp.org, e-mail visit@mdpl.org.

CLEVELANDER HOTEL   Is it a spaceship or a big awning for the car? The "flying saucer sculptures" here look pretty hokey now, but in 1938 they were the rage. Besides, guests at the bar still use them as sunshields. A shady situation, indeed. ~ 1020 Ocean Drive; 305-531-3485; www.clevelanderhotel.com.

CASA CASUARINA   Typical of the Mediterranean architecture sprinkled throughout the area, this majestic building is marked by a marble sculpture of "Kneeling Aphrodite." The three-story manor is the only private home on Ocean Drive. The site of the late designer Gianni Versace's murder, it attracts hordes of morbidly curious visitors. This architectural wonder is fashioned after the Dominican Republic's Alcazar de Colón, which was home to the son of Christopher Columbus. ~ 1116 Ocean Drive; 305-672-6004.

THE CARLYLE   Pink and peach, the nearby Carlyle forms an impressive series of curves, vertical columns and dramatic circular overhangs called "eyebrows." Built in 1941, it is currently being renovated. ~ 1250 Ocean Drive.

CARDOZO HOTEL   Next door, preening with symmetrical cantilevers and precise strokes of cream paint and named after 1930s Supreme Court Justice Benjamin Cardozo, the hotel was featured in the 1996 film *The Birdcage* with Robin Williams and in the 1959 film *A Hole in the Head* starring Frank Sinatra, who was once a regular around South Beach. ~ 1300 Ocean Drive; 305-535-6500; www.cardozohotel.com.

The **Wolfsonian** exhibits an incredible collection of decorative, advertising and propaganda art. Over 70,000 American and European objects produced between 1885 and 1945 are housed in this Florida International University–affiliated museum and study center. A definite stop for art deco and streamliner-era aficionados. Closed Wednesday. Admission. ~ 1001 Washington Avenue; 305-531-1001, fax 305-531-2133; www.wolfsonian.org.

A few blocks south, the MacArthur Causeway leaves South Beach for downtown Miami, passing through Watson Island on the way. This island is home to two noteworthy attractions. More than 1000 beautiful but noisy birds reside at **Parrot Jungle Island**, a classic Miami tourist attraction that opened in 1936. Here parrots reside among 18 acres of tropical foliage and ponds, performing tricks and posing for curious sightseers. A variety of shows feature monkeys, parrots and reptiles—be sure to check out the trained bird performer. Admission. ~ 1111 Parrot Jungle Trail; 305-258-6453, fax 305-400-7290; www.parrotjungle.com, e-mail guestrelations@parrotjungle.com.

Also on Watson Island, **The Miami Children's Museum** is a magical place where children of all ages can play, learn and create. The 56,500-square-foot facility includes 12 galleries, classrooms, an educational gift shop and a 200-seat auditorium. There are hundreds of interactive exhibits and camps tailored to the museum's themes—art, community, communication and culture. Admission. ~ 980 MacArthur Causeway; 305-373-5437, fax 305-373-5431; www.miamichildrensmuseum.org.

Back in South Beach, the **Jewish Museum of Florida** records Jewish life in Florida since 1763. Photos, artifacts, changing exhibits, films and a time line are presented in this museum. The building itself, a restored 1936 synagogue, is on the National Register of Historic Places and features art deco chandeliers. Closed Monday and on Jewish holidays. Admission. ~ 301 Washington Avenue; 305-672-5044; www.jewishmuseum.com, e-mail admin@jewishmuseum.com.

Farther south on **Washington Avenue** lies a strip that, the city will tell you, is "primed" for redevelopment. In other words, the shops are run-down and rows of frame homes haven't seen a coat of fresh paint in years. Still, this area offers a slice of local life. Crusty old Cuban men shoot the breeze on their front porches while dogs laze around the sidewalks. Friendly merchants chat in Spanish to shoppers, pushing specials of the day.

To see neighborhood restoration at its best, head east a block and navigate **Pennsylvania**, **Euclid** and **Jefferson avenues**. Quiet and very intimate, these roadways are rimmed with century-old oaks, massive banyans and flourishing seagrapes. The true colors, though, emanate from the charming deco homes and quaint apartment buildings. Distinct strokes of paint—namely, turquoise, pale yellow, salmon and seafoam green—have been carefully applied to cantilevers and parapets, creating a soothing visual effect. For example, try driving by the **Milfred Apartments** (936 Pennsylvania Avenue), **Rosebloom Apartments** (820 Euclid Avenue) and **Murray Apartments** (750 Jefferson Avenue).

A bit farther north, you'll find the **Jackie Gleason Theater of the Performing Arts,** where Miami's favorite entertainer broadcast his national television series. Another deco design, the 2705-seater has a sleek, rounded facade and serves as the venue for Broadway series performances and major ballet and symphony events. ~ 1700 Washington Avenue; 305-673-7300, fax 305-538-6810; www.gleasontheater.com.

If it's a cloudy day, you might stop off at the **Bass Museum of Art.** A streamlined marble motif, the two-story cultural house contains a limited collection of sculptures, period furniture and objets d'art. More interesting, though, are the rotating contemporary European and American exhibits as well as historic international art. The museum also features a media center and a terrace café. Closed Monday. Admission. ~ 2121 Park Avenue; 305-673-7530, fax 305-673-7062; www.bassmuseum.org, e-mail info@bassmuseum.org.

LODGING

Prices remain at a premium at most Miami Beach highrise hotels. The trick here is not so much where you stay but when. During the summer months, when temperatures soar, hotel rates plummet as much as 50 percent. One exception is South Beach, where a revival of 1930s architecture has spawned small-scale

AUTHOR FAVORITE

The low-key tone at the high-end **National Hotel** is worth a big chunk of my vacation stash. Oh, there may be a celeb or two checking in, but no hoopla. Just an air of calm inside this restored 1940s deco den with lots of original furnishings, including re-upholstered barrel chairs in the lobby and lounge and a 16-arm Roy France chandelier in the oval dining room. My favorite corner of The National universe, though, is the palm-lined infinity pool with a grassy piazza for sunbathing and Miami Beach waiting a few yards beyond. Lincoln Road Mall lies a few blocks outside the front door. The only downside here: the service can range from nonexistent to downright surly. But, hey, this is South Beach. ~ 1677 Collins Avenue; 305-532-2311, fax 305-534-1426; www.nationalhotel.com, e-mail concierge@nationalhotel.com. ULTRA-DELUXE.

hotels with real character. Be prepared, however: The elegant exterior of all deco hotels belies the tiny size of their guest quarters.

The **Park Central Hotel** evokes a real sense of the area's past. An art deco favorite, this 1937 moderne palace is chock full of wonderful black-and-white photos of old Miami. New life has been breathed into the antique terrazzo floors and mahogany ceiling fans throughout the lobby. There are 127 guest rooms—many with ocean views—that are far from fancy; restored '30s furniture and spotless white walls display special care. ~ 640 Ocean Drive; 305-538-1611, 800-727-5236, fax 305-534-7520; www.thepark central.com, e-mail info@theparkcentral.com. ULTRA-DELUXE.

Slipped into one of South Beach's hottest beachfront blocks, **Casa Grande** is as soothing as its neighborhood is hopping. Amid the lobby's softly lit recesses are intimate seating areas and soft seagrass mats to cushion your feet. This Mediterranean-style confection has 34 studios and suites with a primitive chic look: rich Indonesian mahogany and teak furnishings, batik-shaded lamps and French- and Italian-tile floors. Full kitchens are an added perk. Casa Grande is sought out by celebrities, so keep out a careful star watch. ~ 834 Ocean Drive; 305-672-7003, 866-420-2272, fax 305-673-3669; www.casagrandehotel.com, e-mail sales@casagrandehotel.com. ULTRA-DELUXE.

The Clevelander offers a dose of déjà vu; no place else has provided the background for so many fashion shoots, beer commercials and "Miami Vice" reruns. Located next door to the Versace mansion, the hotel is as centrally located as you can get on South Beach's party-all-night Ocean Drive. A historic (and rowdy) swimming pool and no less than five bars on the premises including a sports bar and a hip-hop disco help protect you against a restful night's sleep, but the simple rooms with their dark window shades to keep the daylight at bay are ideal for those who want a convenient place to pass out after all-night partying. No guests under 21. ~ 1020 Ocean Drive; 305-531-3485, fax 534-4707; www.cleve lander.com, e-mail info@clevelander.com. MODERATE.

Beautiful European models frequently stay at the **Cavalier** while filming television commercials. This hostelry features a lobby with mirrored walls, green marble fireplace, dramatic ceilings and wrought-iron couches. The 45 oversized rooms and suites contain a unique combination of period furnishings and high-tech portable phones. ~ 1320 Ocean Drive; 305-531-3555, fax 305-531-5543; www.cavaliermiami.com, e-mail julia@cava liermiami.com. DELUXE.

You'll find a chic crowd at the **Cardozo Hotel**, which is full of romantic decor. The streamlined 1939 design and three floors of sleek cantilevers and delicate strokes of paint have served as a location for films including *A Hole in the Head*, *The Bird Cage* and *There's Something About Mary*. Rooms feature cherry-wood floors, terra-cotta walls and custom wrought-iron furniture. The hotel is owned by singer Gloria Estefan. ~ 1300 Ocean Drive; 305-535-6500, 800-782-6500, fax 305-532-3563; www.cardozohotel.com, e-mail reservations@cardozohotel.com. DELUXE TO ULTRA-DELUXE.

> Just one block from Ocean Drive are two parking garages at the corners of 7th Street/Collins Avenue and 14th Street/Collins Avenue.

Can't get enough neo-deco trendiness? Then the **Royal Hotel** is likely to light you up in neon. Contrasting with the garish-hued lobby, the 42 rooms are bright white plastic and marble accented with subtle shades of lilac, mint, tangerine and baby blue. Curvy beds have headboards that double as bars, complete with stools. Other appointments include computer/TV chaise longues and Italian marble baths. There's a second-floor sundeck with a great city view. ~ 758 Washington Avenue; 305-673-9009, 888-394-6835, fax 305-673-9244; www.royalhotelsouthbeach.com, e-mail info@royalsouthbeach.com. MODERATE.

One of the country's busiest youth hostels has an art deco address and a pretty peach Mediterranean building. At **Clay Hotel Hostelling International—Miami Beach**, wrought-iron balconies buzz with people-watchers, and the lobby is a flurry of activity. A 1920 amalgamation of painted cinderblock and dramatic cantilevers, the stopover is two blocks from the ocean and shares quarters with the Clay Hotel. The hotel offers 120 sparse but tidy private rooms, while the hostel has separate dormitories for men and women with 200 beds. Kitchen facilities provided. ~ 1438 Washington Avenue; 305-534-2988, 800-379-2529, fax 305-673-0346; www.clayhotel.com, e-mail info@clayhotel.com. BUDGET TO MODERATE.

Haute hotelier Ian Shrager's white deco palace by the sea, **The Delano**, is a fantasy fling. An enormous lamp shade hovers over the front desk; a Dali-designed seat with high-heel shoes as feet decorates the "living room" lobby. Outdoors, the "orchard" and "water salon" are Alice in Wonderland places where palm trees parade and grounds are laid with a brass bed, a full-length mirror and a human-sized chess set. Take a seat at the table for two *in* the swimming pool, or at one of the white-cushioned loungers that crowd against its sides. Also on the grounds is Aqua, a rooftop bathhouse where people can indulge in massage, meditation, and other mind- and body-altering therapies. Rooms and suites are all-white affairs—stylish but spare. Go for a spacious poolside bungalow fashioned like those in Beverly Hills. ~ 1685 Collins Avenue; 305-672-2000, 800-555-5001, fax 305-673-0888; www.morganshotelgroup.com, e-mail delano.reservations@morganshotelgroup.com. ULTRA-DELUXE.

Chic and affordable blend together in the **Abbey Hotel**, located just north of South Beach's trendy club area in slightly more peaceful Collins Park. The 50 rooms and suites in this vintage art deco hotel were completely renovated in 2000 in unique decor schemes that range from warm pastel pinks to minimalist black-and-white furnishings set off by burlap-brown walls. A rooftop deck and lounge affords a verdant view of the park around the nearby Bass Museum. ~ 300 21st Street; 305-531-0031, 888-612-2239, fax 305-672-1664; www.abbeyhotel.com, e-mail info@abbeyhotel.com. MODERATE TO DELUXE.

DINING

To dine in South Beach is to relive the fabulous '30s and '40s. Artfully restored pastel buildings provide fairy-tale enclaves for breezy sidewalk cafés and intimate indoor eateries that stretch for 20 blocks along South Miami Beach.

When **Joe's Stone Crab** opened in 1913, it cornered the market on stone crabs, and little has changed since. The local institution at the southern foot of Miami Beach has infamously long lines. Hungry diners allow bibs to be tied around their necks and

AUTHOR FAVORITE

Part of the reason I like to grab an avocado chicken club sandwich or an Asian salad at the **Nexxt Cafe** is historical: of all the European-style sidewalk cafés that line Lincoln Road Mall, the Nexxt was the first. Part of the reason, too, is that the café provides a front-row seat for some of the best people-watching in south Florida. The service can be less than prompt, but the food is worth waiting for and the prices surprisingly affordable. ~ 700 Lincoln Road; 305-532-6643. MODERATE.

subsequently feast on succulent Florida stone crabs dipped in mustard sauce and served with family-portioned hashbrown potatoes. Miamians insist Joe's serves the best Key lime pie in the United States. Since stone crabs are only available mid-October through May, Joe's is usually closed during the summer. No lunch on Sunday or Monday. ~ 11 Washington Avenue; 305-673-0365, fax 305-673-0295; www.joesstonecrab.com, e-mail qanda@joes stonecrab.com. BUDGET TO ULTRA-DELUXE.

In a city where Thai restaurants tend to be average at best, **Royal Thai Kitchen** stands out. The little dining room is stunning with elaborately carved teak tables under glass. The menu is loaded with ginger and curry dishes (the grouper curry deserves high marks) as well as house specialties such as pad thai. Best of all, any dish can be ordered from mild to sizzling hot. ~ 947 Washington Avenue; 305-534-1504, fax 305-534-0916. BUDGET TO MODERATE.

An annual entry on lists of Miami's best restaurants, **Osteria Del Teatro** is a bona fide South Beach tradition. Visiting luminaries and local glitterati vie for the dozen tables and feast on poached stuffed salmon with stone crab and a citrus sauce, hat-shaped ravioli and grilled portobello mushrooms. Reservations are often needed weeks in advance during the winter peak season. Dinner only. Closed Sunday. ~ 1443 Washington Avenue; 305-538-7850, fax 305-534-7887. ULTRA-DELUXE.

Yuca—the name refers both to the tropical root vegetable and to the Young Upscale Cuban Americans who adore the restaurant's inventive cuisine. This mix of new American and Cuban cooking, or "nuevo Cubano," has produced inspiring dishes such as sweet plantains stuffed with cured beef, baby back ribs with spicy guava sauce and braised oxtail in a red wine sauce. ~ 501 Lincoln Road; 305-532-9822, fax 305-673-8276; www.yuca.com, e-mail info@yuca.com. DELUXE TO ULTRA-DELUXE.

La Sandwicherie is a local institution that draws huge crowds of beach- and club-goers alike, thanks to a winning formula of great food offered anytime of the day. As South Beach's only walk-up gourmet sandwich bar, it remains open from 8 a.m. to 5 a.m. Sandwiches are custom-made using fresh, imported ingredients like crusty french bread, brie, *saucisson sec* and salty *cornichons*. Vegetarian ingredients abound. ~ 229 14th Street; 305-532-8934, fax 305-531-9883; www.lasandwicherie.com. BUDGET.

Chefs Andrea Curto and Frank Randazzo ran competing South Beach restaurants until they decided to get married and open their own joint venture. The result is **Talula**, a bistro which local food critics hail as Miami's best, thanks to their "creative American cuisine." American . . . well, maybe; creative, for sure. Try the crispy soft-shell crab, the grilled quail crusted with a cascabel pepper rub or the diced ahi tuna sizzled in chili oil and topped with trout caviar. Dining alone? Check out the row of counter stools in the rear, which offer front-row seating to watch the action in the open kitchen—one of the best dinner shows in town. ~ 210 23rd Street; 305-672-0255, fax 305-672-0768; www.talulaonline.com. DELUXE.

HIDDEN ▶

Want to see the priciest eatery in Florida? It's **Flute**, a champagne bar that gives conspicuous consumption a whole new meaning. The menu consists almost entirely of the finest caviars—beluga, osetra, sevruga, and more—and a dinner-size sampler plate can run $400 to $600, not counting that $290 bottle of 1990 Dom Perignon. For dessert, there are creamy, frosted truffles flown in fresh from La Maison du Chocolat in Paris. Peek in the doorway; it will make a great story when you get home. Then wander up the beach in search of Cuban food, thinking how much beans and rice you could get for $600. ~ 500 South Pointe Drive; 305-674-8680; www.flutebar.com. ULTRA-DELUXE.

On the up-and-coming southern end of South Beach, **Nemo** has ultra-mod decor: chairs and tables done in metal geometrics, animal prints and zinc work. The open kitchen churns out lots of fresh seafood, wok-charred cuisine and sprout salad drenched in soy-lime vinaigrette. A must. ~ 100 Collins Avenue; 305-532-4550, fax 305-532-4187; www.nemorestaurant.com. MODERATE TO DELUXE.

Two blocks west of the ocean in lower South Beach, **Big Pink** is a hip interpretation of a cafeteria, serving gourmet versions of burgers and classic American comfort food. There's a Big Mac–style double burger served on a brioche with hand-cut french fries (your choice of Idaho, sweet potato or polenta). The tuna sandwich is a generous, soy-glazed portion of yellowfin slathered in wasabi mayonnaise. And the "TV dinners" are made from scratch in-house and served in compartmentalized stainless steel trays. ~ 157 Collins Avenue; 305-532-4700, fax 305-532-8982. MODERATE.

Grillfish offers a wide variety of fish dishes and homemade desserts at reasonable prices. Servers don't consider attitude a part of the job. Grilled fish is the specialty, but don't miss the mussels drenched in garlic sauce, the shrimp piccata, chicken and calamari specials and the ponderous choice of desserts. ~ 1444 Collins Avenue; 305-538-9908, fax 305-538-2203; www.grill fish.com. MODERATE.

Tamara is *the* place to go for a French fusion fix in sumptuous surroundings—glamourous red velvet lounge chairs, gleaming silverware and an intricate ceiling mosaic. Menu items include roasted scallops *à l'orange*, magret with *salade verte* and foie gras with caramelized pineapple and port. Dinner outside by the pool is a must. ~ National Hotel, 1677 Collins Avenue; 305-532-2311, fax 305-534-1426; www.nationalhotel. com. DELUXE TO ULTRA-DELUXE.

> There's a great newsstand inside the News Café that sells cigars, suntan lotions and the latest books on Miami.

Sharing the Delano hotel's chic all-white theme, the **Blue Door** is worth writing home about. Its French cuisine with a tropical twist isn't half bad, either, with dishes such as sea bass with sautéed cashews and crêpe soufflé. You can also expect sandwiches, vegetarian and pasta dishes, as well as breakfast staples. ~ The Delano, 1685 Collins Avenue; 305-674-6400, 800-555-5001, fax 305-674-5649; www.chinagrillmgt.com. ULTRA-DELUXE.

Joia is one of the toniest restaurants below 5th Street and its dining patio offers a breezy sanctuary from the Miami heat. The menu leans toward Japanese and Pacific fusion, with items such as river stone–seared Kobe beef and calamari tempura. The crowd is as stylish as the decor. ~ 150 Ocean Drive; 305-674-8871, fax 305-674-0936; www.joiamiami.com. DELUXE TO ULTRA-DELUXE.

The sidewalk fare at **A Fish Called Avalon** is fresh, imaginative and Floridian. From its art deco perch in the restored Avalon Hotel, this sleek eatery offers locally caught fish and shellfish fused with tropical fruits and vegetables. There's something new everyday, though you're apt to find Jamaican jerk grilled chicken served over roasted tomato grits or Guinness barbecued shrimp with saffron potatoes. Chicken and pasta dishes are also tops. White table linens create a minimalist mood that's appropriately beachy—and positively romantic on a windswept night. Live guitar entertainment nightly. Dinner only. ~ 700 Ocean Drive; 305-

532-1727, fax 305-913-6818; www.afishcalledavalon.com. DELUXE TO ULTRA-DELUXE.

At the 24-hour **News Café,** a rather bohemian crowd gathers to sip cappuccino and graze on deli sandwiches and flaky croissants. Serving three meals a day, they also have a full bar, a wine list and grill items. The small outdoor wooden tables and wrought-iron chairs create a perfect people-watching station. ~ 800 Ocean Drive; 305-538-6397, fax 305-538-7817; www.newscafe.com. BUDGET TO MODERATE.

HIDDEN ► For one of those "only in Miami" cultural dining experiences, drop in at **Tap Tap,** a colorful and lively Haitian restaurant in the heart of South Beach. The menu is packed with authentic fare such as *pwason gwosel* (fish in lime sauce), *griyo* (fried pork chunks) and *poul di* (baked chicken) with *kalalou* (okra). Don't worry—it's all delicious after you've knocked back a few *mojitos* with Haitian rum. A party atmosphere prevails here at all times, but the best is Thursday night, when there's live music. A former mayor of Port-au-Prince leads the house band. ~ 819 5th Street; 305-672-2898. MODERATE.

HIDDEN ► Few tourists find their way to **Joe Allen,** a local favorite tucked away under the Venetian Causeway in a gradually evolving former warehouse district. The restaurant's namesake also operates fine restaurants in New York, London, Paris and Ogunquit, Maine. The fare ranges from the mundane—cheeseburgers, pizza and no-fat chicken-vegetable stew—to more ambitious entrées like marinated skirt steak with *chimchurri* sauce and grilled marinated salmon with couscous, arugula and tomato. The decor is chic and modern, the atmosphere is welcoming and the staff is friendlier than is usually encountered in South Beach dining establishments. ~ 1787 Purdy Avenue; 305-531-7007, fax 305-531-7075; www.joeallenrestaurant.com. MODERATE.

> It took less than five years for South Beach to transform from a somewhat dangerous low-rent district to the current sleek urban resort town.

SHOPPING Throughout South Beach, threads of spiffy modern buildings shelter eclectic shops that are perfect for oceanside browsing. Without a doubt, shopping here is sheer entertainment.

Standing apart from the pack is a must in this town of sleek, beautiful people. Belinda Rogers can help you do so with her collection of one-of-a-kind dresses, tailor-made and dyed to your exact specifications. At **Belinda's Designs**, you'll revel in gauzy, fantasy dresses à la Stevie Nicks; you can augment your look with feathered boas, corsets, beaded clothing and flirtatious accessories. Closed Sunday. ~ 917 Washington Avenue; 305-532-0068; www.belindasdesigns.net.

Washington Avenue is quickly becoming the place to drop a buck. Vintage clothing and furniture shops and bohemian and ultra-hip boutiques line this noisy thoroughfare.

Uncle Sam's Music is an independent music store that serves soda, etc., with a music selection that leans heavily toward underground dance and house music. ~ 1141 Washington Avenue; 305-532-0973; www.unclesamsmusic.com.

Back in 1984, when South Beach was in the doldrums and a mostly deserted Lincoln Road Mall was being recolonized by artists in flight from the gentrification of their traditional haunts in Coconut Grove, a group of visual artists founded a cooperative to provide cheap studio and exhibit space in an abandoned department store. Today the **Art Center of South Florida** has grown into a 60,000-square-foot "incubator" that houses 52 artists' studios, chic exhibition galleries and art education classrooms. Everything is open to the public. ~ 800 Lincoln Road; 305-674-8278, fax 305-674-8772.

Walking up Lincoln Road Mall, you're bound to notice two countervailing trends in South Beach fashion: spectacularly bright colors versus stark black-and-white. For bright colors, check out **Britto Central**, the gallery of leading Brazilian painter and serigraph maker Romero Britto, whose works are explosions of saturated hues outlined in broad black lines for maximum effect. ~ 818 Lincoln Road; 305-531-8821. For black and white, visit **White House, Black Market**, where you'll find women's clothing and accessories as well as household furnishings. ~ 1106 Lincoln Road; 305-672-8006.

In keeping with its homage to its art deco past, South Beach has a remarkable number of vintage clothing stores. Among the best, according to buffs of old-fashioned fashion, is **Sasparilla**, where you'll find women's clothing and accessories dating back as far as the 1950s and '60s. Some items are affordable; others cost as much as brand-new designer outfits. ~ 1630 Pennsylvania Avenue; 305-532-6611.

Details is the king of Cool Stuff, packed with one-of-a-kind furniture and *haute maintenant* knickknacks. ~ 1711 Alton Road; 305-531-1325.

Pick up a good read at **Books & Books**, a well-stocked mart that stays open until midnight on weekends. ~ 933 Lincoln Road; 305-532-3222.

Another shopping street in South Beach is **Española Way**, an east–west, two-block-long collection of shops, cafés, boutiques and artists' studios. For international emollients, potions and salves, **South Beach Makeup** stocks body-care goodies from around the world and its own line of makeup. ~ 439 Española Way, Miami Beach; 305-538-0805.

NIGHTLIFE For the hottest nighttime action, head straight to South Beach. This beachside strand is the heart of Miami's entertainment scene. Here a bohemian mood has spawned blocks of avant-garde clubs as well as breezy sidewalk cafés. Most of the action is late-night, with many establishments staying open until dawn. The trend is toward alfresco jazz as well as the more unusual "progressive" clubs, which create a smaller rendition of New York City's avant-garde scene.

Crobar, a theater-turned-nightclub with state-of-the-art light shows, is the setting for high-energy dance, house and hip-hop

---

THE CAUSEWAYS

Dazzling by day and stunning at night, Miami's causeways regularly dispense intoxicating views of Biscayne Bay. In 1913, Miami pioneer John Collins completed the first bridge from downtown to Miami Beach. Now, the gleaming **Venetian Causeway** has taken its place and crosses six islands—San Marino Island, Dilido Island, Biscayne Island, San Marco Island, Belle Isle and Rivo Alto Island. Each with its place in the sun, they lie blanketed with plush residential areas. **MacArthur Causeway**, which joins South Beach with downtown, offers a worthwhile side trip to Watson Island. Here you can watch luxury cruise ships inch their way to and fro in the Port of Miami. The northern causeways, each with a different sumptuous view, are **Julia Tuttle**, **North Bay** (or John F. Kennedy) and **William Lehman**. To the south, **Rickenbacker Causeway** is endowed with two natural spectacles: gorgeous turquoise waters and thin strips of sugary sand. At the end are two more pots of gold—the smaller, less developed Virginia Key and larger Key Biscayne.

concerts. Closed Tuesday and Wednesday. ~ 1445 Washington Avenue; 305-531-8225, fax 305-531-8226; www.crobar.com.

South Beach's largest club, **Mansion**, offers house or hip-hop in one of its two venues. The 40,000-square-foot facility, originally a deco movie palace, features top-of-the-line sound. Cover. ~ 1235 Washington Avenue; 305-532-1525; www.mansionmiami.com.

One of the few jazz clubs on the beach, **Jazid** features live smoky jazz nightly in an intimate club in the thick of the South Beach scene. A teenybopper-free zone. Cover on weekends. ~ 1342 Washington Avenue; 305-673-9372.

A hip, brick-and-glass fandango sprawled on the southern tip of Miami Beach, **Penrod's** is a seafood grill. The adjacent **Nikki Beach Club** has different club nights. ~ 1 Ocean Drive; 305-538-1111; www.penrods.com.

The huge, open-air **Opium Garden** on the southernmost end of South Beach is the club favored by tourists, trendoids, the chicer-than-thous and locals who want to dance, dance, dance. The good news: plenty of nearby parking, a first-rate sound system and ample outdoor seating and darker, intimate areas. The bad news: the cover charge is a bit daunting and the club is a body jam on weekends. Closed Monday and Wednesday. Cover. ~ 136 Collins Avenue; 305-531-5535.

For a shot of South Beach surrealism, head to **Mac's Club Deuce**. Nowhere but here could you hope to see barflies and hipsters rubbing elbows with drag queens. It's a dive bar by South Beach standards—jukebox, pool tables, cheap drinks, cut-offs and cocktail dresses. ~ 222 14th Street; 305-673-9537, fax 305-531-6200. ◄ HIDDEN

THEATER, SYMPHONY AND DANCE For four years, Jackie Gleason broadcast his national television series from a Miami Beach theater. Reopened after an extensive facelift, the 2705-seat **Jackie Gleason Theater of the Performing Arts** offers Broadway musicals, stand-up comics, ballet, and Israeli and Latin dance. ~ 1700 Washington Avenue; 305-673-7300.

Built in 1934 by Paramount Studios, the 465-seat **Colony Theater** is a restored art deco beauty that hosts major ballet and symphony performances as well as contemporary dance and theater. Closed for renovations. ~ 1040 Lincoln Road; 305-674-1040.

To purchase tickets for major productions, call the theaters directly or check with **Ticketmaster** (305-358-5885) outlets.

BEACHES & PARKS

SOUTH POINTE PARK 🏊 🎣 ⛱ ♨ Cloaking the tail of South Miami Beach is this slice of close-cropped grass and meandering sidewalks. Situated near the Port of Miami, the park affords scenic views of cruise ship activity but unfortunately has a small beach. The best section leads around a jutting ledge of boulders and a 300-foot pier, where folks come to swim and snorkelers can explore colorful exotic fish. Just be careful of strong currents. Also, cruise ship traffic stirs up the water sometimes. Anglers fish from the pier or rocks for yellowtail, barracuda and snapper. To the north, the strand and highrises of Miami Beach provide an impressive panorama. Facilities include picnic pavilions and restrooms. ~ On the southern tip of Miami Beach, right off Washington Avenue; 305-673-7730, fax 305-673-7725.

1ST STREET BEACH OR SOUTH BEACH 🚲 🏊 ⛱ 🏄 There's no official name for this beach, but it's *the* sand spot in the Miami area. In fact, more people jam onto this one block of southern beach than in the next five blocks combined. A sprawling sports bar spawns all the action, which spills out over a sandy crest and down into the ocean. Volleyball competitions go on continuously, and loud bar music permeates the salty air. Adding a classy touch, a modern boardwalk winds down toward the ocean, where strong tradewinds and currents churn up great bodysurfing waves. Watercraft rentals are available. It's a good place to swim but it's usually crowded. Bathing suit tops are unofficially optional. ~ At the southernmost block of Miami Beach.

LUMMUS PARK 🚲 🏊 🎣 🏄 Not to be confused with the smaller Lummus Park in downtown Miami, this grassy palm tree plaza wanders along eight blocks of South Miami Beach. Fine white sand stretches 300 glorious feet to the translucent aquamarine ocean. Young Europeans and kite flyers favor this beach, and the stretch between 12th and 14th streets is very popular with the gay crowd. The best thing about the park is that South Beach lies across the street, beckoning beachgoers to its pastel sidewalk cafés. This beach has good windsurfing and excellent swimming; a sandbar extends about 50 yards out. Facilities include restrooms, lifeguards, a playground, shady park benches, a bandshell, bicycle and inline skating rentals, and food and drink vendors. If you hear funny noises above you, look carefully among the palm fronds to catch sight of the wild green parrots that make their home there. ~ On South Miami Beach, between 6th and 14th streets; 305-673-7714, fax 305-673-7717.

South Beach Gay Scene

As with the revitalization of so many historic communities across America—from Boston's South End to San Francisco's Castro District—South Beach owes the success of its amazing comeback to the gay community. Initial efforts to revitalize South Beach came from a mixed group of gay and straight preservationists who shared a love of the historic art deco architecture of the area, and the gay community's contribution had an important impact on the whole development of South Beach.

For this reason, South Beach is a universally gay-friendly destination where gay men and lesbians are woven into the fabric of everything that takes place. Ask any hotel if it's gay or gay-friendly and the man on the other end of the phone will probably laugh and, in the spirit of the old "I'm not gay, but my boyfriend is" joke, will respond with "the hotel isn't, but the staff and I are." In all seriousness, most if not all the hotels in South Beach are gay-friendly, as are the restaurants, shops, nightclubs and beaches.

As the community blossomed, the love of aesthetic beauty became the unifying force for many groups of people. The worldwide fashion industry adopted South Beach as its top shoot location, and beautiful models are seen everywhere. Even those South Beach residents who are not officially models are quite gorgeous. Some are gay, some are straight, but it seems everyone is trying hard to be beautiful—and most are succeeding!

Contrary to some reports, South Beach is not losing its gay identity by becoming "the trendiest community in America." It remains a gathering place, a spot where the gay traveler can come

IN THE KNOW

Gay travelers will find a wealth of information at the **Miami-Dade Gay and Lesbian Chamber of Commerce.** The friendly staff can offer insider tips on everything from where to sleep, eat and play in gay Miami. ~ 3510 Biscayne Boulevard; 305-573-4000, fax 305-751-0068; www.gaybizmiami.com, e-mail info@gogaymiami.com.

for a vibrant visit. From staying at its gay hotels and cruising its fashionable shopping areas to sunning on its gay beaches and dancing in its nightclubs, South Beach still deserves its playful reputation as "America's Gay Riviera."

LODGING Situated five blocks from the beach on a pretty residential street, **European Guesthouse** is a tropical inn for gay men and women, but it welcomes guests from all walks of life. Enveloped in palm trees and painted a sunny yellow, the 1923 wood plank house offers 12 modest rooms with eclectic but inviting decor: checkered floors, bahama fans, reproduction antique furniture and a queen- or king-size bed. There's plenty of privacy, particularly out back, where wood decks wind through a lush garden punctuated by a clothing-optional whirlpool. Rates include an all-you-can-eat buffet breakfast. Discounts are offered for three-night or longer stays. ~ 721 Michigan Avenue; 305-673-6665, fax 305-532-5316; www.europeanguesthouse.com, e-mail info@europeanguesthouse.com. MODERATE TO DELUXE.

HIDDEN ▶ For bed-and-breakfast accommodations consider the **Jefferson House**, set in a 1929 vintage home. Guests stay in a seven-room building, separated from the main house by a lush tropical garden and swimming pool, or in one of the three rooms in the main house. Each room comes with a private bath and is decorated with antique furniture and art deco pieces. A full gourmet breakfast is served on the terrace in the main house. Mostly men, but women are also welcome. ~ 1018 Jefferson Avenue; 305-534-5247, 877-599-5247, fax 305-534-5953; www.thejeffersonhouse.com, e-mail stay@thejeffersonhouse.com. DELUXE TO ULTRA-DELUXE.

To experience the true character of an art deco masterpiece, stay at **The Raleigh Hotel**, a chic 104-room establishment. Guest rooms and penthouse suites combine art deco antiques with the latest technology. Facilities include an award-winning restaurant, a swimming pool, a fitness center and a beach with water-sport facilities. ~ 1775 Collins Avenue; 305-534-6300, 800-848-1775, fax 305-538-8140; www.raleighhotel.com. ULTRA-DELUXE.

Located right in the hub of all the activity is the **Penguin Hotel**, a 44-room establishment that caters to gay men and women. The decor is tropical with a few art deco flourishes. ~ 1418 Ocean Drive; 305-534-9334, 800-235-3296, fax 305-604-0350; www.penguinhotel.com, e-mail info@penguinhotel.com. MODERATE.

For an upscale gay resort away from the hustle and bustle of South Beach, don't miss **Normandy South**. Set in a 1925 Mediterranean deco building located in Miami's upper-east side, this men-only guesthouse features eight spacious rooms and two one-bedroom private apartments. Most of the guest rooms have a private bath. A garden, swimming pool, steam room, workout area and jacuzzi are among the amenities. Clothing optional and nonsmokers only. ~ 575 Northwest 66th Street, Miami; 305-756-9894; www.normandysouth.com, e-mail normandyso@aol.com. MODERATE TO ULTRA-DELUXE.

DINING

The **11th Street Diner** is a favorite with late-night party- and club-goers, serving up old-fashioned diner fare 24 hours a day. It's hard to miss—look for a shiny, silver boxcar that was restored and placed on its Washington Avenue site in 1922. ~ Washington Avenue at 11th Street; 305-534-6373. BUDGET.

> One of the greatest attractions of 12th Street Beach is that South Beach, with its vibrant café scene, lies across the street.

Tucked away on Michigan Avenue, **Ice Box Café** is a hip little eatery that serves up creative Continental cuisine in a casual setting, stylish with simple, clean lines and a stainless-steel open kitchen. The eclectic menu changes daily but always includes fish specials and vegetarian options. On any given day, you might dine on French, Italian or even Asian entrées. A popular dish is grilled skirt steak with *chimichuri* sauce, an Argentinean specialty. Gourmet brunches are served on Saturday and Sunday. ~ 1657 Michigan Avenue; 305-538-8448, fax 305-538-6405; www.iceboxcafe.com. DELUXE.

A laidback dining established offering prime people-watching from its outdoor seating area, **Balans** offers a hodgepodge of international dishes: Asian-inspired Thai salads and crabcakes, fettuccini, British bangers and mash, lobster claws and burgers, among many others. The Alice in Wonderland–inspired decor features zebra-print ceilings, large mirrors throughout the restaurant, and frosted glass bathroom doors. ~ 1022 Lincoln Road; 305-534-9191; www.balans.co.uk. BUDGET TO DELUXE.

The Front Porch is a casual waterfront restaurant that features healthy fare. At breakfast, there are pancakes, omelettes and fresh juices. Lunch includes salads, sandwiches and soups. Turkey meatloaf served with homemade mashed potatoes is a dinner favorite. Most diners eat on the patio, which has delightful views of the ocean. ~ 1418 Ocean Drive; 305-531-8300. BUDGET TO MODERATE.

SHOPPING Although not technically located in South Beach, **Lambda Passages Bookstore** has a large selection of gay- and lesbian-oriented books and videos. ~ 7545 Biscayne Boulevard, Miami; 305-754-6900.

A casual men's clothing shop, **Whittall and Shon** has a clientele that is 80 percent gay. They stock funky hats, funky clothes and funky underwear. ~ 900 Washington Avenue #3; 305-538-2606; www.whittallshon.com.

For the crowd who chooses a canine as the ultimate accessory, the **Dog Bar** on Lincoln Lane is part pooch boutique, part pick-up place where dog owners sniff around for natural dog foods, homeopathic remedies, furniture and toys. ~ 723 North Lincoln Lane; 305-532-5654; www.dogbar.com.

> The Miami Moderne architectural style reflects the romantic vision of the future that originated after World War II and characterized Miami Beach's idea of the shape of things to come in the days of streamlined kitchen appliances and big cars with big tailfins.

NIGHTLIFE One of the beach's best late-night stops, **Twist** boasts no cover charge, a predominantly gay clientele and two floors that include a videobar, pinball machines, a pool table, a small dancefloor and a deejay who spins tunes nightly. Twist has male dancers seven nights a week, an amateur comedy show on Tuesday, complimentary barbecue on Friday starting at 6 p.m., and a drag show on Wednesday and Sunday. ~ 1057 Washington Avenue; 305-538-9478; www.twistsobe.com.

Muscle boys and club kids hang at **Score**, lavishing its dancefloor and five bars with fresh faces and fashion. Some of Miami's favorite deejays spin here; the club also features an attractive patio bar and sidewalk area. Drinks are pricey. Open daily from 3 p.m. to 5 a.m. Occasional cover. ~ 727 Lincoln Road; 305-535-1111; www.scorebar.net.

BEACHES & PARKS **12TH STREET BEACH** This stretch of sand, which is part of Lummus Park, is very popular with the gay crowd. It is a tranquil beach used mostly for bathing and swimming. Facilities include lounge chairs, umbrellas and volleyball nets. Lifeguards are on duty during daylight hours. ~ On South Miami Beach, between 12th Street and Ocean Drive; 305-673-7714, fax 305-673-7717.

21ST STREET BEACH ≈ A one-block enclave of granulated sand wedged between highrises, this spot is frequented by gay men and women. The city's prized two-mile boardwalk, which offers "unobstructed" ocean views behind formidable skyscrapers, commences here and travels northward along a ridge of sand dunes. Swimming is good at this beach, where there are usually lifeguards. The only other facilities are food vendors. ~ On South Miami Beach at 21st Street; 305-673-7714, fax 305-673-7717.

Central and North Beaches

This single stretch of beach—extending generally from 25th Street north to 87th Street—is what put Miami on the big resort map in the 20th century. A drive along the ocean here quickly reveals why. Still the nucleus of Miami's tourism, the area is concentrated with glistening highrise hotels, top-notch restaurants, an unusually wide swath of beach and miles of water on view everywhere.

Though parts of the area had declined during recent decades, a 1990s refurbishment has breathed new life into Central Miami Beach. Today it is quickly gentrifying into something that looks a lot like South Beach. North of the district, Collins Avenue is a virtual wall of freshly painted pastels. Midrise buildings are washed with peach and pink, purple and plum. Streamline eyebrow arches and balconies decorate their facades, and royal palms accent their feet. This is MiMO (Miami Moderne), the most recent historic architectural style recognized by the Miami Design Preservation League. Prime examples of this style are the Fontainebleau and Eden Roc hotels, as well as many condominium complexes in the Central and North Beach area.

SIGHTS

One neighborhood that's seen little change over the years is the one on **La Gorce Drive**. This one-mile jag, north of Arthur Godfrey Road, serves as the primary address for Miami Beach's old money. Here you'll encounter crisp white palatial homes, Mediterranean estates and loads of big, wispy Australian pine trees.

Down the street lies **The Neighborhood,** seven blocks of stores and apartments flanking Arthur Godfrey Road between Pine Tree Drive and Alton Road. This area also serves as a locus for the Hasidic Jewish community. More recently, young professionals have taken to this area, too, transforming many of the older, dilapidated buildings into quaint bungalows nestled along canals.

Queen of Miami Beach hotels, the **Fontainebleau Hilton** ruled the roost during the glitter days of the 1950s and '60s. With their backs to the street, the twin curved buildings have long promised exclusivity for those within their safe bounds. During the hotel's heyday, Bob Hope and Frank Sinatra frequently performed, and its impressive guest list included Joan Crawford, Joe DiMaggio, John F. Kennedy and Richard Nixon. But today, much of that glamour is gone. Its legendary show club, in fact, is now a cabaret with Las Vegas–style shows. But there's still an edge of opulence and nostalgia that makes visiting the Fontainebleau a must. ~ 4441 Collins Avenue; 305-538-2000, fax 305-674-4607; www.hilton.com, e-mail hhonors@hilton.com.

HIDDEN ▶ Populated by a clientele that runs the gamut in age, beauty and girth, the co-ed **Russian and Turkish Baths** is a cavernous succession of steam rooms and saunas (there's also a whirlpool). Treatments include massages and salt scrubs. A juice bar and a small Russian restaurant offer places for the pooped to recupe. Open daily until 11:30 p.m. Admission. ~ At the Castillo del Mar, 5445 Collins Avenue; 305-867-8313.

One especially lovely stretch of Miami Beach, **Indian Creek Drive**, meanders along a spectacular waterway where sparkling luxury houseboats are moored. Get a different perspective of the La Gorce Drive homes across the waterway, their sweeping, well-tended estates flirting with passersby.

Things head downhill here, as "condomania" begins appearing on Collins Avenue along the ocean (but you can't see the water). Blame greedy developers and poor-sighted politicians for this mess along Miami's pristine beach. The reason behind the madness? It provides thousands of people an ocean view while shutting out the rest of the world.

LODGING Towering hotels and condominiums create a virtual concrete wall eclipsing much of Miami's central coastline. If anyone intended to build a cozy motel along this stretch of beach, they never followed through.

A few blocks north of South Beach, you'll find the **Traymore Hotel**. It delights with its cream-colored facade and rows of pink ledges that seem to race around the building. Like many area

CENTRAL AND NORTH BEACHES LODGING

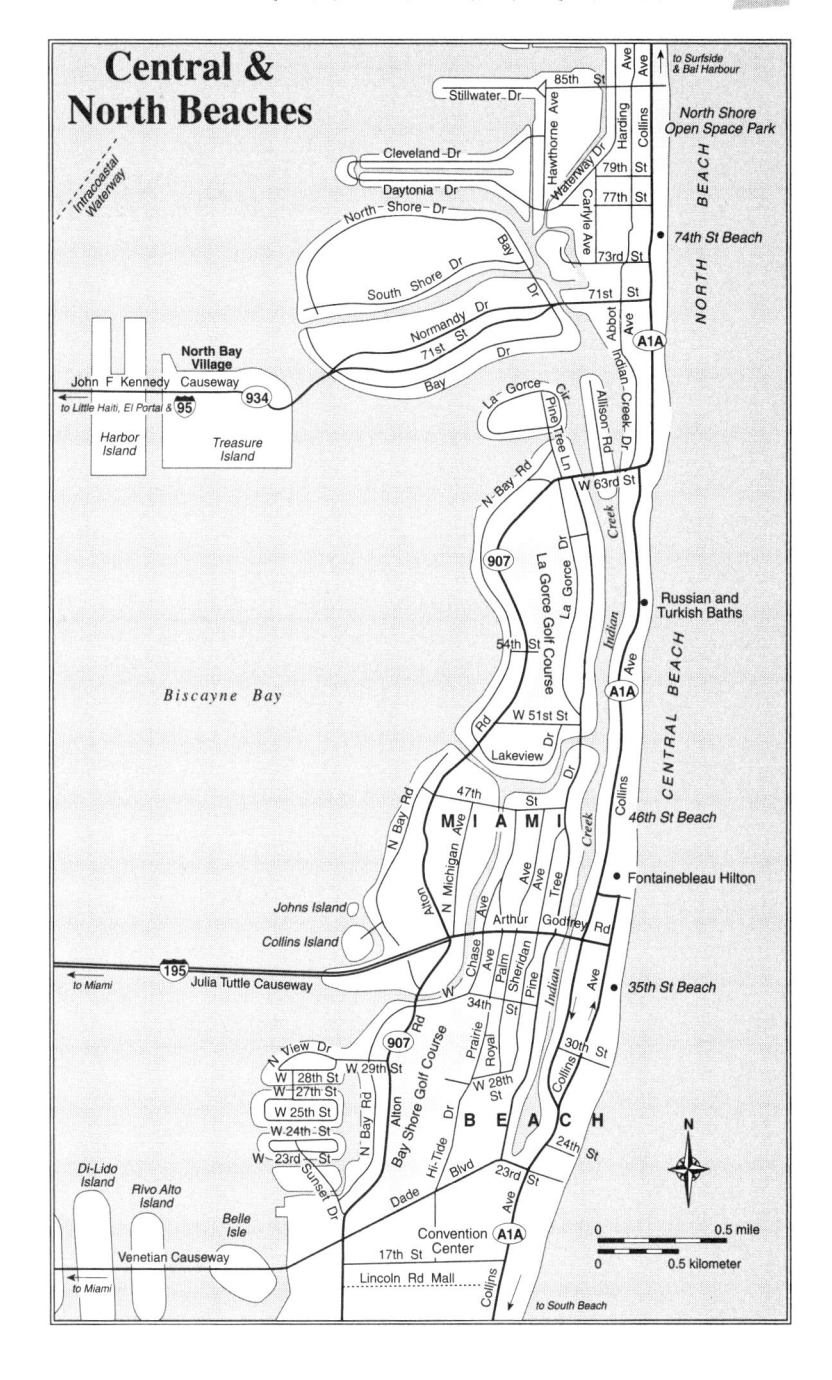

Central & North Beaches

hostelries, the eight-story Traymore has been nicely restored. Shiny terrazzo floors and vast Greek columns grace the lobby, while formica furnishings and pastel schemes adorn the modern rooms. Near the beach, a broad clay-tiled loggia surrounds a Mediterranean-style swimming pool. A free continental breakfast is available. ~ 2445 Collins Avenue; 305-534-7111, 800-445-1512, fax 305-538-2632; www.traymoresouthbeach.com, e-mail stay@traymore.com. ULTRA-DELUXE.

For ocean views at reasonable prices, it's tough to top the **Days Inn Oceanside**. Although it's next to a dingy building, the seven-story hotel saves face with its Grecian lobby and immaculate guest rooms. Amenities include a pool and restaurant. ~ 4299 Collins Avenue; 305-673-1513, 800-356-3017, fax 305-538-0727; www.charlesgrouphotels.net, e-mail reservations@cgh.com. DELUXE.

Restoration worked wonders for the 1950s-era **Best Western**, a classic Miami Beach highrise with a turquoise-and-white veneer. Things here aren't luxurious, but they are contemporary. Follow the marble floors, clusters of comfy couches and water fountains through the lobby, then take the elevator to any of 250 cheery guest rooms, decorated with modern oak furniture, wall-to-wall carpets and seaside paintings. A concrete pool and two restaurants round out the amenities. ~ 4333 Collins Avenue; 305-532-3311, 800-832-8332, fax 305-531-5296; www.bestwestern.com, e-mail lsierra@cghcorp.com. DELUXE.

Leading the pack of luxury highrises is the **Fontainebleau Hilton**, the signature address of Miami Beach. With 900 rooms and nearly as many employees, this place is a city unto itself (the Fontainebleau Tower, its 36-story highrise slated to open February 2005, will feature 460 luxury suites graced with balconies). Two curving, multistory buildings hug a half-mile of beach, creating an alcove for a series of pools with rushing water, hidden rocky caves and palm tree islands. The refurbished lobby, with floor-to-ceiling windows, gigantic crystal chandeliers and magnificent marble staircases, is more opulent than when the hotel opened in 1954. There are ten restaurants and lounges, but then who's counting? Guest rooms are furnished in contemporary Florida styles. The high-end tab is strictly for service and surroundings. ~ 4441 Collins Avenue; 305-538-2000, 800-548-8886, fax 305-535-3299; www.fontainebleauhilton.com. ULTRA-DELUXE.

Wooden cabañas and miles of poolside concrete harken back to the days when Jackie Gleason was a familiar face at the **Eden Roc**. Perched beachside, the T-shaped, 15-story hotel sports a rooftop fixture resembling a steamship visage. Underground shops and a terrazzo lobby with Moorish columns create a time-worn, campy aura. A health and fitness center includes an indoor climbing wall. Expect art-deco furnishings and extra-large closets in each of the 349 rooms. ~ 4525 Collins Avenue; 305-531-0000, 800-327-8337, fax 305-674-5555; www.edenrocresort.com, e-mail maria.cruz@renaissancehotels.com. ULTRA-DELUXE.

> A calm, shallow ocean shelf makes for excellent swimming at 46th Street Beach.

You can easily spot the **Wyndham Resort Miami Beach** by its stark black tower set against a wide spread of sand. Built in 1962, the posh complex has kept pace by adding an extensive fitness center and by refurbishing its 420 guest rooms in plush carpets and pastel colors. There's a heated Olympic-size swimming pool and—for those with bucks to burn—a helicopter pad. ~ 4833 Collins Avenue; 305-532-3600, 800-203-8368, fax 305-535-2787; www.wyndham.com, e-mail lperrino@wyndham.com. ULTRA-DELUXE.

Another beachfront establishment, **The Alexander Hotel** bears an edge of European refinement. The 150 one- and two-bedroom suites are beautifully and individually decorated in styles ranging from classic to modern, and all include full kitchens and wet bars. The private grounds are lush with swirling, boulder-lined pools and myriad flowering plants. ~ 5225 Collins Avenue; 305-865-6500, 800-327-6121, fax 305-341-6553; www.alexanderhotel.com. DELUXE TO ULTRA-DELUXE.

DINING

A palatial Miami institution, **The Forge** has long awed diners with its extravagant rococo designs and reverential Continental cuisine. Massive antique doors, polished brass statues, ten-foot chandeliers and carved wood mantels abound in the restaurant, converted from an actual forge in 1929. There's an out-of-this-world wine list. Reservations are required. Dinner only. ~ 432 Arthur Godfrey Road; 305-538-8533, fax 305-538-7733; www.theforge.com. DELUXE TO ULTRA-DELUXE.

Former Dolphins coach Don Shula operates **Shula's Steak House**, housed in a tony beachfront hotel in Central Miami

Beach. The restaurant pays homage to beef in its usual incarnations and is a shrine to the perfect 17-0 1972 season with memorabilia galore. ~ Alexander Hotel, 5225 Collins Avenue; 305-341-6565. DELUXE TO ULTRA-DELUXE.

The only beachfront restaurant on Miami Beach, **Aquatica** offers casual meals alfresco. The lunch menu is laden with soups, salads, sandwiches and regional specialties. Dinner includes seafood and steak dishes. A modern nautical design and vibrant color evokes the beach. Live music on the weekend. ~ Eden Roc Resort and Spa, 4525 Collins Avenue; 305-531-0000. MODERATE.

NIGHTLIFE Miami's premier Latin cabaret, **Club Tropigala** is a facsimile of a lavish Brazilian samba club. The 650-seat showcase hosts extravagant Las Vegas–style revues as well as orchestra concerts. Closed Monday. Cover. ~ Fontainebleau Hilton, 4441 Collins Avenue; 305-672-7469; www.clubtropigala.com.

The dressy piano bar at **Shula's Lounge** is good for romancing. ~ The Alexander, 5225 Collins Avenue; 305-865-6500.

Jimmy'z is a plush danceclub that attracts an older, upscale clientele. Decked out with comfortable sofas and ottomans, it offers a little for everyone—Latin music, hip-hop and Brazilian nights, among others. Closed Monday and Tuesday. Cover. ~ 432 41st Street; 305-604-9798.

BEACHES & PARKS

35TH STREET BEACH Another one-block respite between highrises, the beach here is narrower than those to the south, and the sand is somewhat shelly. Usually devoid of large crowds and quieter, this site is favored by older people who gather on covered benches along the boardwalk. It's a good place to swim, although seaweed sometimes collects near the shore. Facilities include food vendors and lifeguards. ~ On Miami Beach at 35th Street.

46TH STREET BEACH Our favorite block of Miami Beach, this niche is strategically adjacent to the Eden Roc and Fontainebleau hotels, putting you in arm's reach of some hoppin' beachside activity. The slightly crested swath of white grains is a hot spot for paddleball players and kite flyers. Facilities consist of restrooms, lifeguards, jet ski and sailboat rentals. ~ On Miami Beach at 46th Street.

CENTRAL AND NORTH BEACHES BEACHES & PARKS

74TH STREET BEACH You cross a busy roadway and go over a little ridge to reach this one-block recess on Miami Beach. A single row of palms and lush seagrapes flank the shell-studded sand, which stretches for 150 feet out to the ocean. It's a good place for swimming. The best part of being here, though, is the sweeping southern views of Miami Beach. There are restrooms, showers, lifeguards, food vendors and a playground area. ~ On Miami Beach at 74th Street.

NORTH SHORE OPEN SPACE PARK A slice of lush vegetation between skyscrapers, this eight-block locale flourishes with willowy Australian pines, oak trees and sea oats. Best of all, the ginger-colored sand is as clean as a pin and the ocean affords very good swimming. A boardwalk meanders through the foliage, while people laze in grassy coves adjacent to the beach. Facilities include restrooms, barbecue grills and a picnic area. ~ On Miami Beach between 79th and 87th streets; 305-673-7730, fax 305-673-7074; e-mail recreation@miamibeachfl.gov.

FIVE

Downtown Miami

At ground level, Miami resembles a small Latin American city. You can buy tropical fruit on the street and bargain for merchandise in small shops. Look up, and the future is abuzz overhead, with the Metrorail headed one way, the Metromover headed the other and a skyline of daring modern architecture that would outrage residents of more conservative American cities. It makes Miamians smile. The Centrust Building lights up in different colors on holidays. The Metrorail tracks sport multicolored fluorescent neon. Farther down on Brickell Avenue, buildings are constructed with holes in the middle or painted with every color you'd find in a big box of crayons.

Two decades of immigration have infused this great core with numerous powerful Latin business centers as well as a government in which the majority of top officials are Latino. Exploring the downtown area, you'll hear more Spanish spoken than English and see many Spanish billboards.

Miami is the city of "now you see it, now you don't." Constantly shaping and reshaping its skyline, downtown is a convolution of ultramodern skyscrapers reflecting against beautiful Biscayne Bay. An expansive yet quite conquerable area, the city is served by the Metromover (305-770-3131), an automated double-loop elevated monorail that travels a four-mile route around the perimeter of downtown. It encircles an area of 28 blocks, and every place in the downtown area is within a two-block walk of one of the nine stations along the route. The easiest way to visit downtown is to park in the huge, free lot at Bayside Marketplace, cross Biscayne Boulevard and board the Metromover. For just 25 cents, you can ride around downtown to the Metro-Dade Cultural Center or, if you wish, ride around and around while you eat a take-out picnic lunch.

Occupying the 27th floor of the sleek Barnett Bank Building, the **Greater Miami Convention & Visitors Bureau** will provide you with sightseeing information as well as a good view of the city. ~ 701 Brickell Avenue; 305-539-3000, 800-933-8448; www.gmcvb.com.

Slicing through the heart of downtown, **Flagler Street** is the best place to capture urban life. Jammed with taxi cabs and Latin street vendors, this thoroughfare was first brought to life in the 1920s by some of the city's earliest merchants. Nowadays, brick-lined moderne buildings house noisy electronics shops and discount jewelry centers.

One of the most beautiful buildings downtown, **Gusman Center for the Performing Arts** is a Mediterranean dream world. Built in 1926 for Paramount Studios, the brick-faced theater is wonderfully ornate, resembling an Italian courtyard with twinkling ceiling lights and rolling cloud puffs. It's worth a trip just to experience the surroundings. ~ 174 East Flagler Street; 305-374-2444, fax 305-374-0303; www.gusmancenter.org.

The **Dade County Courthouse** is easily spotted from just about anywhere in the city. A slender building with a striking ziggurat roof, the courthouse is shaped like a rocket poised for lift-off. Inside, beautiful mosaics swirl across the ceiling and ornate brass designs embellish the doors and wall lamps. You can still see court in session at this granddaddy. ~ 73 West Flagler Street; 305-275-1155.

A couple of blocks to the east beats the cultural pulse of downtown. The three-building **Metro-Dade Cultural Center** is a complex of Mediterranean modernism with broad checkered piazzas. ~ 101 West Flagler Street; 305-375-2665.

The most enthralling destination here, the **Historical Museum of Southern Florida**, presents two floors of exhibits that span 10,000 years, carrying you through American Indian camps, boom or bust years and Miami's golden years as the nation's playground. Here you can sit in a 20th-century trolley car, don period costumes or relax on the porch of an old cracker home. Better yet, peruse the thousands of snapshots of yesterday's Florida in the extensive photo library (open five days a week). If you love Florida, you'll adore this museum. Admission. ~ 305-375-1492, fax 305-375-1609; www.historical-museum.org, e-mail hasf@historical-museum.org.

Across the piazza, the **Miami Art Museum** is South Florida's major museum and a showpiece of Mediterranean style. It focuses on international art with world-class exhibits and programs. Closed Monday. Admission. ~ 101 West Flagler Street; 305-375-1700, fax 305-375-1725; www.miamiartmuseum.org.

Rounding out this cultural trio is the four-story **Miami-Dade Public Library**. ~ 305-375-2665; www.mdpls.org.

About four blocks northeast, the **United States Courthouse** is a place where you'll want to spend some time. This stately 1931 building is a masterful work of Spanish Mediterranean revival. Corinthian columns, glass arched doorways and miles of marble floor greet visitors. Around the vine-clad courtyard, artists have taken hold of the hallways, covering them with wild art frescoes. ~ 300 Northeast 1st Avenue; 305-523-5100; www.flsd.uscourts.gov.

For some more heady scenery, stroll around the corner to the **Ingraham Building**, a 1927 study in Italian Renaissance architecture. Its compass arch entrances, heavy bronze doors and sweeping gold ceilings with hand-painted compartments are overwhelming. The building was named for J. E. Ingraham, Henry Flagler's right-hand man. ~ 25 Southeast 2nd Avenue; 305-377-1669.

At the east end of Northeast 4th Avenue, the savvy **Bayside Marketplace** rests primly along the bay, luring just as many sightseers as shoppers to its peach enclaves. ~ 401 Biscayne Boulevard; 305-577-3344, fax 305-577-0306; www.baysidemarketplace.com, e-mail info@baysidemarketplace.com.

Docked at the Bayside Marketplace is the **Heritage of Miami**, a coastal schooner that offers cruises around Biscayne Bay. The majestic tallship is modeled after the early 1900s schooners that traveled between Miami, Cuba and the Bahamas. Offered twice a day, the two-hour cruise provides excellent views of Vizcaya, Key Biscayne and Miami's skyline. Closed in summer. Admission. ~ 401 Biscayne Boulevard; 305-442-9697; www.heritageschooner.com.

If you need some open space, head next door to **Bayfront Park**, 32 acres of subtropical foliage and rock-studded palm tree gardens skirting the bay. This serene fleck of greenery, favored by after-work joggers, is frequently the site of outdoor concerts. ~ 301 North Biscayne Boulevard; 305-358-7550, fax 305-358-1211; www.bayfrontparkmiami.com.

Your most historic stop downtown is several blocks west at the **Lummus Park District**. Here rests Dade County's oldest house, the **Wagner Homestead**. Constructed in 1858 by a struggling pioneer named William Wagner, the simple, four-room pine dwelling has hardily endured hurricanes, wars and the menace of progress. It's not a whole lot to look at, but it signifies a time when this concrete jungle was a mere wilderness. Call for tour information. ~ 404 Northwest 3rd Street; 305-579-6935.

Just south of downtown is Miami's take on Wall Street, a picturesque thoroughfare called **Brickell Avenue**. This impressive collection of ultramodern foreign (and a few domestic) bank buildings juts upward from the roadside, clinging to the skies that rim Biscayne Bay. Along the four-lane road, majestic palm trees and towering oaks create shade and natural sculptures for passing traffic.

Commercial highrises eventually merge with classy residential skyscrapers along this modern roadway. Here you'll spot the cleverly designed **Atlantis** apartment building. The architect built a large square gap into the middle of the building, punctuated the opening with a palm tree and an artsy spiral staircase, and then planted a single, rust-colored triangle atop the building. The Atlantis was completed in the early 1980s to great acclaim from Miami residents. ~ 2025 Brickell Avenue.

In the spirit of competition, the owners of the neighboring **Villa Regina** apartments splashed rainbow colors across their balconies, offsetting them with vertical racing stripes. From Biscayne Bay, the building looks like a painted accordion standing on end. ~ 1581 Brickell Avenue.

Across the street at the **Miami Museum of Science and Planetarium**, heaven and earth meet under one roof. This building boasts creative exhibits for children (and adults, too). Visitors can view birds and reptiles at the wildlife center or catch a celestial or laser light show under the planetarium dome. Admission. ~ 3280 South Miami Avenue; 305-854-4247, fax 305-646-4300; www.miamisci.org, e-mail info@miamisci.org.

LODGING In downtown Miami, ultramodern corporate hotels continue to pop up, helping to shape and reshape the city's skyline. Rates here are deluxe and ultra-deluxe, and they don't fall in the off season. Inland, you'll find sprawling country club resorts and singularly chic addresses intermingled with a few chain motels and even fewer bed and breakfasts.

Rising 34 granite floors from Biscayne Bay, the **Hotel Inter-Continental** takes on a stark look. Catering largely to a business crowd, the hotel features a lobby with marble walls, a grand piano and a canopy of glass. Guest rooms are cushy, with black lacquer oriental armoires, floral print loveseats and granite tables. ~ 100 Chopin Plaza; 305-577-1000, 800-327-0200, fax 305-372-4720; www.interconti.com, e-mail miami@interconti.com. ULTRA-DELUXE.

A definite corporate hotel, the **Hyatt Regency Downtown** has a striking open lobby. The 24-story hostelry is conveniently connected to the Miami Convention Center and offers 612 modernly furnished rooms with contemporary art and good views of the city and river. ~ 400 Southeast 2nd Avenue; 305-358-1234, 800-233-1234, fax 305-358-0529; www.miami.hyatt.com. DELUXE TO ULTRA-DELUXE.

Shoppin' by the Dock of the Bay

Miami's premier shopping mecca, **Bayside Marketplace** (401 Biscayne Boulevard; 305-577-3344, fax 305-577-0306; www.baysidemarketplace.com, e-mail info@baysidemarketplace.com) is a study in cool aesthetics. A festive pink plaza hugging sparkling Biscayne Bay, this open-air mall is a labyrinth of giant ferns, palm trees and brick walkways dotted with white flower carts, strolling musicians and mimes. Though it brims with 120 novel stores and restaurants, Bayside is just as much a people-watching spot as a shopping address. **Coastal Cotton Co.** (305-358-2551) carries T-shirts, shorts and more—all made out of breathable cotton. For a Brazilian flair, **Azteca de Oro** (305-375-0358) has batik resort wear, hand-loomed rugs and the Laurel Birch collection of bags. **Passage to India** (305-375-9504) is where you can pick up fine Indian clothing and bone jewelry. Top it off at **The Hat Attack** (305-373-1428), where you can don baseball caps and all other sports-related crown covers. Kids of all ages will enjoy **The Disney Store** (305-371-7621), with its Mickey and Donald motif toys, games, art and clothing, as well as **Comics** (305-371-7931), with its zany selection of Spider-Man T-shirts, Bob Marley posters and more. **Suncoast Motion Picture** (305-373-6043) carries the largest and most eclectic selection in the Miami area of movies on videocassette and DVD.

Bayside Marketplace has nine restaurants as well as a food court with a dozen different fast-food vendors. For light, heart-healthy Japanese food, try the **Teriyaki Temple** (305-577-3828). BUDGET TO MODERATE. **Lombardi's** (305-381-9580) serves Italian cuisine in an indoor or outdoor setting and has a gelato bar. BUDGET TO MODERATE. **Los Ranchos** (305-375-8188), a South American steakhouse, specializes in *churrasco* (tenderloin) with traditional *chimichurri* sauce made in-house, followed by a serving of *tres leches*—a variation on the carmellike South American favorite, *dulce de leche*. BUDGET. **Kelly's Cajun Grill** (305-375-0222) serves authentic bayou fare such as Bourbon chicken. BUDGET. **Captain Joe's** (305/371-7254) offers seafood, including grilled whole snapper, curried shrimp and fresh Maine lobster, as well as other Caribbean specialties such as jerk chicken. BUDGET.

Bayside Marketplace offers a variety of outdoor entertainment nightly as well as most afternoons. Festivities culminate with a spectacular Saturday evening **Holiday Boat Parade** in mid-December.

Perched nicely on the Miami River, the **Clarion Hotel & Suites** is an elegant hotel offering 16 floors of accommodations. Mahogany furnishings and subdued tones of plum and champagne decorate the guest rooms, many of which overlook the river. There's also a pool that rests waterside. ~ 100 Southeast 4th Street; 305-374-5100, fax 305-381-9826; www.clarionhotelandsuites.com. DELUXE.

HIDDEN ►

If it's charming, indigenous lodging you seek, look no further than the **Miami River Inn**. Set in a courtyard of palms, the Victorian bed and breakfast has been in place since the neighborhood was mostly fishing companies. Its four early-1900s buildings have been splendidly restored, and its bedrooms individually decorated with antiques, carved wood beds and handmade drapes and quilts. Gay-friendly. ~ 118 Southwest South River Drive; 305-325-0045, 800-468-3589, fax 305-325-9227; www.miamiriverinn.com, e-mail miamihotel@aol.com. MODERATE TO DELUXE.

DINING

Sadly, there are but a few choice restaurants to be found in Miami's downtown. In a city where nearly half the people are Latino, the most frequently spotted eatery is the Cuban café. These narrow, oftentimes unkempt pit stops almost always have sidewalk takeout windows, where you can listen to Cuban radio stations while picking up some *sopa de pollo* (chicken soup), *papas fritas* (french fries), *morcillas* (blood sausage) and cold *cervezas* (beer). Stroll bustling Flagler Street, where Latin street vendors offer *empanadas* (fried meat pies) and *batidos de frutas* (fruit milkshakes).

One sizzling lunch locale is **Granny Feelgood's**, where business types hobnob over clever health food creations. Granny's

AUTHOR FAVORITE

I can't think of a better base for exploring the downtown area than the plain, white, 15-story-tall **Riande Continental at Bayside**. The hotel itself is such a standard business-class place that you may get a blast of déjà vu when stepping into your room for the first time, but the location can't be beat. It stands right across the street from Bayside Marketplace and is convenient to the Metromover station and Bayfront Park. If you can get a south-facing room, you can daydream the morning away watching the nearby cruise liners set sail from the world's largest cruise ship port. ~ 146 Biscayne Boulevard; 305-358-4555. MODERATE.

extensive menu features salads loaded with shrimp and chicken, inventive pastas, steamy vegetable soups and freshly squeezed vegetable juices. Breakfast and lunch only. Closed Sunday. ~ 25 West Flagler Street; 305-377-9600. BUDGET TO MODERATE.

Eating on the picnic tables on the back deck of **Garcia's Seafood Grill & Fish Market** means watching oversized freighters getting tugged up the Miami River. It also means eating fresh seafood, Cuban standards, and a fish dip that deserves its own altar. ~ 398 Northwest North River Drive; 305-375-0765; www.garcia seafood.com. MODERATE.

A funky outdoor hideaway tucked among Miami's drab dockside warehouses, **The Big Fish** has a tin roof and an array of mismatched wooden and aluminum tables. The menu, a total of five to six daily items posted on a bulletin board, consists of—you guessed it—fresh fish. A friendly owner introduces diners, a mishmash of crusty old folks and neatly dressed attorneys and financiers. ~ 55 Southwest Miami Avenue Road; 305-373-1770, fax 305-373-0026. MODERATE.

Located a block north of the Miami River, the **River Oyster Bar** serves inventive fresh fish, poultry and meat dishes, and has a raw bar with eight different kinds of oysters. Its happy hour is a secret of the downtown after-work crowd. No lunch on Saturday. Closed Sunday. ~ 650 South Miami Avenue; 305-530-1915, fax 305-577-8500; www.rivermiami.com. MODERATE TO ULTRA-DELUXE.

The lunchtime crowd at **Perricone's Marketplace** is peppered with Brickell Avenue types toting briefcases and hoisting cell phones as they lunch on the wooden deck behind this European gourmet market. Food is adroitly prepared (and winningly priced) yuppie fare: pastas, inventive sandwiches and such. ~ 15 Southeast 10th Street; 305-374-9449; www.perricones.com. MODERATE TO DELUXE.

Everyone loves **S & S Diner**. The Miami institution, immortalized in Mel Kiser and Corky Irick's movie *Last Night at the S & S Diner*, packs 'em in daily with down-to-earth fare such as meatloaf, roast pork, stuffed cabbage, chopped steak with onions, turkey and dressing, and the best mashed potatoes around. After you've waited in line (and wait you will), you can take one of the 23 seats at the horseshoe counter. Save your appetite: Homespun vittles don't get much better than this. Breakfast, lunch and dinner are served on weekdays; no dinner on weekends. ~ 1757 Northeast 2nd Avenue, just north of downtown; 305-373-4291. BUDGET.

SHOPPING James Bond would have loved Miami. Here he could have shopped to his heart's content for a wide array of espionage toys: thumb-sized cameras for sneaking pictures, eyeglasses that let you see who's creeping up behind you, bugs for eavesdropping on your enemies. **Counter Spy Shop** caters to both military personnel and the civilian down the street. Closed weekends. ~ 200 Southeast 1st Street, Suite 700; 305-358-4336.

If diamonds are a girl's best friend, then the **Seybold Building** is her dreamland. Herein lies ten floors of stores abounding with those twinkling jewels as well as gold and silver pieces. The name of the game is bargaining, and most merchants are anxious to strike a deal. ~ 36 Northeast 1st Street; 305-374-7922.

A bustling urban thoroughfare cutting through the heart of downtown, **Flagler Street** is where some of the city's first merchants set up shop during the 1920s. Today, brick sidewalks are rimmed with Latin street vendors and fronted by noisy electronics marts and discount jewelry centers.

Don't miss **Burdines Department Store**, a landmark, 1936 streamlined moderne design that adds a touch of nostalgia to the area. ~ 22 East Flagler Street; 305-577-1500.

NIGHTLIFE Though downtown Miami's club scene may not be as trendy as South Beach's, it is notable for its diversity, from upscale hotel bars to funky, historic hideaways at the river's edge.

Indigo Bar draws a large business clientele for after-work cocktails. ~ Hotel InterContinental, 100 Chopin Plaza; 305-577-1000

One of the best bars around, **Tobacco Road** obtained the city's first liquor license back in 1912. An old speakeasy, "The Road" has a secret closet where illegal booze and roulette tables were once stashed for Al Capone. Upstairs, there's always an impressive lineup of rhythm-and-blues bands. Cover on weekends. ~ 626 South Miami Avenue; 305-374-1198.

Bayside Marketplace is the headquarters for outdoor entertainment, with something going on every evening of the year and most afternoons, too. You'll find reggae, classic rock-and-roll, calypso and Latin bands playing center stage on the waterfront. ~ 401 Biscayne Boulevard; 305-577-3344.

The **Hard Rock Cafe**, with its blazing neon guitar out front, features rock tunes. ~ Bayside Marketplace, 401 Biscayne Boulevard; 305-377-3110.

Located in a dicey neighborhood and decorated like a suburban garage, **Churchill's Hideaway** showcases local bands in this no-frills bar. The three pool tables are always crowded and the cost of a beer won't bend your wallet. Grunge rules for fashion here and much of the crowd is tattooed and body-pierced, though docile. Occasional cover. ~ 5501 Northeast 2nd Avenue; 305-757-1807.

Less groovy and daunting than the clubs on South Beach (and with fewer parking headaches), **Power Studios** in the Design District hosts live music and spun deejay tunes in a setting as comfy as a rec room. Cover. ~ 3701 Northeast 2nd Avenue; 305-576-1336; www.powerstudios.com.

THEATER, OPERA, SYMPHONY AND DANCE   The gorgeous **Gusman Center for the Performing Arts**, an ornate 1709-seat facility, is home to the Florida Philharmonic Orchestra. The Gusman also hosts the popular Miami Film Festival. ~ 174 East Flagler Street; 305-372-0925; www.gusmancenter.org.

The city's prized **Bayfront Park**, which spans 32 acres of waterside palm trees and rolling hills, has a 12,000-person capa-

AUTHOR FAVORITE

While Miami is the largest cruise ship port on earth and has departures practically hourly for destinations like The Bahamas, Jamaica and Cozumel, there's only one place you can go to take a short "cruise to nowhere" for an afternoon or evening. It's the **Casino Princesa**, a 200-foot megayacht that bills itself as the most luxurious vessel in the offshore gaming industry. The *Princesa* sets sail for international waters, just three miles out, where anti-gambling laws don't apply. Although three of the ship's four decks are enclosed and filled with games of chance from slot machines to high-stakes table games, the sea views make the open top deck an inviting place to linger for those who are not inclined to gamble. Tickets, which cost $19 to $25 depending on the day for a five-hour cruise, include lunch or dinner. On Monday, Tuesday and Thursday afternoons, seniors 55 and over can cruise and dine for free. ~ Bayfront Park; 305-379-5825.

city amphitheater for outdoor musical concerts from symphony to rock. ~ 301 Biscayne Boulevard between Northeast 1st and 4th streets; 305-358-7550; www.bayfrontparkmiami.com.

The modern, cylindrical **James L. Knight International Center** is the 4646-seat address of popular Latino, jazz, rock-and-roll and pops concerts. ~ 400 Southeast 2nd Avenue; 305-372-4634; www.jlknightcenter.com.

Larger concerts are held at the 16,500-seat **Miami Arena**, another ultramodern circular facility rimmed with palm trees. The arena is also home to the Miami Manatees, the city's pro hockey team. ~ 721 Northwest 1st Avenue; 305-530-4400; www.miamiarena.com.

Just north of downtown, the **Joseph Caleb Auditorium** presents stellar drama by local artists. The 991-seat facility is also the site of regional orchestra and Shakespearean performances. ~ 5400 Northwest 22nd Avenue, Brownsville; 305-636-2350.

SIX

Little Havana & Other Ethnic Neighborhoods

The term "inner city" doesn't do justice to the exotic residential/commercial neighborhoods close to downtown Miami. Besides the famous Little Havana district, adventurous sightseers in search of Miami's truly "hidden" side will want to seek out the public market in Little Haiti, the shops and cafés of the trendy new Design District, and perhaps such untouristy corners of the city as the Puerto Rican Barrio de San Juan, Overtown's emerging jazz club zone and the huge, bustling Allapattah Produce Market, one of the largest wholesale food shipping points in the United States.

Virtually all the districts mentioned in this chapter are in one stage or another of urban redevelopment. While major thoroughfares and public areas such as parks and markets are heavily patrolled and generally safe, unpopulated back streets can sometimes be risky enough that you wouldn't want to unlock your car doors, let alone walk around. Use judgment and don't flash sizable amounts of money around, and do your sightseeing in the daytime until you're familiar with the neighborhood.

Little Havana

Despite its name, Little Havana bears little architectural resemblance to the Cuban capital, yet it serves as the cultural hub of Miami's Cuban population (which makes up one-third of the entire Miami-Dade County population). Because Spanish is the first language here, Little Havana is also home to many recent immigrants from other Latin American countries, especially Guatemala, Honduras, El Salvador and Nicaragua. Recently, publicists have tried to rename the district the "Latin Quarter," but so far the new name has not stuck.

LITTLE HAVANA & OTHER ETHNIC NEIGHBORHOODS

SIGHTS

Little Havana is situated immediately south of downtown across the Miami River. The main drag is Southwest 8th Street, known locally as **Calle Ocho**, stretching just west of downtown between 27th and 12th avenues (one-way). If you drive your car up Calle Ocho, it will seem like just one long, noisy thoroughfare fringed with discount stores, flashing neon signs, gas stations, restaurants and nightclubs. It wasn't always like this. Back in the 1960s and '70s, Calle Ocho was as exciting and exotic as Old Habana itself. But as many Cubans moved out to more suburban parts of Miami, old-fashioned shops and restaurants closed down and were replaced by fast-food franchises and mini-malls. Historic buildings were demolished with little regard to the mural art on their exteriors. Now, belatedly, the city of Miami is noticing the untapped tourist potential of Little Havana and, along with local community leaders, is promoting a revival designed to attract both local and out-of-town visitors.

The best way to soak in the atmosphere here is to park and walk. The street signs, like the restaurant menus, are mainly in Spanish, but it's fairly easy to find someone who can translate. Old Cuban men in *guayaberas* socialize on street corners, while the younger set strolls the sidewalks with radios blasting Spanish music.

You'll almost always find a crowd at **Parque Máximo Gómez** (commonly called Domino Park), a community center where locals gather for games of chess and dominoes. Photographing people is frowned upon here, perhaps because the park used to be a big drug hangout or perhaps because some locals resent the intrusion of too many tourists; ask first. ~ Southwest 8th Street and Southwest 15th Avenue. The park's big mural commemorating the Summit of the Americas in 1993 is one of the more impressive examples of wall art in the district. Around the corner, running from the park past the nearby McDonald's, don't miss the **Paseo de las Estrellas** ("Walk of the Stars"), a Cubano replica of its Hollywood counterpart but exclusively featuring Latino actors, poets, playwrights and musicians such as Thalia, Gloria Estefan, Julio Iglesias and Maria Conchita Alonso.

Continuing two blocks east, turn south on 13th Avenue to stroll along the two-block **Cuban Memorial Boulevard**, where you'll find a series of busts and other monuments to the Cuban

LITTLE HAVANA SIGHTS 91

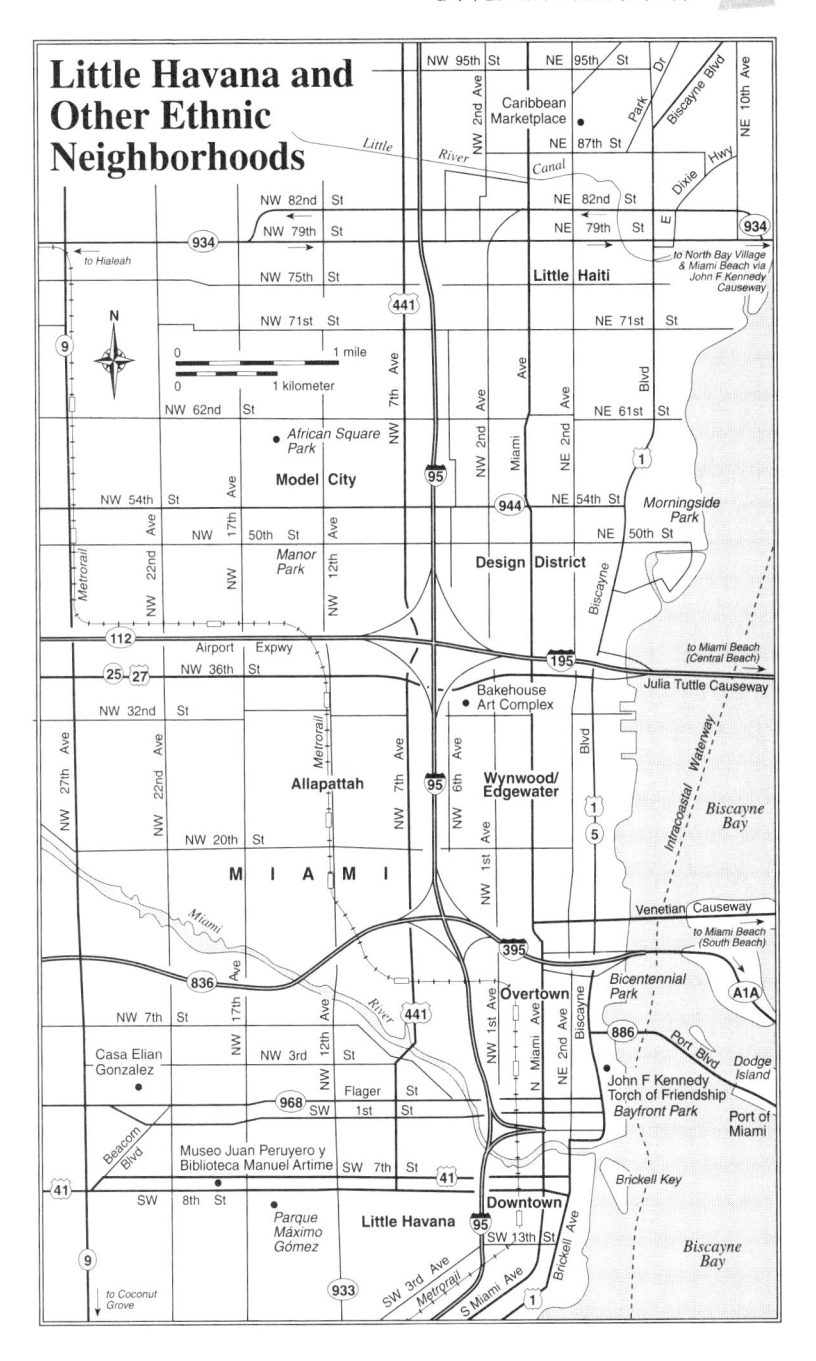

anti-Castro movement. There's a **Memorial to José Martí**, the 19th-century revolutionary poet exiled from Cuba because of his opposition to Spanish colonial rule; a **Memorial to Antonio Maceo**, who led Cuba's war for independence from Spain; the **Memorial Flame** to the martyrs of the Bay of Pigs invasion in 1961; and an **Island of Cuba Memorial** with a life-size sculpture of a peasant with a machete in fighting stance on top. People leave *santería* offerings at the base of the big ceiba tree in Parque Máximo Gómez to honor the heroes who have inspired them.

Three blocks west of Domino Park, the **Museo Juan Peruyero y Biblioteca Manuel Artime** is filled with photos, newspaper clippings, maps and documents about the Bay of Pigs invasion, the ill-fated attempt by CIA-trained Cuban exiles to take back their homeland two years after Castro's revolution. Among the exhibits are photographs—some quite graphic—of virtually every person who participated in the invasion, casualties as well as survivors. Closed weekends. ~ 1821 Southwest 8th Street; 305-649-4719.

On the roadways flanking Calle Ocho, tens of thousands of Cuban immigrants have settled in modest, well-kept neighborhoods. Many residents display the American flag or exhibit bright brass shrines of their favorite patron saint. The most recent addition to the historical sights of Little Havana is the **Casa Elian Gonzalez**, where the five-year-old child cause célèbre lived with relatives from the time he arrived in the United States with a group of Cuban refugees after his mother had drowned during the crossing until U.S. Attorney General Janet Reno returned him to Cuba by armed force six months later. Many Cubans in South Florida believe this controversial outcome caused Al Gore to lose the 2000 presidential election to George W. Bush. The Gonzalez family keeps Elian's room intact, with all the clothing and toys given to him by well-wishers, and has converted the house into a museum filled with photos of the boy. Admission by donation. ~ 2319 Northwest 2nd Street; no phone.

Every March the neighborhood holds the **Calle Ocho Festival**, the country's largest Latino festival, attended by more than one million people, with fabulous food and music and a conga line that continues for blocks.

LODGING   Little Havana doesn't have much to offer in the way of hotels or motels, and the few places there are can attract some seamy clientele, especially late at night. Still, prices are much lower than on the downtown side of the river.

Close to the upper end of the Calle Ocho business district, the modest **El Nido Motel** offers the standard amenities—double bed, phone, TV, shower—and not much more. ~ 3141 Southwest 8th Street; 305-649-8161. BUDGET.

Right next door, the **Tops Motel** offers more of the same. ~ 3151 Southwest 8th Street; 305-642-7663. BUDGET.

A few blocks away and a little classier, the **Miami Executive Hotel** offers suites that feature heart-shaped tubs with jacuzzis. ~ 4350 Southwest 8th Street; 305-443-8464. BUDGET TO MODERATE.

DINING

This haven for thousands of Cuban immigrants is also the settling ground for scores of Cuban eateries offering an abundance of food at incredibly cheap prices.

◄ HIDDEN

For a multicultural fast-food experience, eschew the familiar burger chains up and down Calle Ocho. Instead, drop into **El Rey de las Fritas** for an authentic *frita*, a large, spicy Cuban-style hamburger covered in a huge pile of shoestring potatoes. The burger and fries are intended to be eaten together inside the bun. The casual little eatery, with its gleaming white formica tabletops, also offers other Cuban sandwiches, as well as *batidos* (milkshakes) and flan. ~ 1177 Southwest 8th Street; 305-858-4223. BUDGET.

In a city that seems to have more Cuban restaurants than fashion models (and that's a lot), most people will tell you that the best, most authentic Cuban food to be found is at **El Exquisito**, a modest little family-run restaurant located in the heart of Little Havana that is said to be just like street restaurants in the old

AUTHOR FAVORITE

You'll step back in time when you enter **La Carreta**. Leather-back chairs and heavy wooden chandeliers add a rustic feel to multiple dining rooms, where large color photos of Old Habana adorn the walls. Selections feature traditional Cuban fare such as chicken and yellow rice, pork with black beans and Spanish bean soup. With more than three dozen desserts to choose from, who could resist the final course? Open 24 hours. ~ 3632 Southwest 8th Street; **305-444-7501**, fax **305-444-4889**. BUDGET TO DELUXE.

country. Cubans come from all over Miami-Dade to dine on the house specialty, *bistek de palomilla* (Cuban-style beefsteak smothered in onions), served with *moros y cristianos* (literally "Moors and Christians," black beans and white rice) and fried plantains. Prices are absurdly low, including a full breakfast for under $2. ~ 1510 Southwest 8th Street; 305-643-0227. BUDGET.

> To touch any Santería offerings is considered bad luck, not to mention very bad manners.

Just up the block, **El Pub** offers diners a trip down memory lane as well as a great meal and live entertainment. The walls are littered with post-1959 Cuban memorabilia: paintings, posters, prints and advertisements from the island nation's heyday. The kitchen serves up typical *criollo* or country-style Cuban food such as *lechón* (suckling pig), *pechuga de pollo rellena* (stuffed chicken breast) and *ropa vieja* (literally "old clothes," shredded beef with tomato sauce). El Pub kicks things up a bit on the weekends with a pianist who draws a healthy crowd of revelers. ~ 1548 Southwest 8th Street; 305-642-9942. BUDGET.

A local favorite, **Casa Panza** celebrates Cuba's Spanish heritage in the kind of tapas-and-flamenco tavern you'd expect to find in Barcelona, not Miami. Besides traditional appetizer-size, order-as-many-as-you-want tapas such as garlic mushrooms and grilled shrimp, Casa Panza serves meal-size helpings of paella and a soup called *zarzuela de mariscos* (literally, "operetta of seafood"). ~ 1620 Southwest 8th Street; 305-643-5343. MODERATE.

Your Nicaraguan connection can be made at **Guayacan Restaurant**, a small establishment with counter service and tables in the back. You can sample hen soup with meatballs, *churrasco* and other inexpensive offerings. ~ 1933 Southwest 8th Street; 305-649-2015, fax 305-642-7383. BUDGET TO MODERATE.

HIDDEN ►

One of the more interesting buildings in Little Havana, **Casa Juancho** depicts Spanish Renaissance architecture. A barrel-tiled roof and tan stucco exterior match the brick pillars and wooden beam ceiling inside. Sacks of garlic and ham hocks hang around the open kitchen, where exceptional seafood and game dishes are whipped up. ~ 2436 Southwest 8th Street; 305-642-2452, fax 305-642-2524; www.casajuancho.com, e-mail juancho@casajuancho.com. DELUXE TO ULTRA-DELUXE.

An anomaly in this Latino neighborhood, **Hy-Vong** rightfully takes its place as Miami's best Vietnamese restaurant. With plain white walls and a few wilting plants, the atmosphere is nil, but the food is prepared with great care by one of the owners, a Vietnamese woman who fled Saigon in 1975. The hearty fare includes *thi kho* (pork in coconut milk), *cari tom* (curried shrimp and crab), chicken with jicama and an intriguing squid salad. Dinner only. Closed Monday. ~ 3458 Southwest 8th Street; 305-446-3674, fax 305-662-4128. MODERATE.

Versailles is the epicenter of Cuban cuisine and politics. One of Miami's most famous, revered and kitschy Cuban eateries, it's akin to a Cuban Denny's but offers a true cultural experience. The decor is French rococo (go figure) and the food is nothing short of authentic: *palomilla* steak, *picadillo* and *frijoles negros*, and *platanos fritos* are just a few of the specialties. Be sure to end your meal with *crema catalana* (think crème brûlée) and a *cafecito*. ~ 3555 Southwest 8th Street; 305-444-0240. BUDGET TO MODERATE.

SHOPPING

Miami's Cuban core offers one long street tagged with discount marts where you'll find not only good buys but an intriguing taste of local ethnic life. Focus on Southwest 8th Street, Little Havana's bustling main drag, between Route 95 West and 35th Avenue.

Over at **Lily's Records**, you can find your favorite Latin tunes. Closed weekends. ~ 1260 Southwest 8th Street; 305-856-0536.

La Casa de las Piñatas, a second-story shop in the thick of Calle Ocho, Little Havana's main artery, is wall-to-wall with piñatas of every size for every occasion and a genuine example of the cultural bouillabaisse that is Miami. Closed Sunday. ~ 1756 Southwest 8th Street; 305-649-4711.

For Spanish language books, stop by **Librería Universal**, where the topics range from Cuban-American and Afro-Caribbean issues to ethnic studies, folklore and Latin-American literature. Closed Sunday. ~ 3090 Southwest 8th Street; 305-642-3234; www.ediciones.com.

No expedition to Little Havana would be complete without a trip and a shirt from **La Casa de las Guayaberas**. Tailor Ramon Puig started a phenomenon over 40 years ago when he emigrated to Miami from Cuba and set up shop. Today, he and a fleet of seamstresses churn out some 20 of the pleated, button-down shirts favored by Cuban men (it must be the handy cigar pockets). Buy one off the rack for $15, or splurge on a custom-made one for

$400. As a picture over the cash register attests, even Ronald Reagan picked one up on a campaign stop in Miami. Closed Sunday. ~ 5840 Southwest 8th Street; 305-266-9683.

NIGHTLIFE The prime time to visit Little Havana is the last Friday of any month, which is known as **Viernes Culturales en la Histórica Pequeña Habana** (Cultural Fridays in Historic Little Havana, or just "Cultural Friday"), when several blocks of Calle Ocho are closed to traffic for a street party with live music, dancing and street theater performances that last late into the night.

> Many local artists display their works along the sidewalks of Calle Ocho on Cultural Friday, the last Friday afternoon and evening of each month.

Latino immigrants brought a whole new brand of nightlife to Miami, namely late-night supper clubs with lavish revues. Here on Little Havana's Southwest 8th Street you'll find some of the best.

With seating for 300, **Casa Panza** offers traditional Spanish and flamenco entertainment. On Monday, Wednesday and Sunday the kitchen prepares paella, seafood, *carnes* and octopus dishes until the music stops. Cover on Tuesday, Thursday, Friday and Saturday. ~ 1620 Southwest 8th Street; 305-643-5343.

You'll see top-name Latin musical and comedy shows at the 255-seat **Teatro de Bellas Artes**. ~ 2173 Southwest 8th Street; 305-325-0515.

Strolling musicians serenade diners at **Casa Juancho**. ~ 2436 Southwest 8th Street; 305-642-2452.

Other Ethnic Neighborhoods

Flanking the north side of the downtown area is a series of distinct neighborhoods in transition, most of them undergoing a slow, laid-back, tropical version of urban renewal that is changing some of Miami's worst slums into art districts, entertainment zones and futuristic housing projects. In some areas, such as the back streets of Allapattah or Little Haiti, reasonable people may feel unsafe getting out of the car (or even unlocking the doors). On the other hand, Little Haiti's Caribbean Marketplace and the trendy new Design District beg to be explored on foot.

SIGHTS From 54th to 87th streets, sandwiched between Route 95 and the Florida East Coast Railway tracks, **Little Haiti** is one of the city's most fascinating ethnic neighborhoods. Home to more than 30,000 Haitian refugees who speak Kreyol (pronounced "Creole," Caribbean pidgin French) as their primary language, its business district is along Northeast 2nd Avenue, where you'll find bakeries, hardware stores and clothing shops. The centerpiece of the district is the **Caribbean Marketplace**, a modern replica of Port-au-Prince's landmark Iron Market. The open-air market is filled with stalls selling everything from tropical fruits, herbs and spices, and Voodou candles to bright-hued Haitian-style paintings. The marketplace is undergoing a major renovation and will soon be expanded to include performance spaces. ~ 8927-27 Northeast 2nd Avenue.

◀ HIDDEN

A 12-block area that was formerly the southern part of Little Haiti, bounded by Route 95, 43rd Street, Northeast 2nd Avenue and North Miami Avenue, has been transformed into the **Design District**. The concept is to bring together the finest Miami-style furniture, home and office decor shops together in a single shopping area. While critics and connoisseurs call it one of the five best design districts in the country, retail business has not yet grown to match its potential.

◀ HIDDEN

On the east side of Route 95, the **Wynwood/Edgewater** district has traditionally been home to Miami's Puerto Rican population and is often called the Barrio San Juan. Today, commercialization and urban flight have made the barrio into a transitional neighborhood, at the expense of much of the local color it had in earlier times. A little-known point of interest is the **Bakehouse Art Complex**, an old bakery building that has been converted into a business incubator with studio and exhibition space for 75 of Miami's most promising young artists and craftspeople. Exhibits are open during the afternoon. ~ 561 Northwest 32nd Street; 305-576-2828.

◀ HIDDEN

Just north of downtown, the **Overtown** district dates back to the 1890s, when it was the separate black neighborhood of newly founded Miami. In the early part of the 20th century, Overtown was held up as a flourishing example of a "separate but equal" segregated community, but as the area aged, residents began moving out—first, in the 1930s, to Liberty City. By the 1960s, as all but the poorest residents were moving out to the suburbs, it deteriorated to become one of the most run-down and

Text continued on page 100.

Santería and Voodou in Miami

Afro-Caribbean magic is practiced by millions of people in all walks of life from New York City to Brazil. Nowhere else in the United States is it practiced as widely and openly as in Miami. Cubans call it Santería; Haitians call it Voodou. The differences are matters of linguistics and of the degree of Catholic influence in various sects.

Santería, Voodou and their South American counterparts, Macumba and Candomble, all originated in the Yoruba religions of Nigeria, brought to the Caribbean by slaves in the 17th and 18th centuries. Spanish and French landowners and clergy forced Africans to worship in the European manner, but at the same time people continued Yoruba ceremonies in secret. Over time a New Testament patina transformed the old African religion to a faith unique to the Caribbean.

Santería and Voodou, both of which are formally known as the Rule of Osha, has no bible. Its beliefs are passed along by word of mouth from generation to generation through apprentices using a secret language.

In Africa, the Yoruba religion from which Santería and Voodou derive dates back centuries before the time of Christ, to the era when Greek gods like Zeus, Hera and Aphrodite ruled the cosmos of the Western world. Like the Greeks, followers of Santería and Voodou believe in a multiplicity of gods and goddesses called Orishas, all with their own superpowers, weaknesses and personality quirks. In Santería, each Orisha also has its own Catholic persona, which it originally adopted to escape church persecution. For instance, Olodumare, whose saint persona is Jesus Christ, is all-powerful but elderly and afraid of mice. Obatala, or the Virgin of Mercy, wears only pure white, prefers herbs with white flowers such as datura and responds only to the sacrifices of white goats, chickens or other animals. Orunmila, or St. Francis, wears green and yellow, requires sacrifices of goats who have not given birth, and has a taste for red snapper, yams and plums.

Each Orisha can be entreated through sacrifices to answer certain kinds of prayers. In any authentic Cuban *bodega* in Miami, as well as in Little Haiti herb shops, you will find shelves full of colorful candles to burn as offerings to the various Orishas. They are similar to the saint candles used by Latino Catholics but are painted with the Santería Orishas and bear descriptions of what kind of benefits will come from burning the candle.

Most Santería gatherings are conducted by priests called Santeros or Santeras, while major ceremonies are led by high priests called Babalawo (male) or Iyalocha (female). They involve ecstatic dancing and blood sacrifices of animals or birds, and Orishas may manifest themselves through the consciousness of initiates whom an individual Orisha has "chosen."

Although Santería and Voodou ceremonies are held in secret and are never open to tourists, offerings such as candles and herbs can be encountered in the most unlikely places. It is considered very bad luck to tamper with them.

In one recent Miami money laundering trial, for instance, prosecutors complained that their seats and evidence boxes were covered with a grayish powder. Experts determined that it was "voodoo powder," used in Santería ceremonies to bring good luck, and was intended to sway the jury and court officers in favor of the accused. The prosecuting attorney complained that while he respected all religions, he was tired of getting the dust laundered from his suits.

The dust was apparently overlooked by the court's Voodoo Squad, whose job it is to remove sacrificial chickens and goats from the courthouse grounds.

dangerous areas of the city. The main problem with renovation plans in Overtown is relocating present residents to new project housing areas such as those in Model City.

Today an ambitious urban redevelopment project has been proceeding by fits and starts to demolish Overtown's worst project housing and replace it with nonresidential uses such as the emerging **2nd Avenue Entertainment District**, known for the jazz clubs springing up around the historic **Lyric Theater**, a famed vaudeville venue dating back to 1914 where famed musicians like Ella Fitzgerald, Aretha Franklin and Count Basie performed. The theater itself is undergoing renovation and expansion. ~ 819 Northwest 2nd Avenue; 305-358-1146.

Also in the works is the renovation of **Bicentennial Park**, an underutilized area that was once Miami's main port. Located between American Airlines Arena and Miami's new Center for the Performing Arts, it is envisioned as a blend of museums, restaurants and grassy open space. ~ 1075 Biscayne Boulevard.

North of Overtown and west of Route 95, the **Allapattah** district (the name comes from the Seminole word for "alligator") includes Miami's largest industrial zone as well as a major Hispanic residential area. The **Garment District**, the area's commercial center, along 20th Street between 27th and 17th avenues, is lined with wholesale outlets for the garment shops found along the back streets. Buyers for retail stores come here not only from other East Coast cities but also from all over Latin America.

HIDDEN ▶

In the center of the Garment District, the **Allapattah Produce Center** is the central shipping point for fruits and vegetables, both Florida-grown and imported from the tropics, for all of the southeastern United States. It also supplies the produce for all Miami-area supermarkets and mom-and-pop *bodegas*, as well as for cruise ships. The market was known as a high-crime area until a few years ago, but new law enforcement programs have transformed it into an intriguing place to wander around with a camera.

North of Allapattah is a cluster of quite different communities that used to be the "suburbia" of Miami's early days. On the west side of Route 95, **Model City** includes the pleasant, recently gentrified residential community of **Manor Park**, home to many African-American professionals, as well as big 21st-century housing projects for the elderly and families displaced as older project housing are demolished. The **Edison Center Business District** is a focal point of black entrepreneurship in Miami-Dade County.

Community activities center around **African Square Park**, with its jungle-motif playground, basketball courts and more than 50 acres of lawn and trees. ~ 1400 Northwest 62nd Street; 305-579-3108.

◄ HIDDEN

Have you ever dreamed of eating a Picasso? You can get your chance in the Design District at the **Orange Café + Art**, where the art on the walls is for sale and the sandwiches are all named after artists. The Picasso, for instance, consists of prosciutto and *chorizo* with *manchego* cheese on a crusty baguette. Or try the Gauguin, a wrap with curried chicken and Swiss cheese. ~ 2 Northeast 40th Street; 305-571-4070. MODERATE.

DINING

Among the burgeoning number of small restaurants and sidewalk cafés in the Design District, a standout is **Grass**, a Balinese-themed outdoor restaurant with deejayed background music. The Asian-fusion menu includes such items as Malaysian mixed seafood ceviche and Togarashi pan-roasted sea bass. ~ 28 Northeast 40th Street; 305-573-3355; MODERATE.

By day, the **District Restaurant and Lounge** serves "new American" regional fare, with offerings from the Southwest, Little Italy, the Gulf Coast and other U.S. latitudes. Dine indoors or venture outside to feast around the modernistic, squared-off, colorfully mosaiced fountain in the private courtyard. After dark, the District becomes a trendy stay-out-late disco with a tapas menu. ~ 35 Northeast 40th Street; 305-576-7242. MODERATE.

AUTHOR FAVORITE

The Caribbean Marketplace in Little Haiti is a lot of fun, but for a close-up look at Haitian-American culture, drop in next door at the **Libreri Mapou/Sant Kilterel Mapou**. This multilingual bookstore and cultural center sells gifts ranging from T-shirts to hand-painted ceramics—they even sell homemade Kremas Mapou, a traditional Haitian beverage. Literary events and live performances are often held in the cultural center, and there's a full schedule of classes including arts and crafts, Haitian folk dancing, how to speak Creole, and more. ~ 5919 Northeast 2nd Avenue; 305-757-9922.

HIDDEN ▶ Don't blink or you'll miss the **Secret Sandwich Company**, a hole-in-the-wall place with counter seating for 12, plus take-out options. The menu of soups, sandwiches, salads and deserts has a spy theme: you can order a covert caesar salad, an alibi sandwich (white albacore tuna), a Mata Hari sandwich (lime-marinated spicy chicken breast) or a Bay of Pigs sandwich (Cuban-style roast pork, of course). ~ 3918 North Miami Avenue; 305-571-9990. BUDGET.

SHOPPING The Design District's Caribbean heritage is reflected at **Chelsea Galleria**, a branch of a Trinidad/Jamaica gallery featuring contemporary fine art of the West Indies. ~ 32 Northeast 39th Street; 305-576-2950

Recently relocated to the Design District after 22 years in Soho, the **Bernice Steinbaum Gallery** features contemporary paintings that "deal with the narrative" (as they say in artspeak) by nationally known mid-career artists. ~ 3550 North Miami Avenue; 305-573-2700.

Iran Issa-Khan exhibits the stylish images of the famed photographer whose subjects have included Nancy Reagan, the Baron and Baroness Rothschild, Oscar de la Renta and Paloma Picasso. ~ 180 Northeast 39th Street, Suite 221; 305-573-4614.

One of the oldest boutiques in the Design District, **Susane R.** features French antiques, art deco, 1940s *chinoiserie* oriental rugs, and expressionist paintings. ~ 93 Northeast 40th Street; 305-573-8483.

Holly Hunt displays the product lines of about a dozen "best of class" furniture designers, both traditional and contemporary, in a large showroom. ~ 3833 Northeast 2nd Avenue; 305-571-2012.

Buick Building Gallery showcases large-scale sculptural works and installations in a bare-concrete-walls setting. ~ 3841 Northeast 2nd Avenue; 305-573-8116.

Established in Venice, Italy, over a century ago and recently relocated to Miami, **Bussandri** offers one-of-a-kind reproductions of fine antique furniture and architectural elements from the 15th century through the European art deco period. ~ 4040 Northeast 2nd Avenue; 305-571-1890.

SEVEN

Coconut Grove & Coral Gables

South of downtown Miami and Little Havana you'll find two very different neighborhoods that harken back to the city's early years. Cocoanut Grove, as it was then called, got its start as a ritzy seaside resort. Along its shoreline ever more lavish vacation homes sprouted, inhabited by European nobility and Old Southern gentry, and built and staffed mainly by Bahamian immigrants who lived in the part of the Grove that did not front the water. Like other Miami resort developments, Coconut Grove has had its good and bad times, with its heyday ending in the early 1960s when it, like Miami Beach to the north, fell out of vogue and turned into a low-rent area. It quickly attracted a bohemian-craftsy-hippie counterculture population, as many homes were converted into live-in artists' studios, and Coconut Grove acquired a reputation as a sort of Greenwich Village with sunshine.

Coral Gables, which adjoins Coconut Grove on its inland boundary, was the epicenter of Miami's real estate boom in the 1920s. It centered around developer George Merrick's Biltmore Hotel, which was considered the most luxurious resort hotel in Miami. (Although it was far from the nearest beach, the hotel boasted the largest swimming pool in the United States.) Merrick acquired 10,000 acres of farmland around the hotel and his own coral rock family home, and within five years the entire acreage had been subdivided and sold. Housing construction in Coral Gables represented the culmination of flamboyant, sometimes almost theme-parkish architecture that added to Miami's mystique in the eyes of chilly northerners. Most residences in the area were built in the Mediterranean Revival style that was favored for large mansions in many parts of the United States at that time, but visitors today will also see other homes from the 1920s that were designed in Chinese, French and Italian Provincial, and Dutch–South African Colonial revival styles.

Today, Coral Gables retains a country club feel conducive to driving tours and rubbernecking at peekaboo glimpses of fairy-tale mansions behind walls and groves of trees. Coconut Grove, meanwhile, has become a shoppers' paradise clustered around two big multilevel malls—CocoWalk and Mayfair—that have largely eschewed the standard shopping mall chain stores in favor of trendy, flashy boutiques that sell everything from retro feather boas to sequined motorcycle jackets.

Coconut Grove

Coconut Grove, a turn-of-the-20th-century village, was the area's first real winter resort. Long a nest of quiet homes and quaint stores, the Grove attracted throngs of hippies during the 1960s and now dances to the trendiness of the new century. Though housing prices in the Grove have skyrocketed in the last decade or so, resulting in widespread gentrification, a sizable number of middle-aged artists have resisted the temptation to sell out, choosing instead to stay and temper Coconut Grove's newfound commercialism with a deceptively laid-back creative edge.

SIGHTS

Your first sightseeing opportunity is **Silver Bluff**, an intriguing rock formation extending half a mile along Bayshore Drive between Crystal View and Emathia Street. Carved thousands of years ago by wave action, these knobby white constellations are made of oolitic limestone. Some of the area's first settlers, captured by the beauty of the bluff, built their homes around these rocks overlooking the bay.

Southward around a bend you'll encounter **Miami City Hall**. A two-story gleaming white structure preening on Biscayne Bay, it looks more like a small hotel than a government center. But then, that's typical of Miami. Carvings of little world globes traipse across the facade, hinting that the 1930s building used to be a busy Pan American Airlines seaplane base. ~ 3500 Pan American Drive; 305-250-5300, fax 305-854-4001; www.ci.miami.fl.us, e-mail mannydiaz@ci.miami.fl.us.

The village core lies along **Main Highway** and **Commodore Plaza**, just south of City Hall. Miami's trendiness central, these streets are an experience in contrived aesthetics. Chic shops with bubbled canopies intermingle with towering oaks and nibble at the brick-lined roadways. Fashion-conscious women stroll the sidewalks, laden with perfume and shopping bags.

Coconut Grove pioneer Ralph Middleton Munroe, a true lover and protector of Florida's natural beauty, would have been heartbroken to see throngs of people and automobiles buzzing around what used to be the world's largest hardwood hammock. Quite aptly, the remaining smidgen of nature here is the **Barnacle State Historic Site**, Munroe's serene five-acre estate overlooking Biscayne Bay. An old buggy trail meanders through a lush hammock to the house. This structure, built in stages between 1891 and 1928, is one of the oldest Dade County houses still located on its original site. Reflecting Munroe's devotion to shipbuilding and the sea, the two-story frame building resembles a barnacle and has a large veranda to catch ocean breezes. Many of the 19th-century furnishings are intact, and Munroe's excellent collection of pioneer photographs adorn the walls. On the grounds is an ancient well and a boathouse. Open to the public Friday through Monday; open Tuesday through Thursday for reserved tours. Admission. ~ 3485 Main Highway; 305-442-6866, fax 305-442-6872; www.floridastateparks.org.

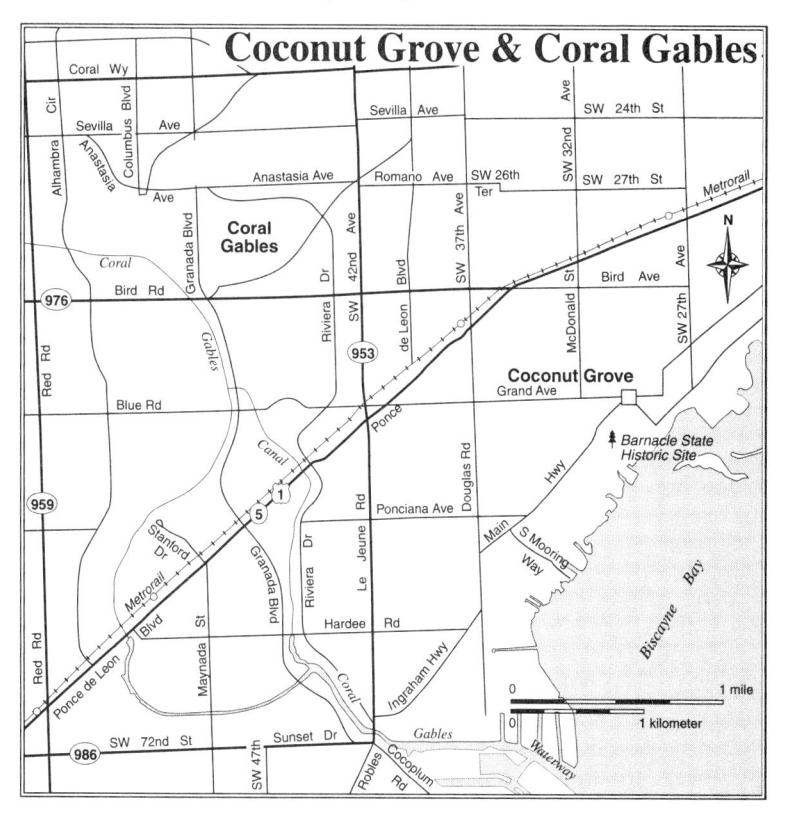

HIDDEN ▶ Another tribute to the area's earlier days, the **Coconut Grove Playhouse** is an inspiring, Spanish-style theater. Constructed in 1926, it was destroyed by the infamous hurricane that year and promptly rebuilt in 1927. Richly ornamented with parapets and twisted columns, the theater now hosts regional, national and international productions and continues to be a fashionable place to go. ~ 3500 Main Highway; 305-442-4000, fax 305-444-6437; www.cgplayhouse.org.

Hidden away from the road in the middle of a private school,
HIDDEN ▶ the **Pagoda of Ransom–Everglades School** is a real find. The 1902 pine building was the entire school until the campus expanded in the 1940s. Now, strolling back to the pagoda is like taking a trip through time. All around, preppy students laze in the grass or sail on the bay, while inside the pagoda's dusty walls rest memories of days past. Chances are, you'll be the only sightseer at this historic stop. ~ 3575 Main Highway; 305-460-8800, fax 305-443-0735; www.ransomeverglades.org.

Located at the north end of Coconut Grove, near where the Rickenbacker Causeway departs the mainland for Key Biscayne, **Vizcaya Museum and Gardens** is a vast Italian villa perched magnificently on Biscayne Bay. The place is the mastermind of farming magnate James Deering. A man infatuated with Renaissance styles, Deering hired 1000 people (one-tenth of Miami's population at the time) in 1916 to build the elaborate estate, a project that took two years and more than $15 million. Here you can wind your way through 34 rooms and halls lavishly adorned with priceless European antiques and paintings, oriental carpets, ornate moldings and spectacular architecture. Outside, stroll the formal Italian gardens, taking in the Great Stone Barge that rests brooding in the bay. The David A. Klein Orchidarium features a

AUTHOR FAVORITE

For a close-up look at the lavish lifestyle of the rich and famous in early-20th-century Miami, no place can quite compare with **Vizcaya Museum and Gardens**. Situated on Biscayne Bay, the European-inspired Vizcaya encompasses the grand winter home of farming magnate James Deering as well as manicured gardens and a historic village. See above for more information.

gallery of orchids. Admission. ~ 3251 South Miami Avenue; 305-250-9133, fax 305-285-2004; www.vizcayamuseum.com.

Just south of the entrance to Vizcaya stands what may be Miami's most impressive monument to Cuban refugees' hope of some day returning to their island home. The **Ermita de la Caridad** ("Hermitage of Charity"), a 90-foot-tall cone-shaped shrine designed to represent a lighthouse with a beacon facing Cuba, was built on a former piece of the Deering estate by the Catholic Church, which offers daily mass there. A panoramic mural around the base depicts the procession of Cuban history from the arrival of the first Spaniards to Castro's revolution. ~ 3609 South Miami Avenue; 305-854-2404.

◄ HIDDEN

One of the area's most unusual hotels, the **Mayfair House** is a work of art. Sculpted mahogany doors, hand-painted tiles and stained-glass panels swirl throughout the small, dark lobby, where guests receive champagne and orange juice upon check-in. The 179 suites, which surround a big, sunlit atrium, are decorated in Viennese art nouveau. Many have antique English grand pianos; all have Japanese hot tubs and all-marble baths. ~ 3000 Florida Avenue; 305-441-0000, 800-433-4555, fax 305-447-9173; www.mayfairhousehotel.com, e-mail mail@mayfairhousehotel.com. ULTRA-DELUXE.

LODGING

A terraced tower overlooking a large yacht basin, the **Doubletree Hotel Coconut Grove** is a casual but stylish kind of place. White marble tiles, hand-hewn cedar paneling and contemporary works of art adorn the lobby, which spills out onto an airy pool deck overlooking a busy avenue. Some of the 192 guest rooms have wet bars and modern furnishings. ~ 2649 South Bayshore Drive; 305-858-2500, 800-222-8733, fax 305-858-5776. DELUXE.

Beautiful jutting terraces brimming with flowering vines signify that you've reached the **Wyndham Grand Bay Hotel**, a very ritzy Miami address. Classical music is piped into a lobby styled with dramatic wood-trimmed glass walls, enormous crystal chandeliers and mirrored ceilings. Most of the 178 accommodations face the Grove's yacht basin and some are aesthetically furnished with period pieces and sunken marble tubs. All units feature breakfast balconies and minibars. A pool deck, restaurant and health spa are just a few of the amenities. Unmatched for service, the Grand Bay even serves you liquid refreshments when you check in. ~ 2669 South Bayshore Drive; 305-858-9600, 800-327-2788, fax 305-859-2026. ULTRA-DELUXE.

DINING

Green Street Café claims the prime people-watching corner and lavishes its outdoor patrons with tall frozen margaritas and green umbrellas to ward off the blazing sun. Burgers, omelettes, pizza and pasta are good for munching. Breakfast, lunch and dinner. ~ 3110 Commodore Plaza; 305-444-0244. BUDGET TO MODERATE.

Formerly an 1800s caretaker's cottage, **Tuscany's** now indulges a trendy clientele that convenes on the outdoor red-brick patio to gaze at a diverse group of passersby. The Italian-style menu includes the traditional selection of pastas, seafood, steak, salads, soups and desserts. ~ 3484 Main Highway; 305-445-0022. MODERATE.

Aptly named **Señor Frog's**, this toad-green stucco formation attracts a lively crowd that gulps huge margaritas and feasts on gringo food as well as tasty traditional Mexican fare. Sepia photos of Mexican heroes, brick floors and a wooden bar set a casual tone. The extensive menu is quite entertaining, warning against a "boring!" consommé and listing an entrée called *arroa cabezón* but saying, "no translation, just order it!" ~ 3480 Main Highway; 305-448-0999, fax 305-529-9598. MODERATE.

A tiny jewel in the midst of chain restaurants, **Le Bouchon du Grove** shines. The service is friendly and intimate—diners can expect a warm greeting from the proprietors at the door. The food is delicious and typical of an authentic French bistro. Musts here are salmon with thyme risotto, duck confit and *moules marinieres et frites*. Le Bouchon serves breakfast, lunch and dinner. ~ 3430 Main Highway; 305-448-6060. MODERATE TO DELUXE.

Café Tu Tu Tango is, quite simply, *the* place to nosh in Coconut Grove. Fashioned after an artist's loft in Barcelona, the wood-floored tapas bar is always crowded and always oh-so-good. Graze on an assortment of chips, dips, and fried tidbits such as calamari and alligator, or opt for a gourmet pizza that's brick-oven baked. ~ 3015 Grand Avenue, in the CocoWalk entertainment plaza; 305-529-2222, fax 305-461-5326; www.cafetututango.com. MODERATE.

Monty's Raw Bar is a perfect place for a dog-day afternoon. This restaurant plays host to swimsuit-clad locals and tourists who soak up the sun and calypso music. Casual tables overlook an expansive marina. Excellent conch fritters, stone crab and those famous Florida oysters on the half shell are featured. Expect bouillabaisse, lobster, steak and seafood on the dinner menu of the upscale upstairs eatery, Monty's Stone Crab Restaurant. ~ 2550 South Bayshore Drive; 305-858-1431; www.montysstonecrab.com. MODERATE TO DELUXE.

SHOPPING

For more than a decade, the Grove's vogue shops have been patronized by trendsetters and those who have money to burn. The best part of browsing these shady glass fronts is eyeing the other shoppers, who love to dress up for the occasion.

The heart of trendiness, **Mayfair in the Grove** has a glass-canopied atrium with savvy written all over it. Shoot up to the second and third floors in glass elevators. Don't miss **Royal**

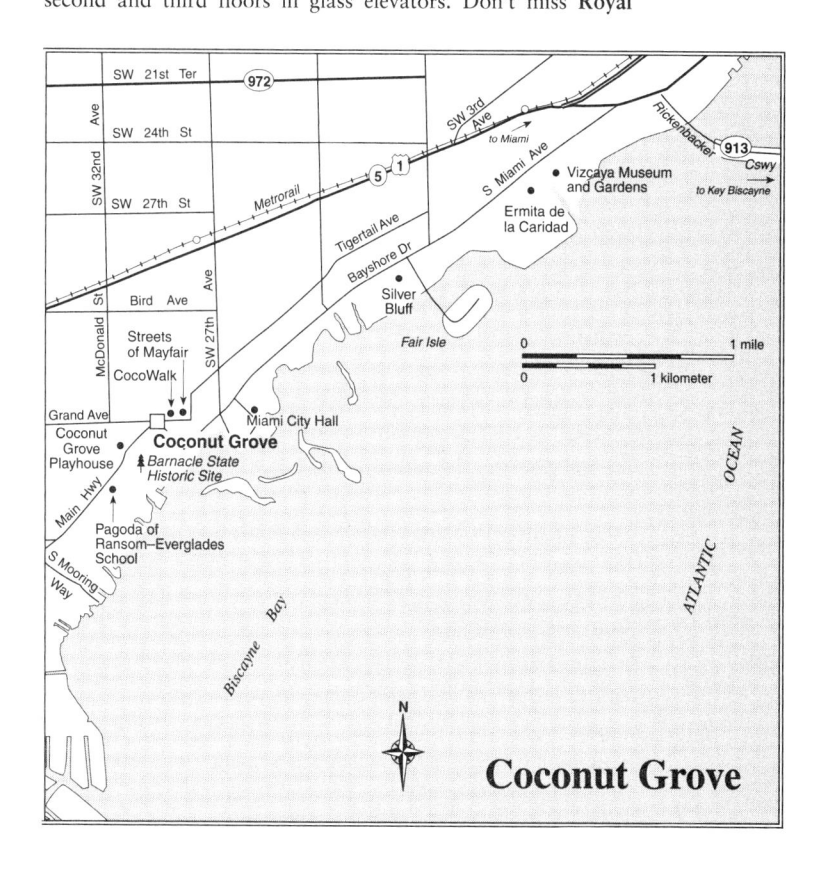

Palaces and Museums (305-774-0009), where the world's best art museums are represented in reproductions of classic art treasures of the Louvre and Prado, plus china, ties, coasters and other items both silly and splendid that borrow motifs from famous paintings. ~ 2911 Grand Avenue; 305-448-1700.

CocoWalk is a multilevel shopping and partying extravaganza, a fanciful version of Spanish stucco and coral rock woven with fountains and balconies and walkways. Among the chic CocoWalk shops is **The White House** (305-446-7747), which caters to the woman who loves white. Suits, sportswear, lingerie, parasols and picture frames are available. And though you probably hadn't considered new eyeglasses as a souvenir of Miami, a visit to **Coco Lunette** (305-441-0457) may change your mind. This optical store disguised as an accessory boutique features frames by famous-name designers like Gaultier, Versace and Moschino. Service is while-you-wait, but always busy. ~ 3015 Grand Avenue.

Maya Hatcha stocks shoes, women's clothing, purses, jewelry, trinkets, artwork and other cool stuff from Indonesia, Thailand, Central America and Africa. ~ 3058 Grand Avenue; 305-443-9040; www.mayahatcha.com.

Even if you thought your safe-sex education was complete, you may discover a thing or two at one of Coconut Grove's most offbeat boutiques, **Condoms USA**, where you'll find the widest imaginable array of prophylactics—male, female, oral, colored, flavored, glow-in-the-dark . . . . ~ 3066 Grand Avenue; 305-445-7729.

Mom will find her string bikini at **Ritchie Swimwear**, a colorful collage of neon, print and striped suits for men, women and children. ~ 3401 Main Highway; 305-443-7919; www.ritchieswimwear.com.

For party wear that is funky, flashy and affordable, check out the wearables at **Via Satelite**, where you can get clothing in chrome lamé, fishnet or faux leopard skin. ~ 3413 Main Highway; 305-648-0059.

Looking for glitzy women's fashions that are sure to get you past the velvet rope at Miami's trendiest clubs? Check out **Ella**, a space-age boutique where the slinky, backless, bright-colored evening gowns are designed to get you noticed. ~ 3444 Main Highway; 305-443-9250.

One of the most original jewelry emporiums in town, **H & H Jewels** offers wildly creative, ostentatiously chunky jewelry in 18-karat gold or sterling silver set with bright-colored precious gems and sold at formidable prices. ~ 3138 Commodore Plaza; 305-442-9760.

If you've watched with envy as all those inline skaters spin and dodge their way along the sidewalks of Miami Beach, maybe you owe yourself a shopping trip to Coconut Grove just to check out **Catch-A-Wave**, the city's largest purveyor of surfboards, skateboards and roller blades—and one of the oldest shops in Coconut Grove. ~ 2990 McFarland Road; 305-569-0339.

NIGHTLIFE

"The Grove" is a hub of nighttime activity. As dusk approaches, the sidewalks teem with shoppers and bar hoppers and a stream of traffic crawls along the village streets.

A shorts-and-flip-flops crowd assembles at **Monty's Raw Bar**, an outdoor, palm-crowned reggae and raw bar overlooking a marina. A live band plays nightly. ~ 2550 South Bayshore Drive; 305-856-3992.

The town's best watering hole is **Tavern in the Grove**, a non-trendy neighborhood spot with a long bar and framed Grove art. Music ranging from classic rock to country to hip-hop resounds from a jukebox. ~ 3416 Main Highway; 305-447-3884; www.tavernmiami.com.

The splendid **Coconut Grove Playhouse** showcases major musical and drama productions as well as comedy acts. Built in 1927, the three-story, Spanish-style building is beautifully ornamented with twisted columns and parapets. ~ 3500 Main Highway; 305-442-4000.

AUTHOR FAVORITE

A Coconut Grove mainstay for a quarter of a century, the **Coconut Grove Farmer's Market** is also a pioneer—it has always been organic, with fresh produce and vegan goods from South Dade's Glaser Organic Farms. The market also boasts a sought-after raw food deli. For those looking beyond food, offerings also include jewelry, handmade clothing and massage therapists. Open Saturdays 10 a.m. to 6 p.m. ~ Intersection of Margaret Street and Grand Avenue; 305-238-7747.

The CocoWalk shopping complex has several options. For great people-watching on a warm night (and what South Florida night isn't?) head over to **Fat Tuesdays**, an open-air bar that serves up frozen alcoholic concoctions from a row of slurpee-like machines. **Café Tu Tu Tango,** a jumping tapas eatery, is also popular for its outdoor bar, a second-story perch above the carnival of downtown Coconut Grove. ~ 3015 Grand Avenue; 305-529-2222; www.cafetututango.com.

Coral Gables

South of Coconut Grove off Route 1, you will find Coral Gables, the dream-come-true city of George Merrick. In the early 1900s, Merrick looked at these backwoods and envisioned grand things. He cleared citrus groves, laid streets and sidewalks, and brought in Mediterranean architecture, touting the spot as the "Miami Riviera." Those who visited Coral Gables, he promised, would find "endless golden sunlight and bronzed people."

Now this pristine, planned town boasts beautiful Spanish-style architecture and miles of country club living. Largely inhabited by wealthy Latinos, the city is a labyrinth of winding streets that unfortunately can make life difficult for the first-time visitor. Refer to maps and even then, plan to spend some time backtracking.

SIGHTS

Set on 19 acres in the midst of Coral Gables, the **Biltmore Hotel** is a stunning 15-story, 280-room Moorish tower built in the '20s as a replica of the Giralda Tower in Seville, Spain. The lobby boasts vaulted frescoes, massive chandeliers, arched courtyards and the country's largest hotel swimming pool. Weekend tours touch on the hotel's role as the showpiece of Coral Gables—the country's first planned posh community. Consider late-afternoon high tea in the lobby, Sunday brunch in the column-encircled courtyard or an evening of live jazz at the Continental-style brasserie. ~ 1200 Anastasia Avenue; 305-445-1926, 800-727-1927, fax 305-913-3159; www.biltmorehotel.com.

Around the time the Biltmore was going up, Merrick donated the land across the street for the **Coral Gables Congregational Church**. An architectural gem, the city's first church is a Mediterranean revival design with barrel tiles and ornate baroque ornaments. Its bell tower, mirroring the Biltmore's, is nearly as stunning. During the 1920s, University of Miami students—protesting school policies—ran the school's first underground newspaper from the tower. More treasures await inside: 16th-century furnishings, chandeliers and beautiful pews carved from native pecky cypress. ~ 3010 DeSoto Boulevard; 305-448-7421, fax 305-441-1836; www.coralgablescongregational.org, e-mail davidr@ucc-cgcc.org.

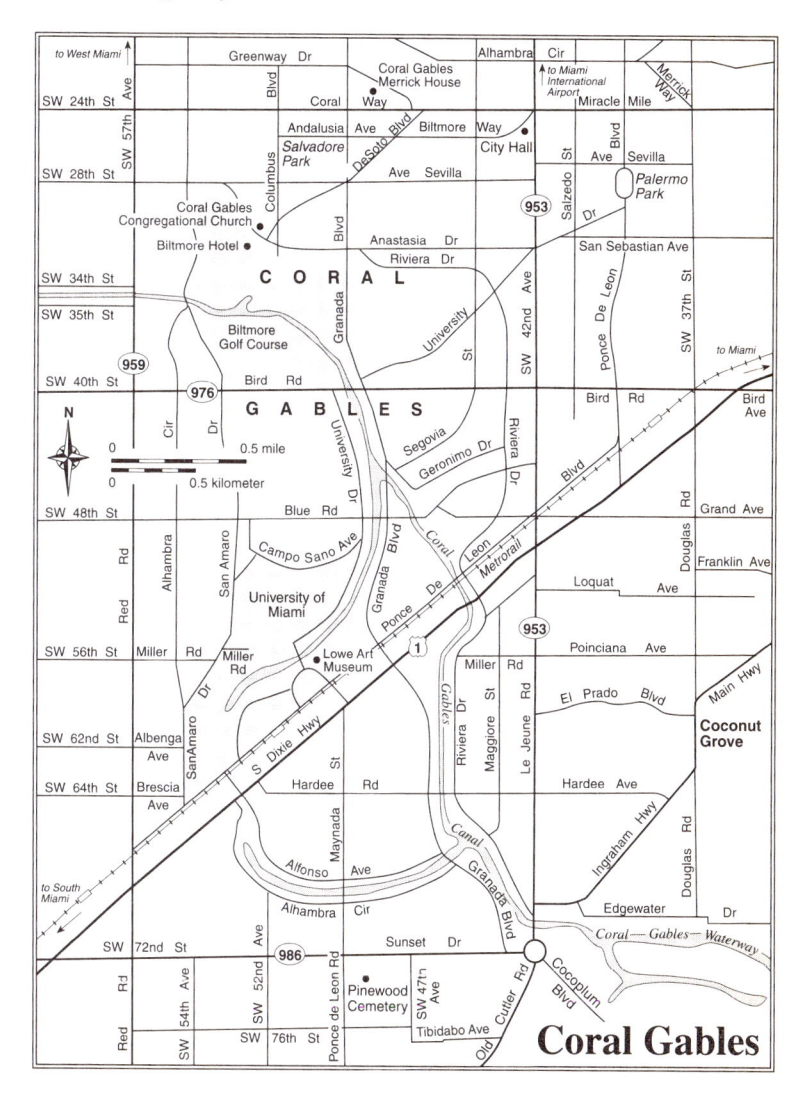

From here, twist your way northeast on DeSoto Boulevard to the **Venetian Pool**. Born out of a rock pit, this Merrick-built retreat is a sprawling lagoon bordered by a Mediterranean villa and the mandatory Miami palm trees. Coral caves, Venetian lampposts and intermittent waterfalls canvas the place, which was the stomping grounds for William Jennings Bryan, Johnny Weissmuller, Esther Williams and other notables. Call for hours. Admission. ~ 2701 DeSoto Boulevard; 305-460-5356.

At the end of DeSoto lies Coral Way, the road where George Merrick spent his boyhood days. The **Coral Gables Merrick House**, where Merrick grew up, has been enshrined by locals and is now a museum. Built around the turn of the 20th century, the coral rock structure and gabled, red-tiled roof gave the home its name. Listed on the National Register of Historic Places, the house is filled with artwork, photos and personal Merrick family treasures. Open Wednesday and Sunday for afternoon tours, or by appointment. Admission. ~ 907 Coral Way; 305-460-5361, fax 305-460-5097; www.coralgables.com, e-mail mbeach@coralgables.com.

Travel eastward on Coral Way and you'll uncover a gold mine known as Miracle Mile. This two-block address of swanky shops and brick-lined streets also houses **Coral Gables City Hall**, an imposing limestone structure that integrates circular and square design. Most impressive is a rounded wing with ornate columns and grotesque carvings true to the mannerist style. Stroll through the building and climb the worn, 1920s-era steps to the third and fourth floors. Along the way, you will see antiques and a brilliantly colored mural that spreads across a rotunda. ~ 405 Biltmore Way; 305-446-6800, fax 305-460-5371; www.coralgables.com.

An easy place to find, the **University of Miami** is south of downtown Coral Gables. Miami's prestigious university has about 15,000 students and a 260-acre maze of low-slung buildings, twisting canals and shady plazas. ~ 1306 Stanford Drive; 305-284-2318; www.miami.edu.

Center of activity here is the **Norman A. Whitten University Center**, where crowds of international students mill around game rooms, cafeterias and a large swimming pool. ~ 1306 Stanford Drive; 305-284-5646; www.miami.edu.

Nearby, student thespians have developed an excellent reputation with performances at the **Ring Theatre**. ~ 1380 Miller Drive; 305-284-3355; www.miami.edu.

Also on campus is the **Lowe Art Museum**, which features a sizable collection of Renaissance and Baroque paintings as well as American Indian, tribal African, Asian and pre-Columbian art. Closed Monday. Admission. ~ 1301 Stanford Drive; 305-284-3535; www.lowemuseum.org, e-mail zenony@miami.edu.

> Animal sculptures perched atop some houses in Chinese Village are meant to bring good luck to residents.

Perhaps more than anything, Coral Gables is a residential village. Winding through its storybook streets, you'll find clusters of private homes with specific architectural designs borrowed from various countries. Called **The Villages**, these 1920s neighborhoods are part of Merrick's scheme to bring in wealthy residents to his model city.

South of Route 1 on Riviera Drive and adjacent streets, **Chinese Village** consists of eight Asian homes styled with carved wooden balconies, curved tiled roofs and a great deal of lattice work.

◀ HIDDEN

Located down Santa Maria are the **Colonial Village** mansions, inspired by the Greek revival period with its tall, white columns, cool verandas, slate roofs and two-story porticoes.

Just off Riviera on Hardee Road are the **French Country**, **French Normandy** and **French City Villages**. Country-style estates resemble châteaux, with rounded and square towers and wrought-iron balconies. The city version features snazzy French town homes surrounded by large walls.

The **Dutch South African Village**, on LeJeune Road, is not African at all but mirrors farmhouses of wealthy Dutch colonists. The quaint L-shaped and T-shaped homes are adorned with scroll work, high domed arches and spiraling chimneys. ~ Call the Historical Resources Department (305-460-5093) for information.

◀ HIDDEN

In the midst of all this gentry is a point lost in time. Abandoned and all but forgotten, the **Pinewood Cemetery** rests in a deserted wooded lot between manicured lawns. Founded in 1855, the oldest cemetery south of the Miami River is overgrown with palmettos and pine trees and sprinkled with pieces of broken headstones. In the center, a single memorial stone pays tribute to more than 200 Miami pioneers buried here. One tombstone that's still intact marks the grave of a Confederate soldier. ~ 47th Avenue just south of Sunset Drive.

LODGING

Granted, there's not much atmosphere at the **Holiday Inn University of Miami**, located across the street from the University of

Miami. But the clean, nicely decorated rooms aren't quite as expensive as others in this pricey town. The three-story, U-shaped building surrounds a standard motel swimming pool. ~ 1350 South Dixie Highway; 305-667-5611, fax 305-669-3153; www.hicoralgables.com, e-mail miaumsc@soundhospitality.com. DELUXE.

The quaint **David William Hotel** offers comfortable accommodations. Slightly camp, with a European flair, the 1964 hostelry has about 45 clean, carpeted rooms and a concrete rooftop pool. ~ 700 Biltmore Way; 305-445-7821, fax 305-913-1933; www.davidwilliamhotel.com. ULTRA-DELUXE.

The **Hyatt Regency Coral Gables** is one of those ultramodern establishments straining to imitate Old World elegance. Designed with a 14th-century Moorish castle in mind, the hotel features 242 rooms fashioned with impressive ten-foot windows, mini-bars and glass coffee tables. Built in 1987, the 14-story pink-and-white hotel takes up an entire city block and features a pool terrace and a gourmet restaurant. ~ 50 Alhambra Plaza; 305-441-1234, 800-233-1234, fax 305-441-0520; www.coralgables.hyatt.com. ULTRA-DELUXE.

Al Capone once slept in the great orange Moorish tower of the **Biltmore Hotel**, and Esther Williams swam in its outsized swimming pool. Today, celebrities still frequent the 1926 Mediterranean grand dame lavished with Old World furnishings, vast arches and columns, handpainted ceiling mosaics, breezeways lined with Italian statuary and perfectly tended gardens and golf greens. The 280 rooms are impeccably adorned—some nearly palatial. The pool is the largest in the country. Two superb restaurants, ten tennis courts, an 18-hole championship golf and a spa and health club make this one of Miami's most desirable resorts. ~ 1200 Ana-

AUTHOR FAVORITE

A rare find in an urban area, **Place St. Michel** possesses all the charm of a French country inn. A mass of clinging ivy obscures the exterior from passing traffic, while inside awaits an unhurried world of carefully chosen antiques, tiled floors, potted flowers and personal service. Built in 1926, the hotel has 27 bedrooms, warmly decorated with hand-loomed rugs, French shag lamps and high, detailed ceilings. Continental breakfast included. ~ 162 Alcazar Avenue; 305-444-1666, 800-848-4683, fax 305-529-0074; www.hotelplacestmichel.com. DELUXE.

stasia Avenue; 305-445-1926, 800-727-1926, fax 305-913-3159; www.biltmorehotel.com, e-mail stephaniekirby@biltmorehotel.com. ULTRA-DELUXE.

Another upscale downtown address, the **Omni Colonnade Hotel** is an impressive tribute to Coral Gables' beginnings. In the lobby you'll find enchanting 1920s town photos and corridors of cathedral windows and pink-and-green marble. The 157 accommodations follow suit, providing formal surroundings with handblown candelabra, mahogany dressers and intricately painted vases. ~ 180 Aragon Avenue; 305-441-2600, 800-843-6664, fax 305-445-3929; www.omnihotels.com. ULTRA-DELUXE.

A misfit along gourmet row, **House of India** promises two things: to provide some of the area's most exotic food, and to give you lots of it. You will encounter large portions of dishes such as *mulligatawny* soup, *navrattan shai korma* (vegetables cooked with spices and cream), curried lamb and an intriguing clay oven–baked bread. Carved wooden dividers create private niches for diners, but the slightly tattered furnishings give a worn look. ~ 22 Merrick Way; 305-444-2348, fax 305-444-0140. BUDGET TO MODERATE.

DINING

In a town renowned for its abundance of French restaurants, **John Martin's** is a welcome change of pace. Run by two Irish childhood buddies, the cultured eatery focuses on European cuisine with Gaelic accents. The old-time decor boasts dark mahogany furnishings and a surprisingly casual atmosphere. Try the Irish stuffed chicken, oak-smoked salmon or Gaelic steak with whiskey-mushroom sauce. There's live music Friday through Sunday nights. ~ 253 Miracle Mile; 305-445-3777; www.johnmartins.com, e-mail info@johnmartins.com. MODERATE TO DELUXE.

You'd sort of expect to find **Restaurant St. Michel** hidden along a hilly road in the French countryside. This splendid little restaurant, situated in a 1926 ivy-clad hotel of the same name, makes you wish the night would linger. Dramatic ceilings, beautiful antiques and elegant draperies punctuated with period furniture create tranquil environs. The New American cuisine is exceptional, with entrées such as sautéed Florida Keys yellowtail with tropical fruit salsa and fried plantains, and crispy Long Island duckling with wild rice and vegetables. Breakfast, lunch and dinner. ~ 162 Alcazar Avenue; 305-444-1666, fax 305-529-0074; www.hotelplacestmichel.com. MODERATE TO ULTRA-DELUXE.

You can order any of the dishes at **Bangkok, Bangkok** with one to five stars, depending on how spicy you like it. Highly regarded by locals, the Thai eatery boasts a full range of fish, beef, seafood and poultry doused in savory and piquant sauces with fruits and vegetables. Two "American" dining rooms are rather plain, but an elaborate Thai balcony has scarlet carpets, redwood walls and carved wood tables with floor cushions. ~ 157 Giralda Avenue; 305-444-2397, fax 305-233-2139. MODERATE.

Just east of Coral Gables, a stretch of road called Coral Way offers a handful of reliable neighborhood restaurants. You'll find the same customers day after day at **Villa Italia**, a simple yet intimate neighborhood café that serves Italian cuisine with gusto. This is food like grandma used to make—thick, hearty spaghetti sauces, bubbling cheesy lasagna, pizza loaded with meat and vegetables, and eggplant parmigiana, a house specialty. A place not to miss! ~ 3058 Coral Way; 305-444-0206, fax 305-441-0971. BUDGET TO MODERATE.

> Free weekday trolley service shuttles shoppers throughout Coral Gables, including the popular Miracle Mile area.

Scenes of Greek fishing ports are splashed on the walls of **Mykonos**, aptly named for its savory Greek fare. A family-run eatery, this diner gets extra noisy when locals pile in for excellent dolmadakia (stuffed grape leaves), moussaka (layered beef and eggplant), spanakopita (spinach pie) and *pastitsio* (Greek lasagna). A Mediterranean treat. ~ 1201 Coral Way; 305-856-3140, fax 305-856-3141. BUDGET TO MODERATE.

SHOPPING A bustling Mediterranean-style city with country club pizzazz, Coral Gables boasts four blocks of shops dubbed **Miracle Mile**. ~ Between Douglas and LeJeune roads.

The Estate Wines & Gourmet Foods has shelves stocked with esoteric edibles from around the world as well as a solid selection of wine. ~ 92 Miracle Mile; 305-442-9915.

At **Rudma Picture Co.** you'll find oils and lithographs from recognized Florida and Cuban artists. ~ 239 Miracle Mile; 305-443-6262.

Coin and stamp collectors will adore **Gables Coin and Stamp**. Rows of rare coins and stamps line the shelves of this eclectic spot. Closed Sunday. ~ 322 Miracle Mile; 305-446-0032.

Satin and lace abound at **Daisy Tarsi**, an exclusive women's formal and bridal wear shop with racks of stunning, custom-made cocktail gowns and bridal accessories. ~ 311 Miracle Mile; 305-854-5557.

Looking for used and out-of-print books? Check out **Books & Books** for art and design, fiction and travel. ~ 265 Aragon Avenue; 305-442-4408; www.booksandbooks.com.

NIGHTLIFE

A local 1 a.m. bar curfew squelched much of the nighttime action in this posh, largely Latino city. However, sprinkled liberally throughout these well-groomed lawns you'll discover some promising area theater.

The 100-seat **New Theatre** hosts both experimental and traditional plays by a resident company. ~ 4120 Laguna Street; 305-443-5909; www.new-theatre.org.

Founded in 1987, the **Actors' Playhouse at the Miracle Theatre** puts on critically acclaimed musical productions for all ages. A former 1950s movie house, the deco venue offers three stages, producing a national children's theater festival, an annual play reading series, conservatories and a summer camp. Its season runs from May to January. ~ 280 Miracle Mile; 305-444-9293; www.actorsplayhouse.org.

Though most of the floor space inside **John Martin's Pub** belongs to the restaurant, the Erin-go-bar downstairs is one of the favored happy-hour stops for much of the Gables business crowd. Irish beer is on tap and Irish newspapers lie on tabletops. The bar is overcrowded on Fridays, but the atmosphere is convivial, the bartenders efficient and the regulars warmhearted. Expect to jig to Irish bands Wednesday through Sunday. ~ 253 Miracle Mile; 305-445-3777.

The **Alcazaba** in the heart of Coral Gables is best on Friday when a live salsa band heats up the place. Popular with an older crowd (anyone not considered a Gen X-er), the small dancefloor is full on weekends and Wednesdays when women drink free champagne. Dress code. Open Wednesday, Friday and Saturday only. ~ Hyatt Regency, 50 Alhambra Plaza; 305-441-1234 ext. 2600.

The University of Miami's **Ring Theatre** has cornered a loyal following with quality student-produced musicals, comedy and drama. ~ 1312 Miller Drive; 305-284-3355.

EIGHT

Key Biscayne & Biscayne National Park

Biscayne Bay extends from the southern tip of Miami Beach down to the northern end of Key Largo, a distance of about 29 miles. Part of the shoreline includes the coast of Coconut Grove and Coral Gables; most of the rest is uninhabited wetlands. The outer limit of the bay, lying six to eight miles offshore, is a chain of long, slender keys, or islands, with an eight-mile gap that hides an underwater reef, between inhabited Key Biscayne on the north and uninhabited Elliot Key and its chain of about 40 smaller islands on the south.

The easiest way to explore Key Biscayne is to drive out the Rickenbacker Causeway to Bill Baggs Cape Florida State Park at the end of Key Biscayne, where you can experience the wild island environment and then stop for lunch and a visit to the Miami Seaquarium on the way back.

The southern half of Biscayne Bay, most of which is set aside as Biscayne National Park, is harder to get to. Ninety-five percent of the park is underwater, and most of the area above the water line is not accessible by car, only by private boat or by tours offered by a park service concessionaire. Besides its abundant bird life and its coral reef teeming with tropical fish and sea turtles, Biscayne National Park is fascinating because it is so close to the big city, yet so wild that it has changed little since the first Spanish explorers laid eyes on it more than four centuries ago.

Key Biscayne

Take the undulating Rickenbacker Causeway across the brilliant turquoise water of Biscayne Bay and you'll land on Virginia Key, a speck of an island smothered in immense Australian pines and quiescent beaches. Although the island has remained very much in its natural state, tourism is beginning to leave its mark here.

Farther down, the larger Key Biscayne is a lush flatland dotted with bushy seagrape trees and willowy pines. A historic crossroads, the barrier island was encountered by Ponce de León in 1513, which is when he dubbed it the Cape of Florida.

SIGHTS

On Virginia Key, you'll encounter seals, Florida manatees, dolphins and a killer whale—but only those living at **Miami Seaquarium**. The 38-acre attraction is flanked by water on three sides and affords a look at local marine and bird life, if you don't mind seeing it in cages and tanks. Get a hug from a sea lion, watch dolphins perform clever moves and listen to the warbles and chirps of native birds. A wet and dry playground will keep the little ones busy. The place is worth visiting, though overpriced. Admission. ~ 4400 Rickenbacker Causeway; 305-361-5705, fax 305-365-0075; www.miamiseaquarium.com.

Crandon Boulevard is Key Biscayne's main drag, cutting two miles through the length of the island. Quaint strip shopping centers, golf fairways and manicured condos line the boulevard.

Tucked obscurely at the island's tip is the 1825 **Cape Florida Lighthouse**, Florida's oldest remaining lighthouse. Oblivious to noisy beachgoers, the white-brick cylinder rises 95 feet from the beach and peers serenely across the Atlantic Ocean, remembering a time when it guided ships through the perilous coastal reefs. Its sturdy walls survived a severe Seminole Indian attack in 1836 as well as an onslaught by Confederate sympathizers during the Civil War. Closed Tuesday and Wednesday. ~ 1200 South Crandon Boulevard in Bill Baggs Cape Florida State Park; 305-361-5811, fax 305-365-0003.

LODGING

The island has only a smattering of hotels, but thankfully each is nestled on a choice slice of beach. The **Silver Sands**, a traditional, L-shaped motel commanding fantastic views, is a departure from fancy oceanfront highrises. This homey, single-story hostelry surrounds a quiet courtyard with a pool and sandy path snaking its way to the beach. Guest rooms are clean and comfortable. Four wooden cottages are the best accommodations. ~ 301 Ocean Drive; 305-361-5441, fax 305-361-5477; www.silversandsmiami.com. DELUXE.

The white, pyramid-shaped **Sonesta Beach Resort** sits crossways and purveys a sense of cool island elegance. The lobby is a mesh of Roman tile floors, glass tables and a waterfall plummeting down an abstract wall design. The resort has a palm tree–studded swimming pool and 292 rooms—all with ocean or island views—furnished with modern decor. An extensive children's program draws lots of families. ~ 350 Ocean Drive; 305-361-2021, 800-766-3782, fax 305-361-3096; www.sonesta.com. ULTRA-DELUXE.

DINING

Eating out on Key Biscayne means trysting with cool blue Biscayne Bay. Arguably, the **Rusty Pelican** has cornered the market on views. Poised on the edge of Key Biscayne and surrounded by water on three sides, the Pelican faces sweeping scenes of downtown and glistening Biscayne Bay. The two-story rustic wooden building is set amidst a sea of palm trees and flowering plants. Inside, you'll find brick floors, stone walls and huge fishing nets draped from the ceiling. Atmosphere is the obvious draw here, since the fare—which focuses on seafood, Continental style—is good but overpriced. Try the coconut shrimp, veal Mediterranean (sautéed, served with sun-dried tomato, pistachio nuts and cream) or spicy lobster and crab pasta. The all-you-can-eat seafood Sunday brunch here is a real treat. ~ 3201 Rickenbacker Causeway; 305-361-3818, fax 305-361-8384. MODERATE TO ULTRA-DELUXE.

> Episodes of "Flipper" were reportedly filmed around Jimbo's, a ramshackle bar built on the edge of the bay.

Bayside Seafood Hut is known by boaties and windsurfers who frequent the Key. The bar and restaurant is a waterside, casual, mostly outdoor place tucked behind the Miami Marine Stadium and a boatyard. Most of the tables sit under a thatched roof. This is a great place at sunset. The smoked-fish dip is a must and the seafood sandwiches are always good. ~ 3501 Rickenbacker Causeway; 305-361-0808, fax 305-361-8840. MODERATE.

If you crave Asian food, you'll love **Two Dragons**. Sit in cozy wicker pagodas and sample traditional Chinese Mandarin and Szechuan as well as some Japanese cuisine. Black lacquered tables and ornate stained glass accented by palm fronds are found throughout the twin eateries. Dinner only. ~ Sonesta Beach Resort, 350 Ocean Drive; 305-361-2021, fax 305-361-3096; www.sonesta.com. BUDGET TO ULTRA-DELUXE.

Sunday's on the Bay is a popular restaurant and bar. On Sunday a reggae band often plays in the waterfront bar. The Sunday brunch is the best draw here; tables are jammed with more than 200 items. The menu is standard fern bar fare (pastas, burgers, salads, seafood) and the crowd is usually predominantly boaties and folks who celebrate watching sunsets. ~ 5420 Crandon Boulevard; 305-361-6777, fax 305-361-8974. MODERATE TO DELUXE.

Jimbo's, hidden on a Virginia Key backroad, is a behind-the-guidebook kind of place that is pure old Florida. A small bar on the water's edge where the bay trickles into the back areas, the brightly painted Caribbeanesque storefronts that line the area around the bar add to the otherworldliness. A bocce ball court

◄ HIDDEN

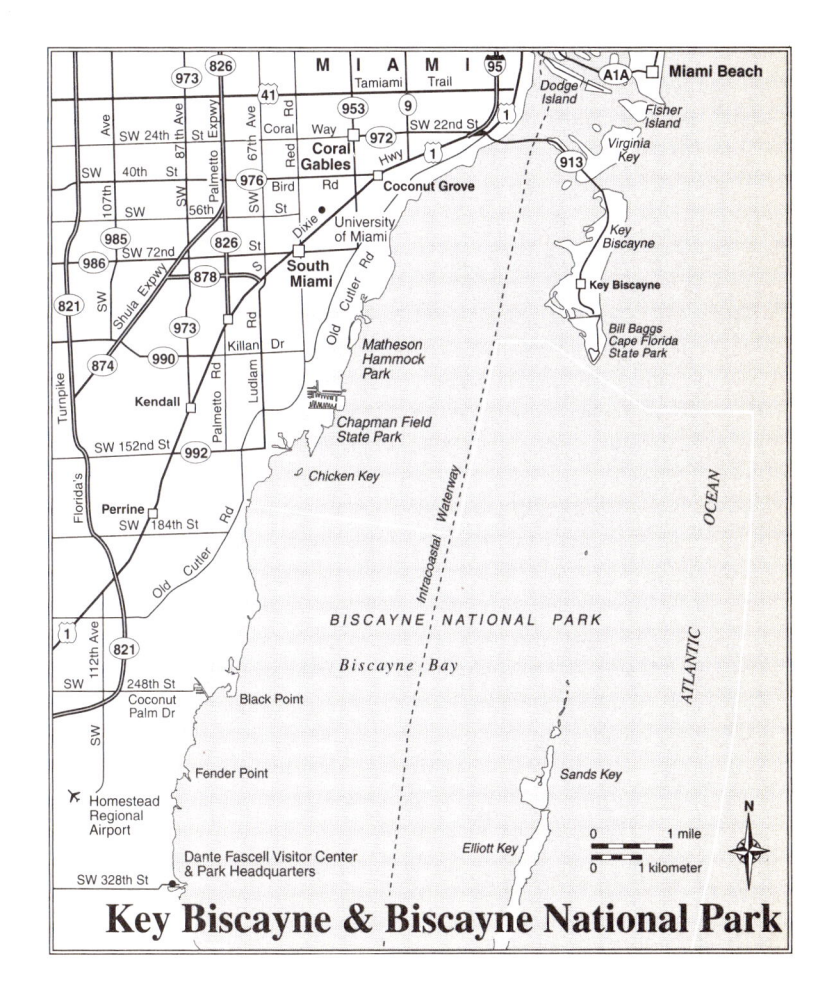

Key Biscayne & Biscayne National Park

draws a fervid group of regulars. Beer is served out of a cooler and patrons park on an old couch outside the tiny place. The smoked fish—its only offering—is sublime. ~ Take the third left after the Miami Marine Stadium on an unmarked street; 305-361-7026. BUDGET.

SHOPPING Key Biscayne is not known for its shopping and has no malls or upscale shopping streets. Most of the commerce focuses on necessities, and the scant shopping is relegated to a couple of strip centers like **KB Galeria** and the **Square Shopping Center** on Crandon Boulevard, the key's main artery.

Next to the Square Shopping Center, the **Pretty Boutique** (305-361-2806) is a store that sells islandy-fashion clothes, shoes and accessories for women and children at very reasonable prices. ~ 328 Crandon Boulevard.

For some of the freshest fish in town, visit the docks at the **Crandon Marina** in the late afternoon as the anglers return with the catch of the day. If you're lucky, they might sell you their surplus catch.

NIGHTLIFE For dance music, from Latin to trance, visit **Stefano's** on Friday and Saturday. While there's no glistening bay in sight, pleasant garden surroundings are an acceptable substitute. ~ 24 Crandon Boulevard; 305-361-7007, fax 305-361-1681; www.stefanos.com. MODERATE TO ULTRA-DELUXE.

BEACHES & PARKS **HOBIE BEACH** A ribbon of fluffy sand along a scenic causeway, this beach gets its name from the hundreds of sailboaters and windsurfers who whiz up and down the coast. Forever windy and spirited, Hobie Beach affords spectacular views of downtown while offering solace under canopies of Australian pines. It's always crowded, especially on weekends, so get here early. When swimming, stay very close to the shore. Otherwise, you'll get plowed down by windsurfers and jet skiers. Facilities include sailboard, sailboat, windsurfing and jet ski rentals and food vendors. ~ Located on the south side of Rickenbacker Causeway.

VIRGINIA KEY BEACH Sugar-fine sand rings most of this quiescent island that's smothered in tall pine trees

Text continued on page 128.

KEY BISCAYNE BEACHES & PARKS

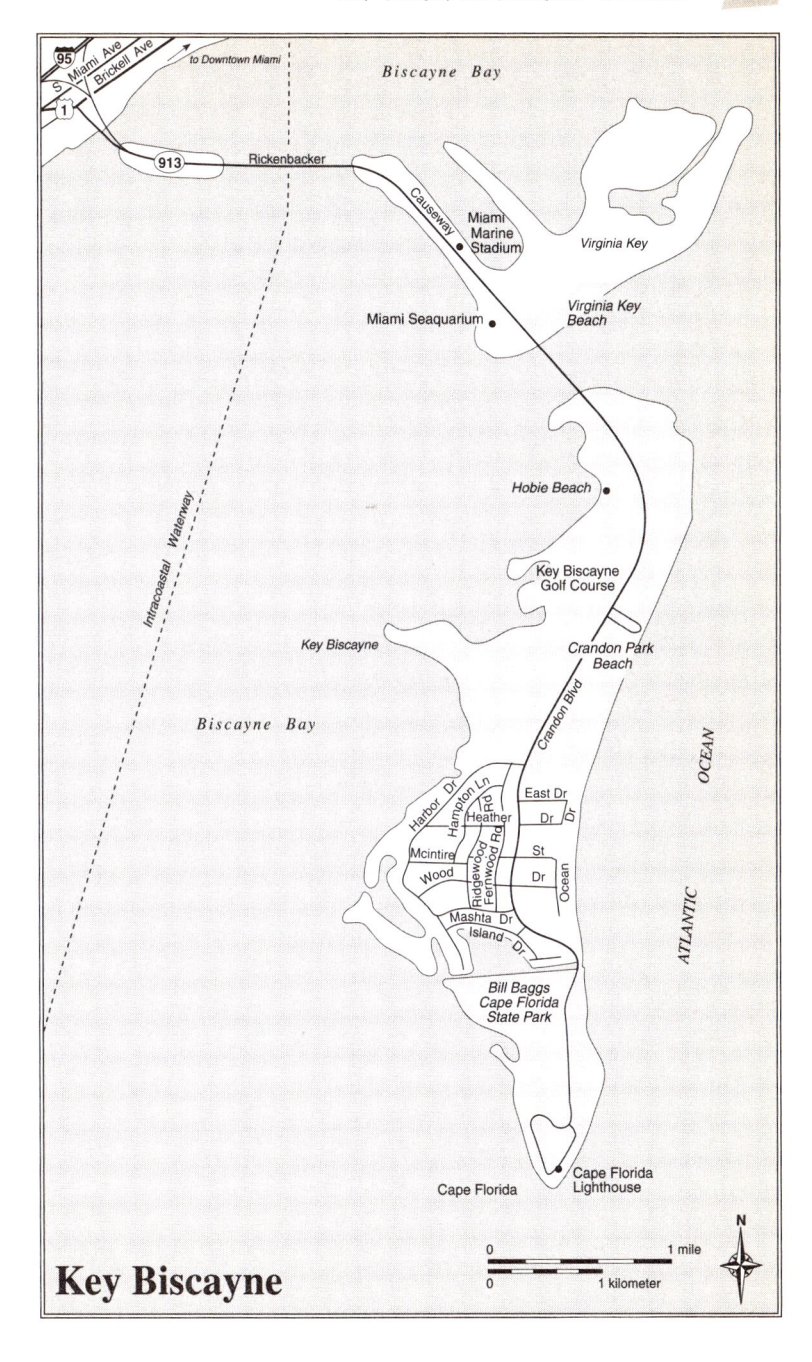

Key Biscayne

Everglades National Park

South of Homestead and Florida City, Everglades National Park begins, almost like a boundary of uneasy truce between people and nature. You quickly forget that Miami is just up the road a piece or that tended gardens lie behind you. Before you lies the mysterious world of what some call "the real Florida," the home of the alligator, the panther, the royal palm and the endangered bald eagle.

There are a number of ways to tackle this area of the park. For help in designing your plan, stop at the **Ernest F. Coe Visitor Center**. Here park staff members will provide you with all sorts of useful information, including weather, trail and insect conditions and listings of the season's varied and informative ranger-guided tours. All visitors centers in the park are wheelchair accessible. ~ 40001 State Road 9336, ten miles southwest of Homestead; 305-242-7700, fax 305-242-7711; www.nps.gov/ever, e-mail ever_information@nps.gov.

Once you have paid your admission and entered the park, you are on the single park road that will eventually arrive at Flamingo, 38 miles away, at the tip of the state on the edge of Florida Bay. This winding, lonely road traverses the heart of the park, meandering among tall pines, through seemingly endless expanses of sawgrass prairie and alongside mysterious dark ponds. Off this road lie a number of paths, trails, boardwalks and waterways designed to give the visitor as wide an Everglades experience as possible.

About four miles into the park (or four miles to the left at the turnoff), watch for signs to the **Royal Palm Visitor Center** on your left. Even if you have already spent a good amount of time at the main center, you should take a stroll down each of the two half-mile trails that begin here. Close together but very different, each plunges into a distinctive Everglades environment. Ranger-led walks are offered here year-round. Most trails are wheelchair accessible.

About seven miles from the main entrance, the half-mile **Pineland Trail** is a mile beyond the Long Pine Key campground; it circles through a section of slash pine forest. Here the ground is dry; occasional fires keep undergrowth in check so the pines can thrive without competition. This is a good place to look at the rock and solution holes formed in the shallow bed of limestone that lies under South Florida. Or just to picnic beside a quiet lake.

About six miles beyond the Pinelands, you come to the **Pa-hay-okee Overlook** (0.25 mile), named for the American Indian word for Everglades, meaning "grassy waters." Walk the short boardwalk and climb the observation tower for a wonderful panorama of the sawgrass prairie dotted with collections of ancient dwarf cypress and small island hammocks of hardwoods. This is one of the best overviews in the park; it's a great place for birdwatching.

Park rangers refer to hammocks as the "bedrooms of the Everglades," the places where so many wild creatures, large and small, find dry ground and shade from the tropical sun. About seven miles from Pa-hay-okee, you can explore one of these magnificent "highlands" that thrive just above the waterlines. The half-mile **Mahogany Hammock Trail** enters the cool, dark, jungle environment of a typical hardwood hammock.

Stop at the **West Lake Trail**, about 11 miles from Mahogany Hammock, for a good close-up look at mangroves. You can walk among the three varieties that thrive here along the half-mile boardwalk trail. With practice you will be able to identify them all—the predominant red mangroves with their arched, spidery prop roofs, black mangroves sending up fingerlike breathing tubes called "pneumatophores" from the mud and white mangroves and buttonwood on the higher, dryer shores of the swampy areas.

As you near the end of the park road, you will pass **Mrazek Pond**, another lovely birdwatching spot, especially rewarding during the winter months. Roseate spoonbills, along with many other common and exotic waterfowl, often come to this quiet, glassy pond to feed.

The road ends at the **Flamingo Visitor Center**, where a remote fishing village once stood. Early settlers could reach the area only by boat, and along with fishing, farming, the making of charcoal and all sorts of other activity—legal and not—went on here. The town is gone now, replaced by a marina, concessions, a motel and cabins, a campground, a gift shop and a visitors center. At Flamingo you can select from a variety of sightseeing opportunities, such as ranger-guided walks, wilderness canoe trips, campfire programs and hands-on activities. Offerings vary with the seasons; check at the visitors center for a schedule. ~ Located 38 miles from the main entrance; 239-695-2945, fax 239-695-3854; www.nps.gov/ever.

To really experience the Everglades, stay at least a couple of nights in the **Flamingo Lodge**. This, the only accommodation in the park, is a plain old motel with window air conditioners and jalousies that can be opened to let in the intriguing watery smells of the 'glades and the shallow bay. Flamingo also offers rustic cottages with fully equipped kitchens. Park entrance fee is not included in the rates. ~ State Route 9336, in the Everglades National Park; 239-695-3101, 800-600-3813, fax 239-695-3921; www.flamingolodge.com, e-mail info-flamingo@xanterra.com. MODERATE.

For more information, consult *Hidden Florida Keys & Everglades* (Ulysses Press, 2004).

and thick brush. At the eastern tip, where most people can be found, flocks of seagulls scurry about the placid shore, leaving their clawed imprints. But here's the real scoop: If you want seclusion, seek out the key's southwestern rim. Park in lot number one, then backtrack through the wooded areas until you find a series of natural coves. This was once a nude beach, and you'll still see a few birthday suits between these crevices. There's not much sand, but the crystal-clear water is an exceptional place to swim. There are picnic tables, restrooms, showers, lifeguards and wooded trails. Day-use fee $3 to $5. ~ Off Rickenbacker Causeway; 305-361-2749.

CRANDON PARK BEACH Key Biscayne's most popular beach sports a very wide swath of tawny sand edged with clusters of palm trees and a sliver of grassy meadow. A concrete path and spacious grassy areas border the mile-long stretch, which is a popular spot for Latino families. Ocean waves purr gently against a knee-deep sand bar that extends nearly 500 yards out, making this a great place to swim. An amusement area showcases an antique carousel, and a nature center provides environmental information on the area. Facilities consist of picnic areas, restrooms, showers, lifeguards, bicycle trails, concession stands and botanical gardens. Day-use fee, $5 per vehicle. ~ Located midway down Key Biscayne off Rickenbacker Causeway; 305-361-5421, fax 305-365-3002; www.co.miami-dade.fl.us/parks.

BILL BAGGS CAPE FLORIDA STATE PARK Situated at the southern end of Key Biscayne and covered in native subtropical vegetation, the 406-acre park offers scenic drives, broad beaches good for swimming and nine fishing piers. Perched in the sand dunes, an 1825 lighthouse still peers across the horizon. In the distance, several stilt houses—built decades ago by fishermen—are clustered together in the Atlantic Ocean, a peculiar spectacle for beachgoers. Today, anglers fish from the seawall on the Biscayne Bay side for snook, red snapper, yellow tail, jack and grouper. Facilities include picnic tables, restrooms, showers, a restaurant and a boardwalk. Day-use fee, $5 per vehicle; walkers, bicyclists $1; motorcycles $2. ~ Located at Key Biscayne's tip, via Rickenbacker Causeway; 305-361-5811, 305-361-8779, fax 305-365-0003.

Biscayne National Park

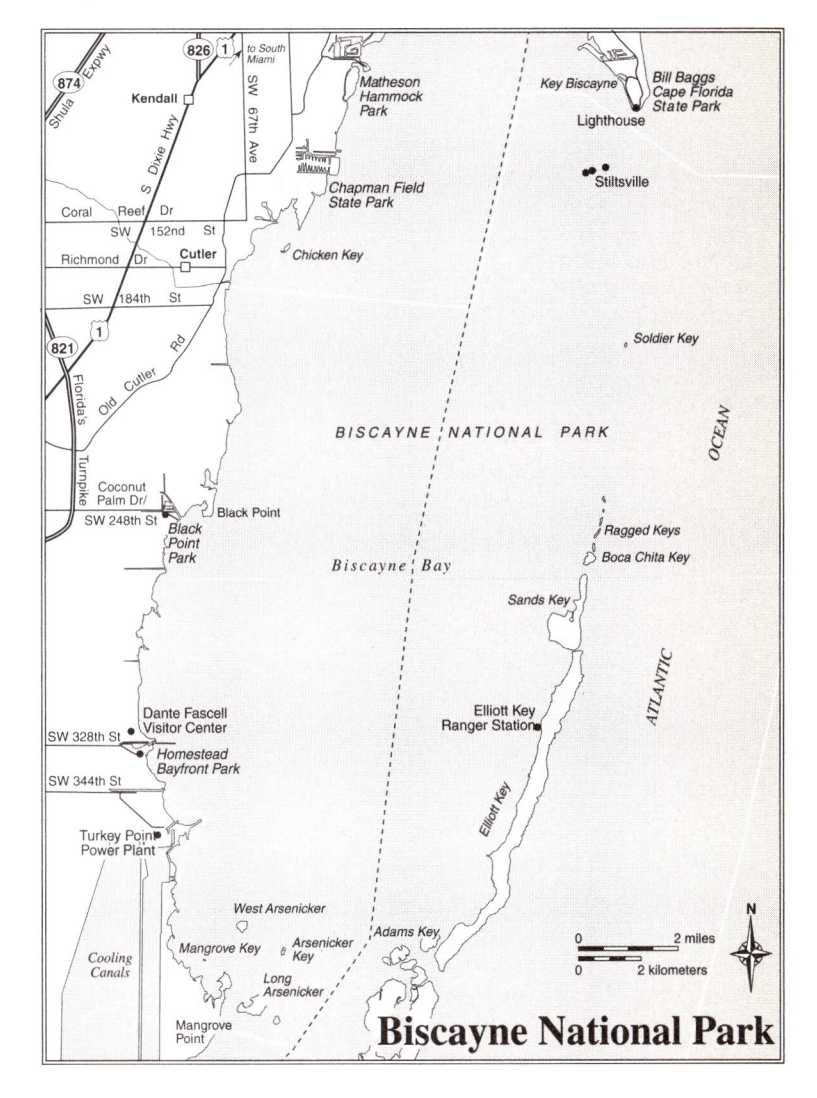

The 173,500-acre Biscayne National Park is the largest marine park in the National Park system, much of it hidden from the average traveler since it lies beneath the waters of Biscayne Bay and the Atlantic Ocean. The shallow, crystalline waters of the bay are actually a marine estuary, where fresh water from the Everglades mixes with Atlantic salt water. The result is an environment where lush beds of turtle-grass, manatee-grass and other sea grasses grow beneath the water, providing a place where young fish and sea turtles can hide from predators until they mature. The bay also provides essential habitat for dolphins and alligators as well as endangered species such as West Indian manatees and rare American crocodiles.

SIGHTS

Biscayne National Park includes a narrow remnant of mangrove shoreline. The mangroves provide shelter for young and small sea creatures, while helping keep the bay clean and clear by filtering the water that flows into it. They also provide nesting habitats and refuge for about 50 bird species including tropicbirds, ibises, roseate spoonbills, wood storks, vultures, eagles and occasional flamingos. Brown pelicans, little blue herons, snowy egrets and a few tropical fish can be seen by even the most casual stroller from the mainland jetty. The mangrove-fringed keys that lie offshore allow discovery of such tropical flora as gumbo-limbo trees, strangler fig and devil's potato.

> Manatees, crocodiles and four types of sea turtles (green, hawksbill, leatherback and kemps ridley) are among the endangered species that inhabit Biscayne National Park.

The **Dante Fascell Visitor Center** has exhibits and a multimedia show that tell about the plants and wildlife in the park; there's also a bookstore and a beautiful veranda with rocking chairs overlooking the bay. Notice the center's curious flagpole: it's shaped like the mast of an old sailing ship, and the American flag flies from its place of honor at the end of the horizontal gaff, not from the tip of the mast as landlubbers might expect. ~ 9710 Southwest 328th Street, Homestead; 305-230-1144, fax 305-230-1120; www.nps.gov/bisc, e-mail bisc_information@nps.gov.

To fully appreciate the beauty of this unusual park, take a three-hour glass-bottom boat tour or go snorkeling or scuba diving around the colorful reef. The park may also be explored by canoe. Daily snorkel, scuba and glass-bottom boat trips to the reef, night dives, and occasional island cruises in the winter are offered by **Biscayne National Underwater Park Tours Inc.**, located at the visitor center. Reservations are required. ~ 305-230-1100; e-mail dive970@aol.com.

If you take the glass-bottom boat cruise or go diving on the coral reef, you'll see some of the **marine archaeological sites**—that is, shipwrecks—that lie submerged within the park boundaries. The oldest date back to the 1700s, and since Spanish shipping lanes from Mexico passed the tip of Florida beginning in the 1500s, experts believe many more wrecked galleons may be buried beneath the sediments and grasses of the bay floor.

Another secret of Biscayne National Park, visible from shore but accessible only by boat, is **Stiltsville**, a strange cluster of buildings constructed on pilings above the shallow water of the bay. The first were fishermen's shacks dating back to the 1930s. Soon larger structures were built and made into clubs, which, during their heyday, attracted boatloads of guests from Miami Beach and Coconut Grove with gambling and other vices. Deeded to the Park Service in 1985, all but seven of the stilt buildings were destroyed in 1992 by Hurricane Andrew; efforts to preserve the others are underway.

◄ HIDDEN

Swimming is not recommended in the bay except on the tiny beaches of **Elliott** and **Sands** keys, where care must be taken to avoid sharp coral rock and spiny sea urchins. Picnic areas, restrooms, canoe rentals and boat tours can be found here.

This park features excellent saltwater fishing in open waters; fishing, however, is prohibited in harbors. Lobster may be taken east of the islands in season. A Florida State saltwater fishing license is required for most anglers.

Tent camping is allowed on Elliott and Boca Chita keys in about 30 sites, boat access only; $15 per night docking fee or $10 per night for camping only. Prepare for mosquitos and other biting insects. The park tour concessionaire offers daily boat shuttles to and from the campgrounds. There is no camping on the mainland.

To get to the park by the most direct route, take Route 1 (the Dixie Highway) south from Miami for about 25 miles to the Goulds exit and follow the park signs out 137th Avenue (Tallahassee Road) and Southwest 328th Street (North Canal Drive—the only road to the park along its entire coastline) to the visitors center. For a slower, more scenic drive, you can follow Bayshore Drive south through Coconut Grove, merge into Old Cutler Drive in Coral Gables and follow it all the way to 137th Avenue in Goulds without ever having to cope with expressway traffic.

NINE
Suburban Miami-Dade

The farther you get from the traditional beach resort areas of Miami Beach and Coconut Grove, the less tourist-oriented Miami is. Yet there are a number of offbeat points of interest in Miami-Dade's sprawling northern suburbs, as the three-hour driving tour outlined in the first half of this chapter will reveal—among them are one of Miami's finest art museums, an old town built in Arabian Nights style, a flamingo colony and traces of an ancient Indian village.

To the south, past the suburb of Kendall en route to Everglades National Park, are a number of venerable old theme parks that capitalize on the South Florida climate to introduce vacationers to a touch of the tropics. Kids will love Parrot Jungle Island and Monkey Jungle, not to mention the outstanding Miami Metrozoo.

Northern Dade County

Without a doubt, the oceanside towns north of Miami Beach are a separate entity from those to the south. Set apart geographically but even more detached in spirit, these communities consider themselves a world away from the hustle of their southern neighbor.

This wide expanse of suburbia stretches above the head of downtown Miami and serves as the living quarters for more than 150,000 people. Most of the terrain here was developed during the 1940s and '50s and includes an amalgamation of posh estates, yacht-filled canals, gleaming strip shopping centers and crowded highways.

Coastside, along the narrow island strand stretching from Bal Harbour to the Broward County line, celebrities and other well-to-do residents enjoy a quiet existence within their highly secured condominiums and estates.

SIGHTS

Starting from Miami Beach, if you follow congested Route A1A (Collins Avenue/Ocean Drive) north on the barrier island between the ocean and the Inland Waterway, you'll pass through a series of villages consisting mainly of highrise condominiums, high-priced shopping districts and golf courses. From south to north, they are Surfside, Bal Harbour, Sunny Isles Beach and Golden Beach These towns are designed more for retirees and snowbirds than short-term tourists. Two of them—Bal Harbour and Golden Beach—don't even have beach access for nonresidents and offer a minuscule amount of public parking for visitors.

A 1930s-era settling ground for French Canadians, **Surfside** is only five blocks long and eight blocks wide. You can pick up maps and information at the **Surfside Tourist Bureau**, a wonderful place for catching up on all the small-town action. The rustic, low-slung complex borders a public swimming pool where old folks lounge under natty green umbrellas. On the adjacent beach, you're apt to encounter topless sunbathing—a tradition among the French and German women who vacation here. ~ 9301 Collins Avenue, Surfside; 305-864-0722, 800-327-4557, fax 305-993-5128.

Cruise down **Harding Avenue**, the main drag where canopied shops and kosher delis nuzzle up to pink sidewalks. Teeming with swimsuit-clad people during the day, the place shuts down at night and resembles a ghost town.

A stone's throw away is the posh 250-acre enclave called **Bal Harbour**. Sculpted lawns, concrete condos and landscaped medians convey a sense of preserved elegance. Center attraction here is the **Bal Harbour Shops**, an open-air collection of designer stores (including Neiman Marcus, Chanel, Prada and Tiffany) and manicured people. ~ 9700 Collins Avenue, Bal Harbour; 305-866-0311; www.balharbourshops.com.

Heading north along the beach, you'll encounter a continuous stretch of sand and ocean with nary a building in sight. **Haulover Beach Park** (see "Beaches & Parks" below) lasts just one and a half miles but affords a peek at natural sand dunes, lush sea oats and unobstructed beach views. ~ 10800 Collins Avenue, Sunny Isles; 305-944-3040.

Up the road stands the **Newport Beach Pier**, built in 1936 and destroyed three times by hurricanes. Like its predecessors, this latest boardwalk is a hotspot for noisy pelicans and local anglers who ply the ocean waters for mackerel, bluefish and jacks. Tackle stores and a food vendor are nearby ~ 16701 Collins Avenue, Sunny Isles; 305-949-1300.

If you cross over the Broad Causeway (Route 922—or 96th street, which marks the divide between Surfside and Bal Harbour and becomes 125th Street after crossing the causeway) to the mainland, you'll find yourself in North Miami. Though certainly not known for its cultural offerings, North Miami does have one crowning jewel: the **Museum of Contemporary Art**. Inaugurated in 1996, MOCA has become one of Miami's finest exhibitors of international art, blending well-known artists with emerging ones. The 12,000-square-foot space offers between eight to ten exhibitions of varied media yearly. The building's architecture, with its movable walls and angular surfaces, will delight even the most discerning contemporary art lover. Closed Monday. Admission. ~ 770 Northeast 125th Street, North Miami; 305-893-6211, fax 305-891-1472; www.mocanomi.org.

It seems ironic that the single true historic sight in northern Miami is indeed the oldest building in the Western Hemisphere. The **Ancient Spanish Monastery** was originally built under the direction of Cistercian monks in 1141 in Segovia, Spain. In 1925, William Randolph Hearst had the cloister disassembled and carted in more than 10,000 crates across the Atlantic Ocean to Miami, where local developers breathed life back into the grand monastery. Now its rough stone walls, ornate columns and buttressed ceilings rest quietly among palm trees and towering oaks. Carvings of crosses, crescents and stars dance across the stone walls, masons' marks etched by skilled craftsmen who originally constructed the building. Admission. ~ 16711 West Dixie Highway, North Miami Beach; 305-945-1461, fax 305-945-6986; www.spanishmonastery.org, e-mail monastery@earthlink.net.

LODGING

The **Thunderbird Hotel** is a large, modest hotel that has one very important thing going for it: a prime oceanfront location.

Decorated with a large mural of a rising phoenix on the building front, it's hard to miss. The rooms are simply furnished but comfortable, and there are two pools and a sunbathing area that leads onto a quiet beach. Heavily frequented by international travelers, the staff is multilingual and accommodating. It's a great place to stay and experience Miami oceanside without draining your wallet. ~ 18401 Collins Avenue, North Miami Beach; 305-931-7700, 800-327-2044, fax 305-932-7521; www.dezerhotels.com, e-mail dezerhotel@aol.com. BUDGET TO MODERATE.

Best Western On the Bay Hotel and Marina has one very important thing going for it: water. The no-frills, family-style accommodations overlook beautiful Biscayne Bay and lie five minutes from the beach. A dramatic wooden ceiling adds character to the tiny lobby. Guest rooms are rather small, but offer clean, standard furnishings. Some rooms include a refrigerator and mi-

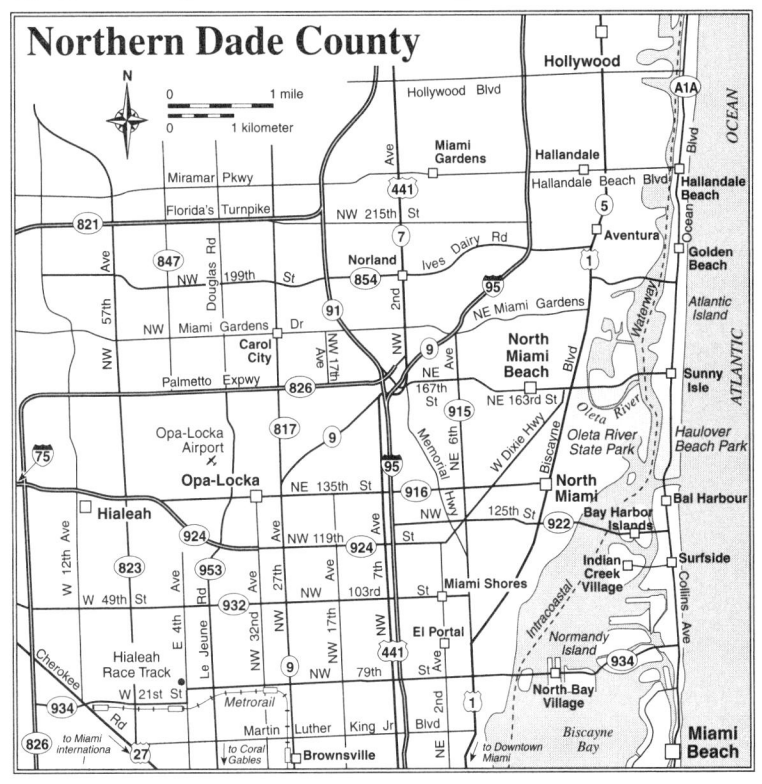

Northern Dade County

DRIVING TOUR
Lost Treasures of Northern Dade

Long before Walt Disney World came to Florida, Miami promoters were busy luring people south. The 1920s saw the construction of the lavishly exotic Opa-Locka neighborhood and the opulent Hialeah racetrack. Nearby, you'll also find evidence of those who first inhabited Florida.

OPA-LOCKA To reach the faded fantasyland of Opa-Locka, continue west through North Miami on 125th Street until you hit Route 95. Take the expressway north for one mile to the 135th Street exit and go westbound on 135th to 27th Avenue. Turn right and you're in Opa-Locka, the showiest of several communities in the Miami area built during the 1920s by pioneer aviator turned real estate developer Glen Curtiss. Here, you'll discover an Arabian Nights theme with architecture patterned after sets used in several silent Hollywood movies such as Rudolph Valentino's *The Sheik* and *The Thief of Baghdad*. The main streets are laid out in the shape of a crescent moon and have Arabic names. Today, Opa-Locka is run-down and a little off-the-beaten-path, so few Miami visitors come to see the magnificently restored **Opa-Locka City Hall**, bedecked with domes, minarets and crenellated palace walls. Closed weekends. ~ 777 Sharazad Boulevard; 305-688-4611. Also worth a look is the **Hurt Building**, an office building with Baghdad-style architecture surrounded by palm trees. ~ 490 Opa-Locka Boulevard.

HIALEAH From Opa-Locka, take 27th Avenue south to 79th Street, turn right and follow 79th west to the second-largest municipality in Dade County, Hialeah, a predominantly Cuban neighborhood interspersed with industrial development. Hialeah was once famous for **Hialeah Park**, a horse racetrack built by Glen Curtiss around the same time as

---

crowave. Continental breakfast included. ~ 1819 79th Street Causeway, North Bay Village; 305-865-7100, 800-937-8376, fax 305-868-3483. MODERATE.

A smaller luxury hotel, the **Beach House Hotel** has 165 cozy rooms and a 200-foot stretch of private beach. Among the special touches here are a hammock grove and an enormous aquarium populated only with seahorses. ~ 9449 Collins Avenue, Surfside; 305-535-8600, fax 305-535-8601; www.thebeachhouse hotel.com, e-mail reservations@rubellhotels.com. MODERATE TO ULTRA-DELUXE.

Opa-Locka. In its 1920s heyday, the 230-acre grounds also included an amusement park complete with a roller coaster, a jai alai fronton and an "Indian village." The race track, one of the most beautiful in the country, continued to operate through the mid-1990s. Although attempts are made intermittently to reopen Hialeah Park for a short racing season, operating costs for the stately old white elephant racetrack seem just too expensive. (The horse racing license issued to Hialeah is now used by Gulfstream Park in Hallendale.) Still, the French Mediterranean–style clubhouse is on the National Register of Historic Places and can't be torn down, and it's open for tours on an irregular schedule. The track's infield is an official bird sanctuary run by the Audubon Society. A flock of West Indian flamingos was imported here from Cuba in the 1930s and multiplied to a peak population of 900. Although many were sold to zoos when the track closed, a free-flying colony of more than 400 remains, and tours are offered during nesting season. ~ 2200 East 4th Avenue; 305-885-8000.

EL PORTAL Returning east on 79th Street from Hialeah will take you back to Miami Beach by way of the John F. Kennedy Causeway. Along the way, a short detour north on 2nd Avenue will take you to a tiny residential enclave called El Portal, a small, pretty, mostly Haitian community of single-family homes and parklike wooded walking trails. Here you'll find rare evidence of ancient human occupation in Miami-Dade County, **Little River Burial Mound**. Four feet high and 16 feet across, this grassy dirt mound marks the site of a Tequesta Indian village that dates back to around AD 500, though the mound itself has been dated to between 1200 and 1500. Though there's not much to see, the connection with South Florida's pre-Columbian people is almost palpable. The name Miami, by the way, is said to have come from the Tequesta word for "sweet water," referring to rivers and streams like the one at El Portal that carried fresh water from the Everglades to the ocean and made habitation possible. ~ 500 Northeast 87th Street.

Claiming a prime, ten-acre oceanside nest in posh Bal Harbour, the **Sheraton Bal Harbour Beach Resort** boasts a 300-foot beach and elaborate grounds with two freeform pools, rushing waterfalls, tennis courts, an underground shop, restaurants and a lounge. In this 645-room showplace you'll also find an impressive lobby with a dramatic glass atrium and twirling mobile artwork. Guest rooms lend a tropical flavor, with rattan furniture, wood paneling and jungle prints. ~ 9701 Collins Avenue, Bal Harbour; 305-865-7511, 800-325-3535, fax 305-864-2601; www.sheraton.com. ULTRA-DELUXE.

Colonial architecture is rarer than snow in these parts, and that's why the **Bay Harbor Inn & Suites** is such a wonderful find. Tucked away along the posh Bay Harbor waterways, this charming restored 1948 hostelry is the pride of the neighborhood. In the main, two-story building, you'll find shiny wooden floors, high beam ceilings, leafy potted plants and turn-of-the-20th-century antiques throughout the lobby and suites. A second, 24-unit building offers Victorian accommodations—all facing the water. This hostelry is a part of Johnson and Wales University Culinary School. The "live classroom" atmosphere supports an educational process while providing luxury service, accommodations and food. ~ 9660 East Bay Harbor Drive, Bay Harbor Island; 305-868-4141, fax 305-867-9094; www.bayharborinn.com. DELUXE.

In an area sadly plagued by deteriorating highrise hotels, the **Golden Strand Ocean Villa Resort** is a real gem. The 152-unit resort, a time-share open to the public, is an oceanfront cluster of four- and five-story stucco buildings fashioned in a private, homelike setting. Guests can stroll the tropical gardens that weave around a large pool and tiki hut or relax at the health spa. Apartments are decorated in tropical styles with wicker furniture, kitchens and spacious balconies. Three-night minimum. ~ 17901 Collins Avenue, Sunny Isles; 305-931-7000, 800-572-4786, fax 305-935-4183; www.goldenstrandresort.com, e-mail info@goldenstrandresort.com. MODERATE.

If you're wondering where members of Miami's upper crust while away their time, you'll find them at **Fairmont Turnberry Isle Resort and Club**, a world of multimillion-dollar yachts, spa treatments, Jaguars and celebrities seeking solace. These heady environs consist of 69 tennis courts, two golf courses, two pools, a private beach club and much more. Hotel suites are cleverly decorated with sleek Italian marble and huge jacuzzis. ~ 19999 West Country Club Drive, Aventura; 305-932-6200, 800-441-1414, fax 305-933-6560; www.turnberryisle.com. ULTRA-DELUXE.

DINING

When you're hankering for a thick, juicy, aged steak, go to **Palm Restaurant**. This cozy speakeasy, a clone of the famed Manhattan steakhouse that opened in 1926, is furnished in wood and tin walls tacked with caricatures of local personalities. Besides delicious beef, Palm also excels in seafood such as jumbo Maine lobster. Dinner only. ~ 9650 East Bay Harbor Drive, Bay Harbor Island; 305-868-7256, fax 305-865-7665. MODERATE.

A yellow neon sign announces **Lemon Twist**, a small restaurant tucked onto the principal North Miami street of commerce—the 71st Street Causeway. An attentive staff serves French offerings. ~ 908 71st Street, North Miami; 305-868-2075. MODERATE TO DELUXE.

Need a health boost? Stop by **Here Comes the Sun**. The health food store/restaurant has an ample selection of salads, sandwiches and hot eats. Try the sunburger, chicken Roma or pasta served with a selection of sauces such as ginger-tamari, orange-sesame or lemon-spice. Heart-studded menu items are fat-, salt- and sugar-free. Closed Sunday. ~ 2188 Northeast 123rd Street, North Miami; 305-893-5711, fax 305-893-0278. BUDGET TO MODERATE.

◄ HIDDEN

Biscayne Wine Merchants is a small restaurant and wine bar serving fresh, hefty sandwiches and salads to a large lunchtime crowd. Wooden table tops, fresh flowers and courteous service greet diners. For dinner, try shrimp dijon, fettuccine carbonara or a special chicken that's stuffed with dill and crabmeat. Closed Saturday for lunch and all day Sunday. ~ 738 Northeast 125th Street, North Miami; 305-899-1997. BUDGET TO DELUXE.

Locals developed a craving for Philly steak sandwiches when **Woody's** opened with curbside service in 1954. Now the roadside stop has expanded and serves twice as many of those cheesy steaks on soft, buttery buns. The plastic tables combined with a view of a gas station make for minimal atmosphere, but the place

AUTHOR FAVORITE

Tucked away in sleepy Surfside, tiny **Cafe Ragazzi** is an exciting find with only a handful of tables to accommodate a long list of patrons. There's always a wait, and it's always worth it. Cafe Ragazzi serves simple but enormously flavorful Italian fare in a bustling yet romantic setting. Choose from a slew of pasta in heavenly sauces, as well as meat, fish and chicken dishes. The service is friendly and efficient. No lunch on weekends. ~ 9500 Harding Avenue, Surfside; 305-866-4495. MODERATE TO DELUXE.

is usually packed. Closed Sunday. ~ 13105 Biscayne Boulevard, North Miami; phone/fax 305-891-1451. BUDGET.

Across from the noisy highway and rickety train tracks is a tin diner that has all the makings of a truck stop. But don't be deceived. Inside the **Gourmet Diner** awaits a plethora of splendid food—carefully prepared delicacies such as chicken *chasseur*, rack of lamb and seafood au gratin. Check the posted chalkboard for more than a dozen daily gastronomic delights. Breakfast served Saturday and Sunday. ~ 13951 Biscayne Boulevard, North Miami Beach; 305-947-2255. MODERATE TO DELUXE.

Wolfie Cohen's Rascal House Restaurant is legendary in the local community. Waitresses in white pinafores scurry to and fro, delivering heaping plates of corned beef, chicken in the pot, kreplaches and stuffed cabbage to diners chatting in Yiddish. Gaudy aqua booths and scuffed terrazzo floors add to the bustling atmosphere. A series of metal railings keeps the perpetual lines of anxiously waiting patrons in order. Breakfast, lunch and dinner are served 24 hours a day. ~ 17190 Collins Avenue, Sunny Isles; 305-947-4581, fax 305-945-8126. BUDGET TO MODERATE.

The contemporary **Bistro Zinc** features Euro-Mediterranean dishes. House specialties include veal chops with shiitake mushroom and a sherry wine sauce, and Chilean sea bass with a portobello demiglaze. Tuna, salmon and imported Dover sole top the seafood entrées. Choose from a decent list of 70 international wines. No lunch on weekends. ~ 17901 Biscayne Boulevard, Aventura; 305-935-2202, fax 305-935-5911; www.bistrozincmiami.com. MODERATE TO DELUXE.

Few restaurants make dining more of an adventure than **Chef Allen's**. Acclaimed South Florida chef Allen Susser, who hails from New York's Le Cirque, works his culinary wizardry in a glassed-in kitchen that allows you an up-close view of his work. The changing menu might feature such extravagances as fire-roasted rack of shrimp or Caribbean antipasto. The food is a tribute to Miami's "tropical fusion" cuisine. Dinner only. ~ 19088 Northeast 29th Avenue, Aventura; 305-935-2900, fax 305-682-9883; www.chefallen.com, e-mail chef@chefallens.com. ULTRA-DELUXE.

SHOPPING The **Mall at 163rd Street** lists more than 150 stores. ~ 1205 Northeast 163rd Street, North Miami Beach; 305-947-9845.

NORTHERN DADE COUNTY NIGHTLIFE

Harding Avenue, a two-block row of colorful canopied shops, comprises the heart of tiny Surfside. The 1930s settling place for French Canadians, Harding Avenue mixes the old and new. **Liborio Cigars & Tobacco** has been in Surfside for 30 of its 40-plus years in business, offering fine cigars, imported cigarettes and a vast line of smoking accessories. Try its signature Liborio Cigar. ~ 9520 Harding Avenue, Surfside; 305-865-0015.

Rafe Sweetheart Beauty Salon is one of those wonderful classic salons where women still line up to chat and relax under long rows of hair dryers. Take a peek for old time's sake, or have a shampoo for the low price of $3. ~ 9437 Harding Avenue, Surfside; 305-865-9179.

The designer capital of the area, **Bal Harbour Shops** houses such upscale caches as Gucci, Cartier, Fendi and Saks Fifth Avenue. Well-groomed crowds meander two levels of open-air alcoves festooned in tropical foliage, tall palms and waterfalls. ~ 9700 Collins Avenue, Bal Harbour; 305-866-0311.

This area possesses one of Dade County's largest malls, which lures beachgoers away from the sand and into its cool confines. **Aventura Mall** offers upscale shopping and rainy-day activities for kids. The indoor playground features a life-size ship; storytelling and art-and-crafts events occur weekly. ~ 19501 Biscayne Boulevard, Aventura; 305-935-1110; www.shopaventuramall.com.

NIGHTLIFE

An urban area littered with strip malls and condominiums, North Miami Beach is a black hole when it comes to nightlife. One of the liveliest and loudest nightspots in the area, however, is **Bermuda Bar & Grill** located in the Intracoastal Shopping Center. This mammoth, multilevel danceteria attracts a younger

---

WHERE IRISH EYES ARE SMILING

If you're in the mood for a frothy Guinness, **Molly Bloom's** is a good place to find one. Somewhat dark and cavernous, this Irish-owned and -operated bar is ripe with local characters and good Irish brew on tap, as well as a dart board, jukebox and pool tables. ~ 166 Sunny Isles Boulevard, North Miami Beach; 305-948-3512.

crowd with energy to expend. Theme nights range from hip-hop, Latin to dance. Typical bar food is available. Closed Monday and Wednesday. Occasional cover. ~ 3509 Northeast 163rd Street, North Miami Beach; 305-945-0196.

Tucked away in a quaint little outdoor mall bordering Greynold's Park, **Martini's Bistro Bar** caters to those who like to mingle. With a gleaming wooden bar, tiled floor and soft lighting, the restaurant turns into a casual nightspot after hours. Closed Monday. ~ 17850 West Dixie Highway, North Miami Beach; 305-931-0262, fax 305-931-1339; www.martinisbistro-bar.com, e-mail martinisbistro@bellsouth.net.

BEACHES & PARKS

SURFSIDE BEACH Wide sweeps of sand behind small hotels, this area offers a respite from the hustle of Miami Beach. French Canadians, who settled in Surfside during the 1930s and '40s, favor this beach, as do European and South American tourists. The swimming here is excellent; ocean waves are calm, breaking far in the distance where a sandbar ledge begins. Most days, you'll see some serious card game action under the beach umbrellas. The only amenities are lifeguards. ~ Collins Avenue, between 88th and 96th streets, Surfside; 305-864-0722, 800-327-4557, fax 305-993-5128; www.town.surfside.fl.us, e-mail surftourbvd@thebeach.net.

HAULOVER BEACH PARK A mile and a half of tropical vegetation with skyscraperless views, this beach got its name in the early 1900s when residents had to "haulover" their boats over surrounding swamplands to reach the ocean. During the 1800s, the barefoot mailman traveled this firm-packed shoreline along his South Florida route. Laden with thick carpets of grass, hilly sand dunes and chestnut-colored sand,

---

ENDANGERED RESIDENCES

Dade County's northernmost beach possesses one of Miami's true rarities: oceanfront homes. To see these endangered species, travel northward along Ocean Boulevard through **Golden Beach**, where two miles of palatial, Venetian-style estates blanket the shoreline. The so-called public beach here welcomes only town residents.

Haulover is a real beauty and a good place to swim. The jetty is where anglers fish for snapper, grunt, mackerel and yellowtail, and where other folks go to enjoy the southern panorama of Miami Beach. The most popular area of the beach, located at the north end, is clothing optional. You'll find picnic tables, restrooms, lifeguards, concession stands, a golf course, tennis courts and a marina. Day-use fee, $5 per vehicle. ~ Along Collins Avenue in south Sunny Isles; 305-947-3525, fax 305-948-2802; e-mail haulover@miamidade.gov.

OLETA RIVER STATE PARK A real gem, this 1044-acre park is nestled at the top of Biscayne Bay near the Intracoastal Waterway and the Oleta River. It bursts with wide open spaces yet shelters dense mangrove preserves. Opossums, raccoons, rabbits and foxes can be spotted frequently, along with native birds such as osprey and great blue heron. Though the 1200-foot beach is manmade, the sand consists of white crystals and borders a calm inlet that's ideal for swimming. There's great fishing for snapper, shad and sheepshead from the seawall or dock. There are picnic areas, concession stands, restrooms, 14 miles of bike trails and canoe/kayak rentals. Day-use fee, $3 to $5 per vehicle. ~ On Northeast 163rd Street (also State Road 826) and 34th Avenue, North Miami Beach; 305-919-1846, fax 305-919-1845.

▲ There are 14 primitive cabins that each sleep four; $40 per night. Reservations: 800-326-3521.

SUNNY ISLES BEACH AND NEWPORT BEACH Extending for two miles in back of condominiums and hotels, these beaches are capped with rocky sand and dotted with small tiki huts. Swimming is the primary activity at Sunny Isles. The rougher surf and perennial winds at Newport Beach draw windsurfers and sailors. The hot spot is in front of the Holiday Inn, where wall-to-wall lounge chairs and pretty people line the beach. For picturesque southerly views, stroll the **Newport Pier** where anglers regularly gather. Built in 1936, the boardwalk here was destroyed three times by hurricanes but has new life again. Facilities consist of food vendors, and windsurfing, sailboat, parasailing and jet ski rentals near the pier. ~ On Collins Avenue, between 163rd and 192nd streets.

Southern Dade County

Across Dade County's southern reaches lie burgeoning residential developments that—aching for more space—creep through farmlands and citrus groves and back up to the Everglades. Meandering through this extensive spectrum you'll find miles of beautiful old and new homes nestled against pick-it-yourself spots and fruit fields.

The epitome of sprawling suburbia, Kendall is home to several hundred thousand yuppies who navigate the traffic-clogged roadways to downtown each workday. Nearby, Cutler Ridge and Perrine are 1950s neighborhoods originally christened "Big Hunting Ground" by the area's only real natives, the Seminoles. Farther south and seemingly worlds away, Homestead is a congenial farming town where the daily grind takes a back seat to enjoying life.

SIGHTS

Scattered throughout the southwest reaches of Dade County lie modern subdivisions, pick-it-yourself produce fields and a few attractions worth the 45-minute drive from Miami.

HIDDEN ►

For a horticulture treat, travel south of Coral Gables on Old Cutler Road to **Fairchild Tropical Botanic Garden**. An 83-acre series of quiescent lakes, perfectly formed foliage and carpeted lawn, this place is a quiet reprieve from the surrounding hubbub. Here you get to look and touch. Admission. ~ 10901 Old Cutler Road, Coral Gables; 305-667-1651; www.ftg.org.

Across the street and shrouded among shrubs is a historical marker in front of a **sausage tree** (*kigelia pinnata*). The tropical tree, born of a seed sent from Egypt in 1907, grows not sausages but rare fruit that looks like—you guessed it—a sausage. Weighing up to 20 pounds and measuring three feet long, the fruit are commonly used as sturdy doorstops. If you continue south on Old Cutler Road for a mile, you will see several taller sausage trees on the east side of the street. ~ 10400 Old Cutler Road, Coral Gables.

HIDDEN ►

The bayfront **Charles Deering Estate** offers a sublime look at the area's past. Deering, the half-brother of Vizcaya's James Deering, built the retreat in the 1920s to "escape the hubbub of downtown Miami." Next to a simple, three-story pine homestead built when the town of Old Cutler occupied the site, Deering constructed a spacious stone building to house his art collection. On the grounds are more than 396 acres of virgin pineland, hammock and mangrove areas. There is also a Tequesta Indian burial mound and fossil site. Admission. ~ 16701 Southwest 72nd Avenue; 305-235-1668, fax 305-254-5866; www.deeringestate.org.

Airplane fanatics will think they've reached heaven at **Wings Over Miami Aviation Museum**. A public education vehicle, Wings also pays an impressive tribute to veterans and aviators who contributed to civilian and military aviation. Tours lead through a huge hangar filled with fully restored vintage planes. Closed Monday through Wednesday. Admission. ~ 14710 Southwest 128th Street in Tamiami Airport; 305-233-5197, fax 305-232-4134; www.wingsovermiami.com, e-mail wingsovermiami@aol.com.

More than 400 animals wander about **Metrozoo**, a 290-acre cageless habitat separated by watery moats. Don't miss the adorable koalas and the white Bengal tiger. Also check out the Asian river life exhibit and aviary featuring southeast Asian birds. Admission. ~ 12400 Southwest 152nd Street; 305-251-0400, fax 305-378-6381; www.miamimetrozoo.com.

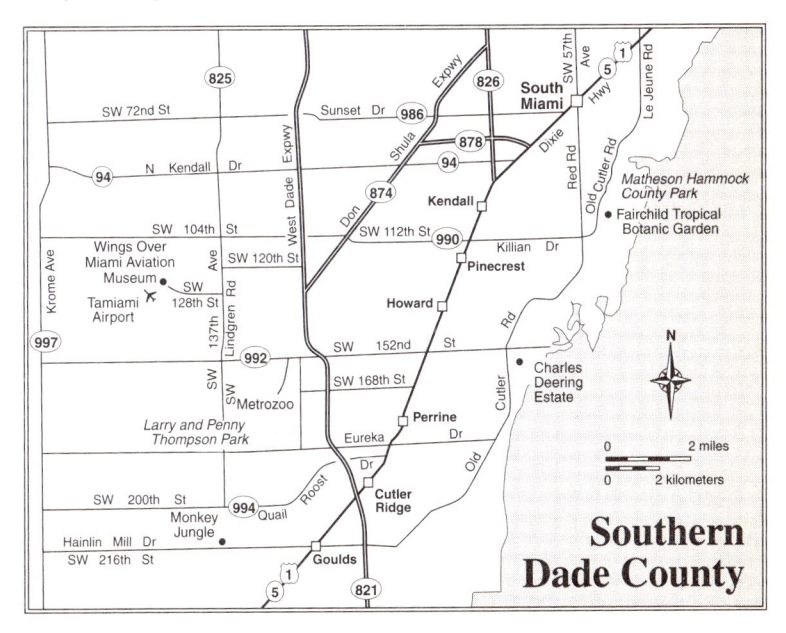

Next door is the interesting but often overlooked **Gold Coast Railroad Museum**. Like a ghost town of train yards, the nearly deserted outpost possesses rows of historic trains. Climb through the fancy *Ferdinand Magellan*, a 1942 Pullman car built exclusively for U.S. presidents, or the streamlined *Silver Crescent*, built in 1948 for the California Zephyr. You can also cruise around on a compressed-air locomotive. Admission. ~ 12450 Southwest 152nd Street; 305-253-0063, fax 305-233-4641.

Go ape at **Monkey Jungle**, a partially cageless primate habitat situated in a lush South Florida hammock. Hundreds of chimpanzees, gorillas, baboons and orangutans swing through trees and perform tricks such as skindiving. Parrots and other tropical creatures abound. One of South Florida's largest fossil beds has been discovered here—teeth and bones from the saber tooth tiger, dire wolf and Pleistocene camel are on display. Admission. ~ 14805 Southwest 216th Street; 305-235-1611, fax 305-235-4253; www.monkeyjungle.com.

HIDDEN ▶

Several miles farther south, just off Route 1 (the Dixie Highway), **Coral Castle** was built by Latvian immigrant Edward Leedskalnin, supposedly in an attempt to win back the heart of a 16-year-old girl who jilted him. Beginning in 1920, the 5-foot-tall, 97-pound Leedskalnin spent 28 years building the place out of coral oolite rock, which he quarried, moved and put in place at night so that no one could see how he did it. Some of the oolite blocks weighed up to nine tons, a total of 1100 tons of rock went into the building, and the result baffles architects and engineers to this day. Always more tourist attraction than residence, the "castle" is filled with fanciful sculptures and stone benches and tables, including one huge table carved in the shape of the state of Florida, but it has never had a roof. Admission. ~ 28655 South Dixie Highway; 305-248-6344; www.coralcastle.com.

LODGING

Largely a corporate hotel, the **Miami Marriott Dadeland** is situated along a busy highway but affords picturesque views of downtown Miami and close proximity to one of the area's largest shopping malls. The 24-story building houses a spacious seventh-floor pool deck and guest rooms with large windows, contemporary artwork and burgundy carpets. Marble floors and tables give the lobby a modern edge. Some rates include a continental breakfast. ~ 9090 South Dadeland Boulevard; 305-670-1035, 800-228-9290, fax 305-670-7540; www.miamidadelandmarriott. ULTRA-DELUXE.

DINING

Sumptuous portions of creative and traditional Japanese fare are in store at **Kampai**. This venue, which overlooks the inside of the historic Bakery Center, has clusters of shiny wooden tables and a

HIDDEN ▶

wonderfully fresh sushi bar. Sample the sashimi, *sunomono*, crunchy chicken wings or intriguing grilled *unagi* (eel), all arranged decoratively in pretty wooden trays. ~ 8745 Sunset Drive; 305-596-1551. MODERATE.

Shibui is a wonderful place to eat sushi. The shrimp, salmon and California rolls are outstanding, but best of all, they're served in a cozy upstairs sushi bar. You can also dine on cushions in a dimly lit loft or downstairs beneath a high wood ceiling. The regular menu features delicious tempura, teriyaki, stirfry and sukiyaki. Dinner only. ~ 10141 Southwest 72nd Street; 305-274-5578, fax 305-274-4153. MODERATE.

> A coconut plantation in the early 1900s, Matheson Hammock is now the only real "local" beach park left in Dade County.

Shorty's has long established a reputation as one of the best barbecue joints around. The log and brick cabin, which rests along a buzzing highway, is jammed with rustic wooden tables and decorated with neon beer signs. Folks come here to slurp up Shorty's scrumptious hickory sauce, which covers smoked ribs, chicken and beef. The service is extra friendly, but lines tend to be long during lunch. ~ 9200 South Dixie Highway, Kendall; 305-670-7732, fax 305-670-7733; www.shortys.com. BUDGET TO MODERATE.

SHOPPING

Although not generally recognized as a shopping destination, the town of South Miami offers a three-block stretch of eclectic stores that are worth perusing. You'll find these marts along Sunset Drive, between Southwest 57th and Southwest 59th avenues.

Keep an eye out for unusual and traditional antique jewelry at **Five Golden Rings**. A solid gold cigar ash preserver, Italian cameos and intricate Victorian jewels are a few of the finds. Closed Sunday and Monday. ~ 5843 Sunset Drive; 305-667-3208.

Brilliantly blooming azaleas, orchids and bromeliads beckon from inside **The Garden Gate**. Dainty wicker baskets are also found at this fragrant stop. Closed Sunday. ~ 5872-B Sunset Drive; 305-661-0605.

Along Route 1 near Kendall you'll discover two of the area's most talked-about malls. **Dadeland Mall** is like a city unto itself, with over 180 stores and restaurants in a sleek motif of gray, cream and navy blue, glass atriums and ficus trees. Several major department stores as well as chain shops offer everything from chic attire and furnishings to gourmet chocolate and nifty toys. ~ Route 1 and North Kendall Drive; 305-665-6226.

Cascading fountains, rock gardens, breezy gazebos and steep price tags await at **The Falls**, a ritzy collection of more than 100 unique shops and chain stores. This open-air setting is a popular strolling destination, even after the shops have closed at night. ~ Route 1 and Southwest 136th Street; 305-255-4570.

NIGHTLIFE The South Dade party scene is minimal at best, and most of what you'll find are hole-in-the-wall taverns or well-established sports bars. **Hooligan's Pub & Oyster Bar** has all the trappings of a sports bar—billiards, darts, a lively bar scene and TVs every which way you turn. A small dancefloor comes in handy for those nights when live music and deejays are featured. Sports bar image aside, the kitchen does turn out some surprisingly good food; the all-you-can-eat grilled rib-eye steak is a tasty way to experience it. Occasional cover. ~ 9555 South Dixie Highway, Kendall; 305-667-9673, fax 305-667-1005; www.hooliganspub.com.

BEACHES & PARKS

MATHESON HAMMOCK COUNTY PARK Situated along the shoreline south of Coral Gables, this area is favored by families who picnic, swim and fish. Winding trails crawl through more than 100 acres of thick mangrove hammock that blankets the area. There are picnic tables, restrooms, showers, a restaurant, lifeguards, a marina with an on-site sailing school and nature and bike trails. Day-use fee, $4 per vehicle; RVs and campers, $20, boat launch, $10. ~ Off old Cutler Road, just south of Coral Gables; 305-665-5475, fax 305-669-4008; www.metro-dade.com/parks.

LARRY AND PENNY THOMPSON PARK This nucleus of activity is set among the agricultural fields in southern Dade County and offers one of the few large campgrounds around Miami. Here you'll find a crystal clear lake dotted with swimmers, paddleboats, a manmade waterslide and 270 acres of crisscrossed jogging paths lined with saw palmetto trees. Freshwater fishing is good from lake banks, and swimming is good during the summer. There are picnic areas, restrooms and showers; laundry facilities are provided for campers. ~ 12451 Southwest 184th Street near Metrozoo; 305-232-1049, fax 786-293-4529.

▲ There are 270 RV sites, all with hookups and a five-acre area for tents; $10 per night for tents, $22 for hookups. Reservations required.

TEN

Fort Lauderdale Area

Fort Lauderdale's beginnings can be traced to at least A.D. 1450, when the aboriginal Tequesta tribe is believed to have begun roaming the area around the New River. After the Spanish "discovered" northern Florida, an increasing tide of colonization forced the Seminole tribe south into the area.

It was during the Seminole Wars in 1837 that one Major William Lauderdale was commissioned to establish the fort—long since crumbled into oblivion—for which the city would one day be named. Eventually, the fledgling settlement was enhanced by people of vision and skill such as Frank Stranahan. He arrived at the New River in 1893, established a ferry system and opened a trading post with the American Indians. His home as well as those of other early citizens of prominence form the centerpiece of Fort Lauderdale's historic district today.

The towns and small cities that have grown up since the 1920s around the hub of Fort Lauderdale have their own personalities. Hallandale and Hollywood, for instance, resemble nearby Miami, with their highrise oceanfront condominiums and low-priced motels.

A wonderland of T-shirt and sunglasses shops, Hollywood is perhaps best known for its dog racetrack, the only one in the greater Miami area. Adopting retired greyhounds has become so "in" among trendy South Beachers that Hollydogs, the greyhound rescue center, has a long waiting list.

Fort Lauderdale owes its reputation to two bursts of media notoriety. First, the 1960 film *Where the Boys Are* put it on the map as the spring break destination of choice for generations of college students. Second, the city's sprawling marina—the largest in Florida—was the home port for Travis McGee, the enormously popular fictional boat bum detective whose creator, the late John D. MacDonald, originated the subgenre of offbeat South Florida mystery novels.

Fort Lauderdale still has more than its share of spring breakers and boat bums, amid the kind of anything-goes atmosphere promoted by bars that sponsor mud wrestling and wet T-shirt contests. But other factions—retirees in their condos and upscale merchants along Las Olas Boulevard—clamor for legal measures to discourage the partiers and vagrants in a struggle for the city's soul that has been going on for nearly half a century.

Hollywood and Hallandale

From Flamingo gardens to jai alai, South Broward County offers another of the Sunshine State's intriguing destinations. Here you can find American Indian villages and beachfront promenades, pythons and miniature golf courses.

Hollywood, home to no movie studios, owes its moniker to one Joseph Young. During the 1920s, Young selected a swath of South Florida swamplands and—dreaming of his beloved Southern California—dubbed it Hollywood.

Today, Hollywood and its southern neighbor, Hallandale, are home to about 163,000 warm-weather loyalists and hard-core beach bums. Set apart from Fort Lauderdale both geographically and in personality, these twin cities exhibit a reserved style of living. The area's many retired residents while away their time on the beach or socializing downtown. Architecture harkens back to the 1950s, with rows of older, highrise condominiums taking center stage throughout the region.

Hollywood's subdued style, together with its colorful beach boardwalk, fine restaurants and quaint motels draw thousands of tourists seeking a pace slower than in Fort Lauderdale.

SIGHTS

To get a feel for the area, travel on **Hollywood Boulevard** between Dixie Highway and the Atlantic Ocean. You'll pass through Hollywood's downtown, an area that's enjoying rejuvenation as dilapidated buildings slowly become rows of colorful canopied stores and restaurants. Stroll the lush, landscaped medians of this quiet city, then head east toward a scenic stretch of quiescent homes flanked by huge palm trees.

The height of activity takes place along the **Broadwalk**, which hugs the beach for over two miles between Simms and Georgia streets. Mom-and-pop motels, beer shacks and souvenir shops crowd along the promenade, creating a mood that's delightfully tacky. It was originally built of coral rock dredged from the Intracoastal Waterway. Long ago it was paved over with asphalt, and today it is peopled with bicyclists, joggers, senior citizens and women in itsy-bitsy bikinis.

The **Art and Culture Center of Hollywood** features revolving exhibitions of contemporary art in an airy two-story building. The center also houses theater, dance and music performances throughout the year, featuring local and national artists. Closed Monday. Admission. ~ 1650 Harrison Street, Hollywood; 954-921-3275, fax 954-921-3273; www.artandculturecenter.org, e-mail info@artandculturecenter.org.

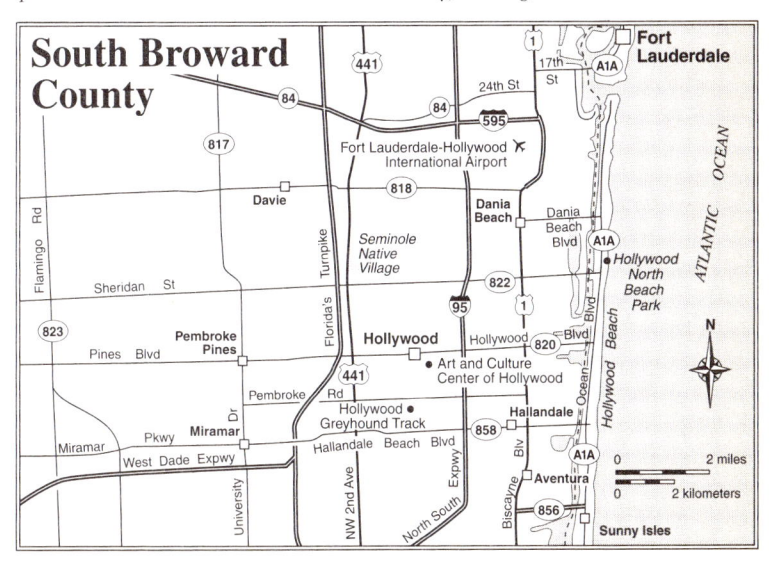

If your entertainment tastes lean toward the dangerous, don't miss the alligator wrestling and snake shows at the **Seminole Native Village**. Here you'll see the centuries-old Seminole technique of chasing and nabbing a man-size alligator. In between the shows, which are held throughout the day, you can tour a wildlife area that's home to bobcats, panthers and crocodiles. Here, children have the opportunity to hold a baby alligator. An art exhibit displayed in the museum's gift shop traces the history, legends and lifestyles of the Seminoles. The artist, Guy LaBree, is a white man who, as a child, befriended the American Indians and spent weekends on their reservation. He is known across Florida as the "barefoot artist" because—like those early Seminoles—he prefers to live shoeless. Admission. Additionally, the alligator and snake shows are separate admissions. ~ 3551 North State Road 7, Hollywood; 954-961-4519, fax 954-961-7221.

The five-story **Hollywood Greyhound Track** is a Gold Coast landmark. During the season (December through May), an average crowd of 5000 racing fans turns out for the evening to watch greyhounds race around the oval track at speeds of up to 40 m.p.h. During the rest of the year you'll find simulcast racing. A sports bar, a restaurant and a poker room round out the attractions. ~ Federal Highway and Pembroke Road, Hallandale; 954-924-3200, fax 954-457-4229; www.hollywoodgreyhound.com.

LODGING

A stone's throw from the broad sands and bustle of the Hollywood Beach boardwalk, the **St. Maurice Inn** has much more going for it than its prime location. A tiny hotel in the old-Florida vein, it's somewhat reminiscent of a wedding cake with brilliantly colored icing—the facade is a pale yellow, the awning blue, the walls skirting the property brick red. Rooms are clean and modern with cool, gleaming tiles and pastel-colored walls; some boast fully equipped kitchenettes. A quaint, shaded courtyard provides respite from sweltering south Florida afternoons. Daily maid service extra. ~ 310 Michigan Street, Hollywood; 954-925-0527, 866-809-9330, fax 954-925-9491; www.stmaurice-inn.com. BUDGET.

With its desert-colored stucco trimmed in brilliant teal awnings, **Sheldon Ocean Resort** stands out on the beach. This midrise hotel is decorated with terrazzo floors and a kitschy wall mural in the lobby, while 42 small but tidy guest rooms feature ceiling fans, popcorn ceilings and carpeting. Three efficiencies with kitchenettes and one apartment are also offered at this oceanside spot. ~ 1000 North Surf Road, Hollywood; 954-922-6020, 800-344-6020, fax 954-922-6218. MODERATE.

DINING

On the water in Hollywood, the top floor of **Martha's Supper Club** commands a breathtaking ocean view and sports a menu of American-Continental cuisine heavy on the seafood dishes. Downstairs, there's live entertainment and dancing nightly. ~ 6024 North Ocean Drive, Hollywood; 954-923-5444, fax 954-923-9697; www.marthasrestaurant.com. MODERATE TO DELUXE.

Tucked away in downtown Hollywood, the **Coral Rose Cafe** serves up a healthy variety of breakfast and lunch plates that run the gamut from grain burgers and chicken sandwiches to salads, soups and hummus plates. A favorite with the locals, the fresh fruit and homemade bread make up for a somewhat generic atmosphere of formica tabletops and Florida prints. No dinner. ~ 1840 Harrison Street, Hollywood; 954-925-4414. BUDGET.

For an informal, inexpensive evening out, a good place to remember is **Mott Street**, a friendly Chinese restaurant with low lights and high spirits. Two aquariums and a sleek lacquered screen dress up this long narrow room, but the point here is the variety of selections such as snapper steamed with ginger, scallions and black beans, orange-peel beef and salt-and-pepper squid. ~ 1295 East Hallandale Beach Boulevard, Hallandale; 954-456-7555, fax 954-456-7551. BUDGET TO MODERATE.

◄ HIDDEN

If you feel like slumming it, check out the divey shops along Hollywood's **Broadwalk**. The neon-lit cubbyholes advertise "big sales" and have everything to satisfy the tourist in you. ~ On the ocean between Simms and Georgia streets.

SHOPPING

Most of the non-beach shopping in Hollywood is located east of downtown on decidedly bohemian Harrison Street and Hollywood Boulevard. Here, quaint brick-lined sidewalks boast a bevy of antique and second-hand stores, trendy boutiques, specialty stores and art galleries. **Jeweled Castle** carries all manner of ethereal jewelry, prints, candles, decorations and incense. ~ 1920 Hollywood Boulevard; 954-920-2424. **Havana Boys Tobacco Outlet** has imported cigars, cigarettes, smoking accessories and humidors. Closed Sunday. ~ 1832 Harrison Street; 954-367-3402. If browsing through a bookstore is your idea of relaxation, **Trader John's Books** is the place to go. You'll find hundreds of used titles, records, CDs and cassettes. ~ 1907 Hollywood Boulevard; 954-922-2466.

GLAD RAGS

It's known locally as **Schmatta** (Yiddish for "rag") **Row**, a stretch of Dixie Highway in the warehouse district of Hallandale, where designer labels are sold for discount prices. BMWs, Bentleys and Rolls Royces vie for space in warehouse parking lots. Inside in about a dozen stores, women fondle high-end merchandise at cheaper-than-retail prices. ~ Dixie Highway, just north of Hallandale Beach Boulevard, Hallandale.

The 88-acre **Swap Shop** is a great discount haven where more than 800 vendors ply clothing, hardware, kitchen items, jewelry and much more. ~ 3291 West Sunrise Boulevard; 954-791-7927; www.floridaswapshop.com.

NIGHTLIFE The vanguard of South Florida blues and jazz plays nightly at the perennially popular **O'Hara's Jazz & Blues Cafe**. A showcase for local and national talent, the mix is enlivened with the occasional bop, swing or R&B group. Two-drink minimum. Closed Monday. ~ 1903 Hollywood Boulevard, Hollywood; 954-925-2555, fax 954-925-4119; www.oharasjazzcafe.com.

BEACHES & PARKS

HALLANDALE BEACH The municipal beach at the eastern edge of Hallandale is so tiny that it is easily overcrowded. Soft dark sand extends from a rock outcropping north to the border of Hollywood Beach, which is a short distance indeed. On a typical day, visitors range from seniors to teenagers and families with small children. Swimming is good in areas where there are no submerged rocks. Lifeguards are on duty daily. Facilities include a playground, volleyball and tetherball courts, picnic areas, restrooms, showers and concession stands. ~ Located at the end of Hallandale Beach Boulevard off Route A1A south of Route 824; 954-457-1409, fax 954-457-1467; www.ci.hallandale.fl.us, e-mail ctymgr@ci.hallandale.fl.us.

HIDDEN ▶ **HOLLYWOOD BEACH** This seven-mile-plus swath of pale sand is larger than some islands. Sprinkled with palm trees, it is one of the most beautiful beaches on the entire Gold Coast. It is also one of the neatest, which, given its immense popularity, is a pleasant surprise. For much of its length, it is bordered by Broadwalk, a wide strip of pavement closed to automobile traffic and open only to bikes and inline skating at certain hours. There are also specific areas designated for beach games. The beach itself consists of medium-soft sand, good for walking but a little soft for jogging. Swimming is excellent everywhere along the beach. Surf anglers should check with lifeguards for safe areas. Facilities consist of picnic areas, restrooms, showers, lifeguards and concession stands. ~ There are dozens of access points off Route A1A, from Greenbriar Street to Sherman Street; 954-921-3460, 954-921-3423, fax 954-926-3369.

HOLLYWOOD NORTH BEACH PARK 🚶 🚴 🏊 ⛱ 🎣 ⚓ It's easy to drive right past this 56-acre park sandwiched between Hollywood Beach and Dania Beach. Much of the park is a greensward planted with 500 species of vegetation, including oak trees and broad-leafed seagrapes. To protect the dunes, several crossovers have been built along the park's mile-long beach access area. You can jog or walk along Broadwalk, the two-mile walkway that extends from Georgia Street to Simms Street. It's an excellent place to swim, and people fish for snapper, jack and snook from the pier on the intracoastal side. A pleasant change from most coastal parks, North Beach also operates a protection and relocation program for sea turtles. There are many facilities including picnic areas, barbecue pits, restrooms, showers, lifeguards, concession stands, a 60-foot observation tower, bicycle and rollerblade paths and a volleyball court. Day-use fee, $4 per vehicle; $2 per vehicle after 2 p.m. ~ At Route A1A and Sheridan Street; 954-926-2444, fax 954-926-3336.

Fort Lauderdale

Fort Lauderdale's reputation as a spring break haven has sadly led many visitors to overlook some of the splendid sights the city has to offer. Though it boasts 23 miles of balmy beaches, the city's beauty goes well beyond its shoreline. Traveling through the area, you will quickly discover majestic estates lush with foliage, handsome commercial centers, hardwood hammocks, an impressive maze of clean waterways and a general feeling of the laidback tropics.

> Some of Fort Lauderdale's original buildings were forged with wood culled from shipwrecks.

Though much of its history barely trickles back 100 years, you will still find plenty of historical intrigue. Tales of sunken treasure and pirates are interwoven into the architecture and the personalities that gave birth to this carefree locale.

Most of Fort Lauderdale's sights are spread out, so it's essential to navigate by car. The good news is, the roadways are a near-perfect gridwork of east–west and north–south thoroughfares, so it's easy to get around.

SIGHTS

Meander along 17th Street Causeway east to the ocean and then wend your way north along Fort Lauderdale's infamous **Strip**.

This five-mile stretch of road, which extends northward to Sunrise Boulevard, pulses with life, as the sidewalks and beach are a constant flurry of activity. Reminiscent of commercial areas along San Francisco's Fisherman's Wharf, the Strip is a series of T-shirt shops, fast-food joints, seedy pool bars and lowrise hotels. This byway seems devised for "cruising," and that's exactly what takes place 24 hours a day. Most nights, traffic is gridlocked along the beach.

This animated stretch of beach—bashed by locals ever since spring break brought it to life—is now nearly void of college vacationers and instead is peopled by a curious mix of families, gays and high school students. In an effort to attract an upscale crowd, city leaders began a massive revitalization of the area. The beach now has a sleek new look. Pretty brick promenades and gas lamps line the street and Moorish pillars invite access to the beach. Palm trees divide the roadway and new paint covers several facades.

The **International Swimming Hall of Fame** displays artifacts such as wool, early-20th-century bathing costumes, sweatshirts that once belonged to such Olympic champions as Mark Spitz and Janet Evans, and swim-related works by artists from Honoré Daumier to Norman Rockwell. Admission. ~ 1 Hall of Fame Drive; 954-462-6536, fax 954-522-4521; www.ishof.org, e-mail ishof@ishof.org.

For a peek at true Fort Lauderdale living, travel west on **Las Olas Boulevard** and explore the finger islands that protrude from the roadway. These tiny isles provide waterfront berths for thousands of residents and their extravagant yachts. Just west of this area is a row of posh downtown shops where pricey furs and priceless paintings peep from beneath bright awnings. At night the area comes alive with sidewalk cafés and jazz clubs.

The free Fort Lauderdale **City Cruiser** shuttle goes downtown through the entertainment district to the beach. Just wave and the shuttle will stop for you. Buses run about every 15 minutes Friday and Saturday nights, 6 p.m. to 1:30 a.m. Free route maps and schedules are available on the buses, or the Transportation Management Association. ~ 954-761-3543, fax 954-761-3402; www.citycruiser.org, e-mail dfltma@lsouth.com.

Several former private residences in this area are now open for touring. Built in the 1920s as an idyllic family retreat, the

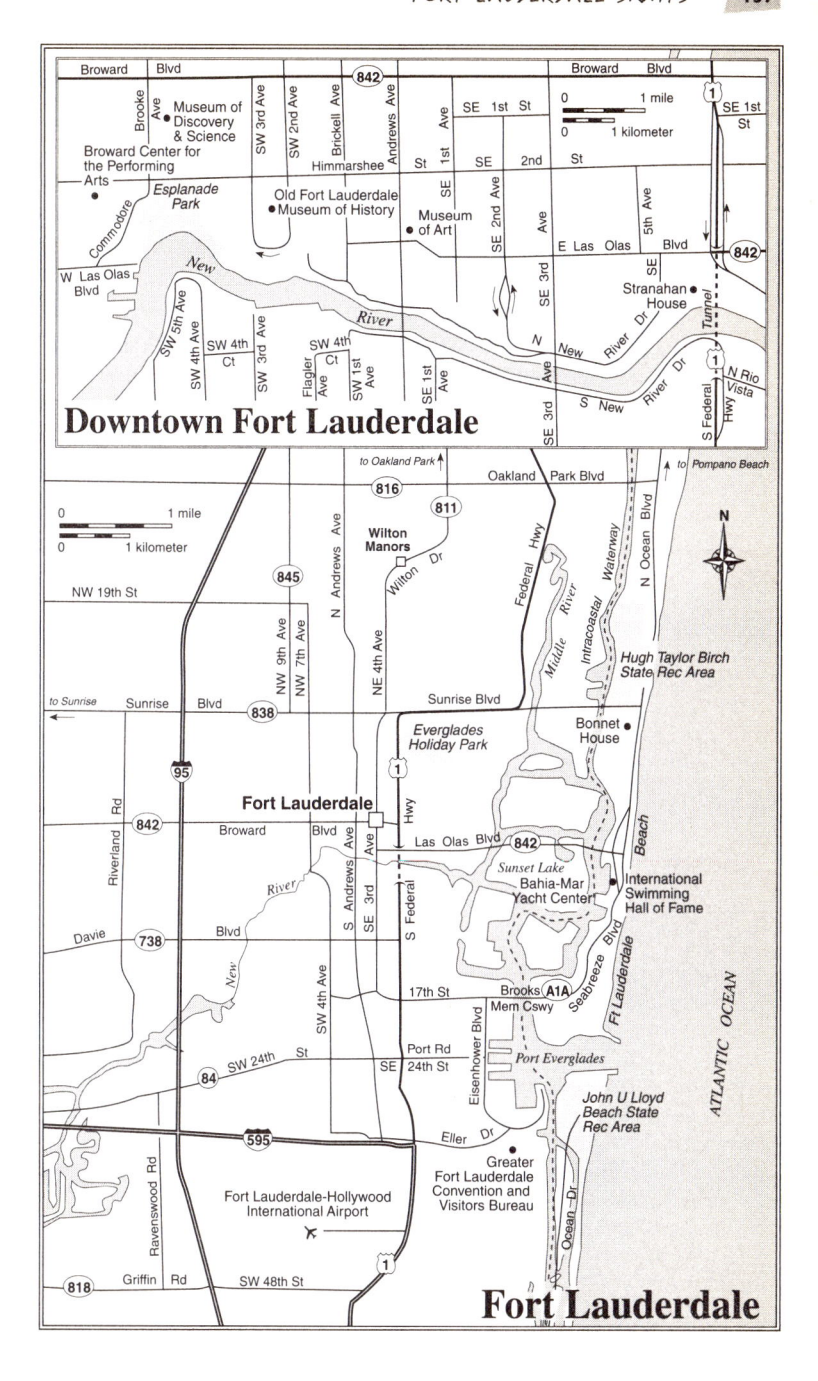

FORT LAUDERDALE SIGHTS

Downtown Fort Lauderdale

Fort Lauderdale

charming **Bonnet House** remains an oasis on 35 acres, sheltered from all signs of modern-day urban life. Tours of the beautifully preserved two-story house and various nature trails are open to the public year-round. The Shell Room, with its inlaid shells and an impressive collection of paired specimens, is worth a trip all by itself. Also not to be missed is the studio of Frederic Bartlett (who built the estate); many of his original paintings remain on display. White swans swim in a peaceful lagoon, and Brazilian squirrel monkeys cavort in a forest of trees in this enchanting enclave, which also fronts 700 feet of the Atlantic Ocean. Closed Monday and Tuesday from May through November, and Monday from December through April. Admission. ~ 900 North Birch Road; 954-563-5393, fax 954-561-4174; www.bonnethouse.org.

The Museum of Art, Fort Lauderdale houses pieces from its permanent collection of 20th-century American and European paintings and sculpture by Dali, Andy Warhol, Frank Stella and Picasso, as well as temporary shows. The museum is especially noted for its extensive collection of American impressionism, and for having the largest collection in the United States of artwork from Copenhagen, Brussels and Amsterdam. Closed Tuesday. Admission. ~ 1 East Las Olas Boulevard; 954-763-6464, fax 954-524-6011; www.moafl.org, e-mail info@moafl.org.

If you like old-fashioned things, the most attractive building in all of Fort Lauderdale may be the **Stranahan House**. This two-story frame structure was built in 1901 by the city's first citizen, Frank Stranahan, who saw it evolve from a trading post to a

AUTHOR FAVORITE

I hadn't thought much about the lifespan of butterflies until I took the spellbinding tour at **Butterfly World**, a short, pleasant sidetrip north of Fort Lauderdale. Protected in this paradise for flying insects, some of the 2000 specimens often survive here for as long as 14 days—twice their normal lifespan in the wild. The iridescent blue-banded eggfly, the Ecuadorian metalmark, and more than 100 other types of butterflies and moths flutter amid ten acres landscaped with beautiful nectar-producing plants. The Tropical Rain Forest, an 8000-square-foot screened structure, houses specimens from all over the world. Admission. ~ Tradewinds Park South, 3600 West Sample Road, Coconut Creek; 954-977-4400, fax 954-977-4501; www.butterflyworld.com, e-mail gardens@butterfly world.com.

family home. Constructed of Dade County pine, the house eventually sprouted bay windows, electric wiring and modern plumbing—all signs of the times—as well as of the Stranahan family's prominence. The house is now restored to the 1915 period, furnished with appropriate examples of Victorian furniture and open to guided tours (except in September, when only private tours are given). Closed Monday and Tuesday. Admission. ~ Las Olas Boulevard at the New River Tunnel; 954-524-4736, fax 954-525-2838; www.stranahanhouse.org, e-mail stranahan1@aol.com.

The best way to see the most beautiful residential areas of Fort Lauderdale is via the city's intricate network of waterways. There are several ways to experience the waterways, but the easiest is simply to ride the bus. A water bus, that is. **Water Taxi** possesses a fleet of bright yellow skiffs that—for a moderate fare—shuttle passengers to 20 locations along the Intracoastal Waterway and New and Middle rivers. Look for the schedule at its stops along the New River and the Intracoastal Waterway. ~ 651 Seabreeze Boulevard; 954-467-6677, fax 954-728-8417; www.watertaxi.com, e-mail info@watertaxi.com.

If you prefer to travel en masse, try the **Jungle Queen**, a 538-passenger riverboat that meanders through downtown, past Millionaire's Row and up the New River to an island village for a look at native trees, monkeys and birds. A nightly dinner cruise features a variety show and an occasional sing-along. ~ Bahia Mar Yacht Center, 801 Seabreeze Boulevard; 954-462-5596, fax 954-832-9923; www.junglequeen.com, e-mail jungle@bellsouth.net.

For additional information about the area, maps and free brochures, stop by the **Greater Fort Lauderdale Convention and Visitors Bureau**. Closed Saturday and Sunday. ~ 100 East Broward Boulevard, Suite 200; 954-765-4466, 800-227-8669, fax 954-765-4467; www.sunny.org, e-mail gflcvb@broward.org.

LODGING

In Fort Lauderdale you'll find a number of highrise hotels belonging to major chains, as well as some individually owned facilities on the south end of town. The "strip" of motels, bars and stores along Route A1A, across from the beach, is something of an eyesore, so most of our recommendations are located further afield. Thanks to a local ordinance, there is no construction whatsoever between Route A1A and the heart of the long beach. Since

WALKING TOUR
Along the Riverfront

Downtown Fort Lauderdale's riverfront, abandoned over recent decades, has undergone a revival. The city's Riverwalk features meandering footpaths, gazebos and manicured gardens and parks. Stroll along the New River between Southeast 2nd Avenue and Southwest 7th Avenue and discover this area's treasures.

ESPLANADE PARK This is a real highlight, featuring a science exhibit complete with giant kaleidoscopes, a rain gauge and sextant, and plaques honoring the world's famous mathematicians and scientists. You'll find the park next to the gleaming **Broward Center for the Performing Arts**. ~ 201 Southwest 5th Avenue; 954-462-0222 (tickets).

OLD TOWN Part of the renovated Old Fort Lauderdale complex, the **King-Cromartie House** is a 1907 home that now serves as a turn-of-the-20th-century museum furnished with period antiques. Several surrounding historical buildings and a replica of an 1899 schoolhouse are also open to the public. Tours of the King-Cromartie House are available Saturday and by appointment. Admission. ~ 219 Southwest 2nd Avenue; 954-463-4431; www.oldfortlauderdale.org.

---

ocean views are a rarity elsewhere, however, it's better to base your lodging selection on other factors.

Graced with a small lagoon on one side and a spectacularly wide private beach on the other, **Lago Mar Resort and Club** offers a beautiful setting. In fact, with 204 rooms and suites, two swimming pools, spa, tennis courts, a putting green, three restaurants and a lounge, Lago Mar could enter in the resort category. A variety of accommodations are available in buildings designed to catch those gorgeous Gold Coast sunrises. A typical room has soft textured wallpaper, off-white furniture with brass handles, faux stone lamps and accents of rose and forest green throughout. ~ 1700 South Ocean Lane; 954-523-6511, 800-524-6627, fax 954-524-6627; www.lagomar.com. ULTRA-DELUXE.

Hyatt Regency Pier 66 looks like a cylindrical spaceship dreamed up by a 1960s sci-fi writer. Topped off with a 17th-floor revolving lounge, it dominates the coastal skyline and offers unsurpassed upper-level views. Spacious accommodations (380 rooms and suites) with subdued tropical color schemes sport

LOCAL HISTORY   The **Old Fort Lauderdale Museum of History** is the best clearinghouse for information on this historic district, which extends roughly from the nearby railroad tracks east of here to 5th Avenue, and from the New River north to 2nd Street. The exhibits here are not extensive, though they're nicely done. They include a large collection of historical photographs and a room devoted to locally produced films such as *Cape Fear* and *Where the Boys Are*. The museum features an excellent selection of regional books. Closed Monday. ~ 231 Southwest 2nd Avenue; 954-463-4431, fax 954-463-4434; www.oldfort lauderdale.org.

NEW FRONTIERS   A few blocks away is the **Museum of Discovery & Science**. Chock-full of entertaining and educational exhibits, this is the kind of place where you could spend an entire day (with or without children). Exhibits include a real coral reef with sea creatures and tropical fish, a musical kaleidoscope that lets you conduct sound with a laser beam wand, a simulated space flight and landing, and a gravity-free moon walk. The museum also houses an IMAX theater with a five-story screen on which visitors can view adventure films on such subjects as the tyrannosaurus rex and African elephants. Admission. ~ 401 Southwest 2nd Street; 954-467-6637, fax 954-467-0046; www.mods.org.

---

small lanais that overlook the Intracoastal Waterway, the city, the ocean and 22 lushly landscaped acres. The amenities include restaurants, tennis courts, swimming pools, a spa and a health club. ~ 2301 Southeast 17th Street Causeway; 954-525-6666, 800-233-1234, fax 954-728-3551; www.pier66.hyatt.com. ULTRA-DELUXE.

A great deal—even in season—**The Bermudian Waterfront Motel & Apartments** fronts the Intracoastal and is a block from the ocean. Fourteen guest rooms include one- and two-bedroom apartments and efficiencies, some with French doors that overlook the pool. Children under 12 stay free. ~ 315 North Birch Road; 954-467-0467; www.bermudian-tropical.com, e-mail bermudiansm@aol.com. BUDGET TO DELUXE.

Two blocks off the beach in a veritable motel heaven, Fort Lauderdale–style, of course, you'll find **Sea Château Motel**. Each room is decorated individually with an eclectic assortment of antique and wicker furniture. Efficiencies with full kitchens are available. A pool and garden patio add to the charm. ~ 555

North Birch Road; 954-566-8331, 800-726-3732, fax 954-564-2411. BUDGET TO MODERATE.

The gentility is almost palpable at the **Riverside Hotel**. Visitors here find a residential ambience: most of the 105 rooms and suites have comfy beds and solid oak furniture. The views are of tree-lined Las Olas Boulevard, the garden or the boat-bedecked waters of the New River. Coral fireplaces and terra-cotta floors in the lobby add a Spanish flavor. Two restaurants, a bar and a pool round out the amenities. Children are free with one or two adults in a room. ~ 620 East Las Olas Boulevard; 954-467-0671, 800-325-3280, fax 954-462-2148; www.riversidehotel.com, e-mail info@riversidehotel.com. DELUXE TO ULTRA-DELUXE.

GAY LODGING For gay men only, **The Blue Dolphin** rests in the prettiest of buildings just two blocks from the ocean. One-bedroom suites, efficiencies and spacious motel rooms are available; suites and efficiencies have kitchens. There's a heated swimming pool on the grounds (clothing optional), and grocery stores nearby for do-it-yourselfers. A large fence surrounds the grounds, ensuring privacy for the guests. ~ 725 North Birch Road; 954-565-8437, 800-893-2583, fax 954-565-6015; www.bluedolphinhotel.com, e-mail dolphinftlaud@aol.com. MODERATE TO DELUXE.

Expect plush accommodations at **The Royal Palms Resort**, which regularly earns *Out & About*'s Editor's Choice award. This predominantly gay clothing-optional establishment outfits its contemporary-styled rooms with tasteful artwork. You'll also find refrigerators, VCRs and CD players at your disposal. Four suites boast even more luxurious amenities—separate dining areas, private decks; some have full kitchens. All this in a tropical setting just three blocks from the beach, complete with palm trees and myriad exotic plants, a pool, a spa, a sundeck and a tiki bar. Complimentary continental breakfast is included. Four-night minimum stay required during the peak season. ~ 2901 Terramar Street; 954-564-6444, 800-237-7256, fax 954-564-6443; www.royalpalms.com, e-mail info@royalpalms.com. DELUXE TO ULTRA-DELUXE.

The Bamboo Resort offers intimate, clothing-optional accommodations in a casual atmosphere. The five smoke-free hotel rooms and one studio apartment reflect today's Florida decor and are located in a safe area of town within walking distance to gay bars, shopping and restaurants. The grounds feature a solar-heated pool. ~ 2733 Middle River Drive; 954-565-7775, 800-479-1767; www.thebambooresort.com, e-mail info@thebambooresort.com. MODERATE TO DELUXE.

The **Rustic Inn Crabhouse** is so far inland that first-time visitors are astonished to find a waterway right out back. It's famous locally for its garlic crab, best eaten over a table covered in newspapers. Fancier fare is also available, including Florida lobster, crab cakes, Key West shrimp and fresh fish. No lunch on Sunday. ~ 4331 Ravenswood Road; 954-584-1637, fax 954-584-5005; www.rusticinn.com. MODERATE.

DINING

Insiders know that the place to go for succulent, explosively hot barbecue is **Ernie's Bar B Que and Lounge**. A plain building with few adornments in the one high-ceilinged dining room, Ernie's relies on a dynamite sauce for its draw. Meat choices include chicken, pork and ribs, each of which can be accompanied by corn on the cob, cole slaw and gallons of iced tea. ~ 1843 South Federal Highway; 954-523-8636, fax 954-523-1245. BUDGET.

◄ HIDDEN

Grille 66 & Bar is an absolutely delightful spot with great views and a menu that emphasizes beef. Spacious dining areas are staggered, affording views of the marina action beyond. Dinner only. ~ At the Hyatt Regency Pier 66, 2301 Southeast 17th Street; 954-728-3500, fax 954-728-8255; www.grille66.com. MODERATE TO ULTRA-DELUXE.

It's difficult to get reservations at the **15th Street Fisheries**, but locals swear it's always worth the trouble. This out-of-the-way waterfront restaurant offers excellent views and two levels of dining, both literally and figuratively. Go for the upstairs, where weathered wood walls are festooned with shrimp nets and

AUTHOR FAVORITE

I have to award the city's toniest shopping street, Las Olas Boulevard, first place in the people-watching category. At **Indigo**, in the historic Riverside Hotel, the alfresco eating affords fabulous sociological info and the seafood-based menu is delicious. ~ 620 East Las Olas Boulevard; 954-467-0671, 800-827-1585, fax 954-462-2148; www.riversidehotel.com. MODERATE TO DELUXE.

there are small marble tables. Seafood is king here: blackened tuna, dolphin and snapper are usually available, but veal and steak dishes are, too. ~ 1900 Southeast 15th Street; 954-763-2777, fax 954-763-2830; www.15streetfisheries.com, e-mail fisheries15@aol.com. MODERATE TO ULTRA-DELUXE.

The hip way to arrive at the **Southport Raw Bar** is via private boat, but it's acceptable to come by land as well. This dockside joint is mighty lively, with loyal patrons sliding down oysters and clams, conch salad, excellent clam chowder, crisp crab cakes and fried shrimp. A great place to drop by for a snack in the middle of the afternoon. ~ 1536 Cordova Road; 954-525-2526, 877-646-9808, fax 954-523-9342; www.southportrawbar.com, e-mail buddy@southportrawbar.com. BUDGET.

HIDDEN ►

One of the Fort Lauderdale area's best restaurants would seem to have two strikes against it. **By Word of Mouth** is very hard to find and does no advertising. But word of mouth has, indeed, worked very well. And no wonder, given the quality and variety of its gourmet Continental cuisine. The setting is as fresh as the concept: ceiling fans cool the two airy rooms rimmed by windows and white lace curtains. A typical day's offerings include raspberry jalapeno pork, lobster lasagna and coconut-crusted snapper with mango rum sauce, to name only a few. Lunch Monday through Friday, dinner Wednesday through Saturday. Reservations are suggested for dinner. ~ 3200 Northeast 12th Avenue, Oakland Park; 954-564-3663, fax 954-564-1901; www.bywordofmouthfoods.com, e-mail ellenbwm@bellsouth.net. ULTRA-DELUXE.

HIDDEN ►

The hours just prior to sundown are the most beautiful at **The Sea Watch**, one of the very few oceanfront restaurants on the Gold Coast. Hidden between condominium buildings, The Sea Watch offers fabulous views of the beach. You can stave off hunger pangs with seafood appetizers while you peruse a varied menu of fish, scampi, chicken and beef dishes. Rough wood and an expanse of glass add to the romantic atmosphere. ~ 6002 North Ocean Boulevard; 954-781-2200, fax 954-783-1382. DELUXE TO ULTRA-DELUXE.

SHOPPING

The best-known shopping address in Fort Lauderdale is **Las Olas Boulevard**. This tree-lined street in a residential area is home to a wide variety of stores, mostly one-of-a-kind boutiques.

Audace caters primarily to the gay man who likes his undergarments soft, clingy and pricey. Swimwear and sportswear round out the selection here. ~ 813 East Las Olas Boulevard; 954-522-7503; www.audace.com.

One local attention-getter, the **New River Gallery**, carries modern pieces by artists such as Dino Rosin, Alberto Dona and M.L. Snowden. Works here span a variety of media. You'll find paintings, sculptures and drawings. ~ 914 East Las Olas Boulevard; 954-524-2100; www.newrivergallery.com.

> Highlights of Riverwalk include outdoor jazz brunches, water taxis and cruises along the meandering river.

Palm Produce Resortwear carries the very latest in beach attire, including colorful rayon dresses, straw hats, flip-flops and Florida T-shirts that thankfully aren't tacky. ~ 300 Southwest 1st Avenue; 954-525-4744.

Within **The Galleria** are over 100 shops and restaurants, anchored by several major department stores and dozens of chain outlets specializing in best sellers, polo shirts, safari clothing and imported soaps. ~ On East Sunrise Boulevard just west of North Atlantic Boulevard; 954-564-1015; www.galleriamall-fl.com.

Sightseeing on the Gold Coast leads to some interesting finds such as the **Explore Store**. The store, located at the Museum of Discovery & Science, spills over with kites, kaleidoscopes and treasures like inexpensive magnifying glasses, tops, books, games and playing cards depicting endangered species. ~ 401 Southwest 2nd Street; 954-467-6637.

The Seminole Indian Reservation, located in west Fort Lauderdale, is home to a few shops with American Indian crafts. At the **Anhinga Indian Museum and Art Gallery** you'll find a large stock of clothing, turquoise and silver jewelry, woven rugs, dolls made from palm bark, and potholders in traditional Seminole patchwork designs. ~ 5791 South State Road 7; 954-581-0416.

NIGHTLIFE

Fort Lauderdale has a teeming nightlife scene that's much more relaxed and much less pretentious than South Beach. The bulk of its hot spots are located on the **Riverwalk**—a downtown center for the arts, entertainment, shopping and dining. Winding along the banks of the New River, Riverwalk extends from trendy Las Olas Boulevard to the Broward Center for the Performing Arts. Although Riverwalk has something for everyone, certain areas have a definite fraternity vibe to them, thanks to the bar hoppers equipped with their beers wandering through the streets.

The **Poor House** is a watering hole with great beer on tap and live blues nightly. The laidback atmosphere and bartenders have earned it a loyal following among the locals. A pub-crawl favorite. Occasional cover. ~ 110 Southwest 3rd Avenue; 954-522-5145.

The casual **Tarpon Bend** restaurant attracts a raucous crowd of young professionals during happy hour. Decorated with a distinct fishing theme, the walls are covered with nets, fishing trophies and real world records of the International Game Fishing Association. An outdoor seating section offers a prime people-watching spot, while live entertainment and dirt-cheap drink specials keep the lively crowds coming back for more. ~ 200 Southwest 2nd Street; 954-523-3233.

> Fort Lauderdale sparkles with 250 miles of waterways, earning it the nickname, "Venice of America."

Boasting 10,000 square feet of dance space, **Voodoo Lounge** caters to those who want to see and be seen. The upscale club features tapestries, cushy furniture and an elegant VIP lounge for those seeking a more intimate experience. Here you can dance 'til daylight on any one of its theme nights or catch one of the popular drag shows. Closed Monday, Tuesday and Thursday. Cover. ~ 111 Southwest 2nd Avenue; 954-522-0733; www.voodooloungeflorida.com.

THEATER, OPERA AND DANCE Broadway shows, including some performed by nationally known actors, are the main fare at the **Parker Playhouse**. Plan to reserve tickets well in advance. ~ 707 Northeast 8th Street; 954-763-2444.

The Gold Coast's newest cultural gem, **Broward Center for the Performing Arts** has an impressive dependable lineup of Broadway plays, regional opera and drama, and dance. ~ 201 Southwest 5th Avenue; 954-462-0222; www.browardcenter.org.

GAY SCENE Fort Lauderdale is a popular destination for gays. As more move into the area, more businesses, like those listed below, open to serve this growing segment of the visiting and resident populace. While there is no single gathering spot, certain beaches (such as the middle part of both John U. Lloyd Beach State Recreation Area in north Hollywood and Fort Lauderdale's Strip), restaurants, hotels and nightclubs cater to a gay clientele.

At the **Coliseum,** anything goes. Catering largely to young men, this non-stop party 'til dawn is a tribute to the ancient Roman Empire; think huge doric columns and wall murals. A popular danceteria, it boasts a video bar, a hip-hop room, and a high-tech dance floor with intelligent lighting. Open Thursday, Friday and Saturday nights. Cover. ~ 2520 South Miami Road; 954-832-0100; www.coliseumnight.com.

For over a decade, **The COPA** has been the city's most popular gay bar. Cool, clean and rambling, it features numerous rooms and a sprawling Key West–style patio bar strung with tiny lights. The extravagant entertainment runs 'til 4 a.m. Cover. ~ 2800 South Federal Highway; 954-463-1507; www.copaboy.com.

The casual upscale elegance and piano bar at **Chardees** draws a crowd that enjoys listening to old standards, show tunes and audience requests. A good choice for cocktails and dancing, Chardees also serves dinner (steaks and seafood) and Sunday brunch. ~ 2209 Wilton Drive; 954-563-1800.

JOHN U. LLOYD BEACH STATE RECREATION AREA

BEACHES & PARKS

As soon as we passed the guard station to this park, we could feel it was something special. A mile-long, tree-lined road leads past several beach access areas, each with its own personality. A narrow white-sand beach extends 11,500 feet up to a jetty, the tip of which offers a sweeping view of the oceanfront to the south. Most beachgoers make a little nest between the high-water mark and the seagrass, which gives them a proprietary feeling that is one of the park's greatest appeals. Within these 310 acres is a self-guided nature trail meandering through a semitropical coastal hammock that takes about 45 minutes roundtrip. Bird life is abundant and manatees are spotted in the shallows of Whiskey Creek. The gentle surf makes swimming a pleasure. Fishing is excellent off the jetty at the north end of the park; you can also try the Intracoastal Waterway. Facilities include picnic areas, barbecue grills, restrooms, showers, canoe rentals and a restaurant/gift shop. Sea turtles nest here; "sea turtle walks" are available by reservation in June and July. Day-use fee, $3 per single-occupant vehicle; $5, two to eight people, per vehicle; $1 for walk-ins. ~ North of the intersection of East Dania Beach Boulevard and North Ocean Drive; 954-923-2833, fax 954-923-2904.

FORT LAUDERDALE BEACH Many moviegoers of a certain age got their first impressions of Fort Lauderdale from the 1960 film *Where the Boys Are*, which prominently featured the glorious palm-fringed beach. The same film also started a trend among college students, who descended upon the beachfront every year for spring break. The city is discouraging these hordes, but Route A1A in Fort Lauderdale remains one of the most developed strips on the Gold Coast. Since hotel construction is limited to the inland side of the highway roughly from Las Olas Boulevard to Northeast 18th Street, most of the three-and-a-half-mile beach of crushed shells and slightly coarse beige sand lies in full view. There is a promenade wall where beachgoers walk, bike and rollerblade. The least-crowded area is **South Beach Park**. It's not well-known, thus its relative peacefulness. Plus, it's an excellent place to swim. Surf angling is allowed from sunset to sunrise. To the north, the highrises along Galt Ocean Mile shade the narrow beach, which offers little public access anyway. Facilities consist of showers and lifeguards. ~ Located in front of the major hotels south of South Route A1A. Major access street ends are Sunrise Boulevard and Oakland Park Boulevard; 954-828-4595, fax 954-468-1582; www.ci.ft laud.fl.us.

HIDDEN ▶

HUGH TAYLOR BIRCH STATE RECREATION AREA Within sight of highrise condominiums lie 180 protected acres of green trees and fresh water. The facility includes a coastal hammock, mangroves, freshwater lagoons and underground access to a pristine stretch of beach. The long, narrow park occupies an almost rectangular portion of barrier island between the Atlantic Ocean and the Intracoastal Waterway. Established in 1942, when Fort Lauderdale was still a small city, this peaceful sanctuary still offers visitors a glimpse of old Florida in its natural state. The swimming is wonderful and saltwater angling on the Intracoastal Waterway is often rewarding. Surfers try the waves just north of the park. Facilities include picnic areas, barbecue grills, restrooms, a nature trail, canoe rentals and an exercise course. Day-use fee, $4 per vehicle, $1 for walk-ins. ~ 3109 East Sunrise Boulevard, Fort Lauderdale; 954-564-4521, fax 954-762-3737.

Index

African Square Park, 101
Afro-Carribean magic, 98–99
Air travel, 19–20
Allapattah district (Miami), 100
Allapattah Produce Center, 100
Amtrak, 20
Ancient Spanish Monastery, 134
Animals, 25–26, 27
Art and Culture Center of Hollywood, 151
Art Deco Welcome Center, 52–53
Atlantis apartments, 82
Aventura: dining, 140; lodging, 138; shopping, 141

Bakehouse Art Complex, 97
Bal Harbour: lodging, 137; shopping, 141; sights, 133
Bal Harbour Shops, 133; shopping, 141
Barnacle State Historic Site, 105
Barrio San Juan (Wynwood/Edgewater district), 97
Bass Museum of Art, 55
Bay Harbor Island: dining, 138–39; lodging, 138
Bayfront Park, 80; nightlife, 87–88
Bayside Marketplace, 80; dining, 83; nightlife, 83, 86–87; shopping, 83
Beach Patrol Station (Miami Beach), 52
Beacon Hotel, 52
Bed and breakfasts. *See* Lodging
Bicentennial Park, 100
Biking, 32–33
Bill Baggs Cape Florida State Park, 121, 128
Biltmore Hotel, 112; lodging, 116–17
Birds, 26
Biscayne National Park, 129–31; camping, 131; map, 129; sights, 130–31; visitor information, 130
Biscayne National Underwater Park Tours, 130
Boating, 27–28
Boca Chita Key, 131
Bonnet House, 156, 158
Brickell Avenue (downtown Miami), 81–82
Broadwalk (Hollywood), 150–51; shopping, 153
Broward Center for the Performing Arts, 160; nightlife, 166

Broward County (south): map, 151. *See also* Fort Lauderdale area
Bus travel, 20
Butterfly World, 158

Calendar of events, 9–11
Calle Ocho, 90
Calle Ocho Festival, 92
Cape Florida Lighthouse, 121
Car rentals, 20–21
Car travel, 19
Cardozo Hotel, 53; lodging, 57
Caribbean Marketplace, 97
Carlyle Hotel, 53
Casa Casuarina, 53
Casa Elian Gonzalez, 92
Causeways (Miami Beach), 64
Central and North Beach area, 71–77; beaches & parks, 76–77; dining, 75–76; events, 9–11; map, 73; nightlife, 76; sights, 71–72
Charles Deering Estate, 144–45
Children, traveling with, 14–15
Chinese Village (Coral Gables), 115
City Cruiser shuttle (Fort Lauderdale), 156
Clevelander Hotel, 53; lodging, 56
Clothing to pack, 12
Coconut Creek: sights, 158
Coconut Grove, 104–12; dining, 108–109; lodging, 107–108; maps, 105, 109; nightlife, 111–12; shopping, 109–11; sights, 104–107
Coconut Grove/Coral Gables area, 8, 103–19; events, 9–11; maps, 105, 109, 113; outdoor adventures, 26–33. *See also* Coconut Grove; Coral Gables
Coconut Grove Farmer's Market, 111
Coconut Grove Playhouse, 106; nightlife, 111
Colonial Village (Coral Gables), 115
Commodore Plaza (Coconut Grove), 104; dining, 108; shopping 111
Coral Castle, 146
Coral Gables, 112–19; dining, 117–18; lodging, 115–17; maps, 105, 113; nightlife, 119; shopping, 118–19; sights, 112–15, 144
Coral Gables City Hall, 114
Coral Gables Congregational Church, 112–13

170

Coral Gables Merrick House, 114
Crandon Boulevard (Key Biscayne), 121; dining, 122–23; nightlife, 124; shopping, 124
Crandon Park Beach, 128
Crobar (theater), 50; nightlife, 64–65
Cuban Memorial Boulevard, 90, 92

Dade County (northern), 132–43; beaches & parks, 142–43; dining, 138–40; driving tour, 136–37; lodging, 134–38; map, 135; nightlife, 141–42; shopping, 140–41; sights, 133–34, 136–37
Dade County (southern), 144–48; beaches & parks, 148; camping, 148; dining, 146–47; lodging, 146; map, 145; nightlife, 148; shopping, 147–48; sights, 144–46
Dade County Courthouse, 79
Dante Fascell Visitor Center, 130
Deering (Charles) Estate, 144–45
Design District (Miami), 97; dining, 101; shopping, 102
Dining (overview), 13–14. *See also* Dining *in area and town entries; see also* Dining Index
Disabled travelers, 17
Diving, 28
Domino Park (Parque Máximo Gómez), 90
Downtown Miami. *See* Miami downtown
Dutch South African Village (Coral Gables), 115

Edison Center Business District (Miami), 101
El Portal: sights, 137
Elian Gonzalez house, 92
Elliott Key, 131
Ermita de la Caridad, 107
Ernest F. Coe Visitor Center, 126
Española Way (Miami Beach), 50; shopping, 64
Esplanade Park, 160
Euclid Avenue (Miami Beach), 54
Events, 9–11
Everglades National Park, 126–27; lodging, 127; visitor information, 126, 127

Fairchild Tropical Botanic Garden, 144
Fauna, 25–26, 27
1st Street Beach, 66
Fishing, 26–27
Flagler Street (downtown Miami), 79; shopping, 86
Flamingo Visitor Center, 127
Flora, 23–25

Fontainebleau Hilton, 72; lodging, 74
Foreign travelers, 17–18
Fort Lauderdale, 155–68; beaches & parks, 167–68; dining, 163–64; lodging, 159–63; map, 157; nightlife, 165–67; shopping, 164–65; sights, 155–59, 160–61; visitor information, 159; walking tour, 160–61
Fort Lauderdale area, 8, 149–68; events, 9–11; maps, 151, 157; outdoor adventures, 26–33; visitor information, 159. *See also* Fort Lauderdale; Hollywood/Hallandale area
Fort Lauderdale Beach, 168
Fort Lauderdale–Hollywood International Airport, 19–20
Fort Lauderdale Old Town, 160
46th Street Beach, 76
French Country and City Villages (Coral Gables), 115
French Normandy Village (Coral Gables), 115

Garment District (Miami), 100
Gay-friendly travel, 15–16; beaches & parks, 66–67; lodging, 84, 162–63; nightlife, 166–67; shopping, 165. *See also* South Beach gay scene
Geology, 22–23
Gold Coast Railroad Museum, 145–46
Golden Beach, 142
Golf, 30, 32
Gonzalez (Elian) house, 92
Gusman Center for the Performing Arts, 79; nightlife, 87

Hallandale. *See* Hollywood/Hallandale area
Hallandale Beach, 154
Harding Avenue (Surfside), 133
Haulover Beach Park, 133–34, 142–43
Heritage of Miami (ship), 80
Hermitage of Charity (Ermita de la Caridad), 107
Hialeah: sights, 136–37
Hialeah Park, 136–37
Historical Museum of Southern Florida, 79
History, 34–39
Hobie Beach, 124
Hollywood Beach, 154
Hollywood Boulevard (Hollywood), 150; shopping, 153
Hollywood Greyhound Track, 152
Hollywood/Hallandale area, 150–55; beaches & parks, 154–55; dining, 152–53; lodging, 152; nightlife, 154; shopping, 153–54; sights, 150–52

Hollywood North Beach Park, 155
Hostels, 57
Hotels. *See* Lodging
Hugh Taylor Birch State Recreation Area, 168
Hurricanes, 7, 23
Hurt Building, 136

Indian Creek Drive (Miami Beach), 72
Ingraham Building, 80
Inline skating, 30
International Swimming Hall of Fame, 156
International travelers, 17–18
Island of Cuba Memorial, 92

Jackie Gleason Theater of the Performing Arts, 55; nightlife, 65
Jefferson Avenue (Miami Beach), 54
Jewish Museum of Florida, 54
Jogging, 29–30
John F. Kennedy Causeway (North Bay Causeway), 64
John U. Lloyd Beach State Recreation Area, 167
Julia Tuttle Causeway, 64
Jungle Queen (riverboat), 159

Kendall area: dining, 147; nightlife, 148; shopping, 147
Key Biscayne, 120–25, 128; beaches & parks, 124, 128; dining, 122–24; lodging, 121–22; maps, 123, 125; nightlife, 124; shopping, 124; sights, 121
Key Biscayne area, 8, 120–25, 128–31; events, 9–11; maps, 123, 125, 129; outdoor adventures, 26–33; visitor information, 130. *See also* Biscayne National Park; Key Biscayne
King-Cromartie House, 160

La Gorce Drive (Miami Beach), 71
Larry and Penny Thompson Park, 148
Las Olas Boulevard (Fort Lauderdale), 156, 158–59; dining, 163; shopping, 164–65
Lesbian travelers. *See* Gay-friendly travel
Little Haiti, 96–97; dining, 101
Little Havana, 89–96; dining, 93–95; lodging, 92–93; map, 91; nightlife, 96; shopping, 95–96; sights, 90–92
Little Havana area and ethnic neighborhoods, 7, 89–102; events, 9–11; map, 91; outdoor adventures, 26–33; santería & voodou, 98–99. *See also* Little Havana; Miami's ethnic neighborhoods
Little River Burial Mound, 137

Lodging (overview), 12–13. *See also* Lodging *in area and town entries*; *see also Lodging Index*
Lowe Art Museum, 115
Lummus Park, 66–67
Lummus Park District (downtown Miami), 81
Lyric Theater, 100

MacArthur Causeway, 64
Maceo (Antonio) memorial, 92
Mahogany Hammock Trail, 127
Main Highway (Coconut Grove), 104–106; dining, 108; nightlife, 111; shopping, 110
Main Post Office (Miami Beach), 52
Manor Park: sights, 100–101
Martí (José) memorial, 92
Matheson Hammock County Park, 148
Memorial Flame, 92
Memorial to Antonio Maceo, 92
Memorial to José Martí, 92
Merrick (George) House, 114
Metro-Dade Cultural Center, 79
Metromover, 19
Metrorail, 19
Metrozoo, 145
Miami (overview), 1–46; animals, 25–26, 27; areas, 7–8; cuisine, 40–41; dining, 13–14; events, 9–11; geology, 22–23; history, 34–39; itinerary, suggested, 4–5; lodging, 12–13; map, 3; natural habitats, 26; outdoor adventures, 26–33; people, 39, 42–46; plants, 23–25; transportation, 19–21; visitor information, 11–12; weather, 8–9. *See also specific areas and towns*
Miami Art Museum, 80
Miami Beach, 7, 47–77; causeways, 64; events, 9–11; maps, 49, 51, 73; outdoor adventures, 26–33; visitor information, 52–53; walking tour, 52–53. *See also* Central and North Beach area; South Beach; South Beach gay scene
Miami Beach Post Office, 52
Miami Children's Museum, 54
Miami City Hall, 104
Miami-Dade Public Library, 80
Miami-Dade suburbs, 8, 132–48; events, 9–11; maps, 135, 145; outdoor adventures, 26–33; visitor information, 133. *See also* Dade County (northern); Dade County (southern)
Miami Design and Preservation League, 52–53
Miami downtown, 7, 78–88; dining, 84–86; events, 9–11; lodging, 82, 84; map, 81; nightlife, 86–88; outdoor

adventures, 26–33; shopping, 83, 86; sights, 79–82; visitor information, 79
Miami International Airport (Wilcox Field), 19
Miami Museum of Science and Planetarium, 82
Miami Seaquarium, 121
Miami's ethnic neighborhoods, 96–102; dining, 101–102; shopping, 101, 102; sights, 96–97, 100–101
Milfred Apartments, 54–55
Model City: sights, 100–101
Monkey Jungle, 146
Mrazek Pond, 127
Murray Apartments, 55
Museo Juan Peruyero y Biblioteca Manuel Artime, 92
Museum of Art, Fort Lauderdale, 158
Museum of Contemporary Art, 134
Museum of Discovery & Science, 161; shopping, 165

Natural habitats, 26
The Neighborhood (Miami Beach), 71–72
Newport Beach, 143
Newport Beach Pier, 134
Newport Pier, 143
Norman A. Whitten University Center, 114
North Bay Causeway, 64
North Bay Village: lodging, 135–36
North Miami: dining, 139–40; sights, 134
North Miami Beach: dining, 140; lodging, 134–35; nightlife, 141–42; shopping, 140; sights, 134
North Shore Open Space Park, 77
Northern Dade County. *See* Dade County (northern)

Oakland Park: dining, 164
Ocean Drive (Miami Beach), 50
Old City Hall (Miami Beach), 52
Old Fort Lauderdale Museum of History, 161
Older travelers, 16–17
Oleta River State Park, 143
Opa-Locka: sights, 136
Opa-Locka City Hall, 136
Outdoor adventures, 26–33
Overtown district (Miami), 97, 100

Packing, 12
Pagoda of Ransom–Everglades School, 106
Pa-hay-okee Overlook, 126–27
Parasailing, 29
Park Central Hotel, 52; lodging, 56

Parque Máximo Gómez, 90
Parrot Jungle Island, 54
Paseo de las Estrellas, 90
Pennsylvania Avenue (Miami Beach), 54
People, 39, 42–46
Pineland Trail, 126
Pinewood Cemetery, 115
Plants, 23–25
Price ranges used in book: dining, 14; lodging, 13
Public transit, 21

Restaurants. *See* Dining
Rickenbacker Causeway, 64
Ring Theatre, 114; nightlife, 119
Rosebloom Apartments, 55
Royal Palm Visitor Center, 126
Russian and Turkish Baths, 72

Sailing, 29
Sand Key, 131
Santería, 98–99
Sausage trees, 144
Schmatta Row, 153
2nd Avenue Entertainment District (Miami), 100
Seminole Native Village, 151–52
Senior travelers, 16–17
74th Street Beach, 77
Shipwrecks, 130–31
Silver Bluff, 104
Skating, 30
Skindiving, 28
South Beach, 49–67; beaches & parks, 66–67; dining, 58–62; lodging, 55–58; map, 51; nightlife, 64–65; shopping, 62–64; sights, 50–55; visitor information, 52–53; walking tour, 52–53
South Beach (1st Street Beach), 66
South Beach gay scene, 67–71; beaches & parks, 70–71; dining, 69–70; lodging, 68–69; nightlife, 70; shopping, 70; visitor information, 67
South Miami Beach. *See* South Beach
South Pointe Park, 66
Southern Broward County. *See* Broward County (southern)
Southern Dade County. *See* Dade County (southern)
Sportfishing, 26–27
Sports, 26–33
Stiltsville, 131
Stranahan House, 158–59
The Strip (Fort Lauderdale), 155–56
Suburban Miami-Dade. *See* Miami-Dade suburbs
Sunny Isles: dining, 140; lodging, 138; sights, 133–34

Sunny Isles Beach, 143
Surfside: dining, 139; lodging, 136; shopping, 141; sights, 133; visitor information, 133
Surfside Beach, 142

Tamiami Airport: sights, 145
Taxis, 21
Tennis, 32
35th Street Beach, 76
Train travel, 20
Transportation, 19–21
Trees, 23–25
12th Street Beach, 70
21st Street Beach, 71

United States Courthouse (downtown Miami), 80
University of Miami, 114–15; nightlife, 119

Venetian Causeway, 64
Venetian Pool, 114
Villa Regina apartments, 82
The Villages (Coral Gables), 115

Virginia Key: beaches & parks, 124, 128; dining, 123–24; sights, 121
Virginia Key Beach, 124, 128
Visitor information, 11–12. *See also* Visitor information *in area and town entries*
Vizcaya Museum and Gardens, 106–107
voodoo, 98–99

Wagner Homestead, 81
Washington Avenue (Miami Beach), 54; dining, 58–59; nightlife, 64–65; shopping, 62–63
Water safety, 31
Water Taxi, 159
Waterskiing, 29
Weather, 8–9
West Lake Trail, 127
Wilcox Field (Miami International Airport), 19
William Lehman Causeway, 64
Windsurfing, 28–29
Wings over Miami Aviation Museum, 145
Wolfsonian (museum), 53
Women travelers, 15
Wynwood/Edgewater district (Miami), 97

Lodging Index

Abbey Hotel, 58
Alexander Hotel, 75

Bamboo Resort, 162–63
Bay Harbor Inn & Suites, 138
Beach House Hotel, 136
Bermudian Waterfront Motel & Apartments, 161
Best Western (Miami Beach), 74
Best Western On the Bay Hotel and Marina, 135–36
Biltmore Hotel, 116–17
Blue Dolphin, 162

Cardozo Hotel, 57
Casa Grande, 56
Cavalier, 56–57
Clarion Hotel & Suites, 84
Clay Hotel Hostelling International—Miami Beach, 57
The Clevelander, 56

David William Hotel, 116
Days Inn Oceanside, 74
The Delano, 57–58
Doubletree Hotel Coconut Grove, 107

Eden Roc, 75
El Nido Motel, 93
European Guesthouse, 68

Fairmont Turnberry Isle Resort and Club, 138
Flamingo Lodge, 127
Fontainebleau Hilton, 74

Golden Strand Ocean Villa Resort, 138

Holiday Inn University of Miami, 115–16
Hotel InterContinental, 82
Hyatt Regency Coral Gables, 116

Hyatt Regency Downtown, 82
Hyatt Regency Pier 66, 160–61

Jefferson House, 68

Lago Mar Resort and Club, 160

Mayfair House, 107
Miami Executive Hotel, 93
Miami Marriott Dadeland, 146
Miami River Inn, 84

National Hotel, 55
Normandy South, 69

Omni Colonnade Hotel, 117

Park Central Hotel, 56
Penguin Hotel, 68
Place St. Michel, 116

Raleigh Hotel, 68
Riande Continental at Bayside, 84
Riverside Hotel, 162
Royal Hotel, 57
Royal Palms Resort, 162

St. Maurice Inn, 152
Sea Château Motel, 161–62
Sheldon Ocean Resort, 152
Sheraton Bal Harbour Beach Resort, 137
Silver Sands, 121
Sonesta Beach Resort, 121–22

Thunderbird Hotel, 134–35
Tops Motel, 93
Traymore Hotel, 72, 74

Wyndham Grand Bay Hotel, 107–108
Wyndham Resort Miami Beach, 75

Dining Index

Aquatica, 76

Balans, 69
Bangkok, Bangkok, 118
Bayside Seafood Hut, 122
Big Fish, 85
Big Pink, 60
Biscayne Wine Merchants, 139
Bistro Zinc, 140
Blue Door, 61
By Word of Mouth, 164

Cafe Ragazzi, 139
Café Tu Tu Tango, 108
Captain Joe's, 83
Casa Juancho, 94
Casa Panza, 94
Chef Allen's, 140
Coral Rose Cafe, 152–53

District Restaurant and Lounge, 101

El Exquisito, 93–94
El Pub, 94
El Rey de las Fritas, 93
11th Street Diner, 69
Ernie's Bar B Que and Lounge, 163

15th Street Fisheries, 163–64
A Fish Called Avalon, 61–62
Flute, 60
The Forge, 75
Front Porch, 69–70

Garcia's Seafood Grill & Fish Market, 85
Gourmet Diner, 140
Granny Feelgood's, 84–85
Grass, 101
Green Street Café, 108
Grille 66 & Bar, 163
Grillfish, 61
Guayacan Restaurant, 94

Here Comes the Sun, 139
House of India, 117
Hy-Vong, 94–95

Ice Box Café, 69

Indigo, 163

Jimbo's, 123–24
Joe Allen, 62
Joe's Stone Crab, 58–59
John Martin's, 117
Joia, 61

Kampai, 146–47
Kelly's Cajun Grill, 83

La Carreta, 93
La Sandwicherie, 59
Le Bouchon du Grove, 108
Lemon Twist, 139
Lombardi's, 83
Los Ranchos, 83

Martha's Supper Club, 152
Monty's Raw Bar, 108–109
Mott Street, 153
Mykonos, 118

Nemo, 60
News Café, 62
Nexxt Cafe, 58

Orange Café + Art, 101
Osteria Del Teatro, 59

Palm Restaurant, 138–39
Perricone's Marketplace, 85

Restaurant St. Michel, 117
River Oyster Bar, 85
Royal Thai Kitchen, 59
Rustic Inn Crabhouse, 163
Rusty Pelican (Key Biscayne), 122

S & S Diner, 85–86
Sea Watch, 164
Secret Sandwich Company, 102
Señor Frog's, 108
Shibui, 147
Shorty's, 147
Shula's Steak House, 75–76
Southport Raw Bar, 164
Sunday's on the Bay, 122–23

Talula, 60

Tamara, 61
Tap Tap, 62
Teriyaki Temple, 83
Tuscany's, 108
Two Dragons, 122

Versailles, 95

Villa Italia, 118

Wolfie Cohen's Rascal House Restaurant, 140
Woody's, 139–40

Yuca, 59

HIDDEN GUIDES

Adventure travel or a relaxing vacation?—"Hidden" guidebooks are the only travel books in the business to provide detailed information on both. Aimed at environmentally aware travelers, our motto is "Where Vacations Meet Adventures." These books combine details on unique hotels, restaurants and sightseeing with information on camping, sports and hiking for the outdoor enthusiast.

PARADISE FAMILY GUIDES

Ideal for families traveling with kids of any age—toddlers to teenagers—Paradise Family Guides offer a blend of travel information unlike any other guides to the Hawaiian islands. With vacation ideas and tropical adventures that are sure to satisfy both action-hungry youngsters and relaxation-seeking parents, these guides meet the specific needs of each and every family member.

Ulysses Press books are available at bookstores everywhere. If any of the following titles are unavailable at your local bookstore, ask the bookseller to order them.

You can also order books directly from Ulysses Press
P.O. Box 3440, Berkeley, CA 94703
800-377-2542 or 510-601-8301
fax: 510-601-8307
www.ulyssespress.com
e-mail: ulysses@ulyssespress.com

HIDDEN GUIDEBOOKS

___ Hidden Arizona, $16.95
___ Hidden Bahamas, $14.95
___ Hidden Baja, $14.95
___ Hidden Belize, $15.95
___ Hidden Big Island of Hawaii, $13.95
___ Hidden Boston & Cape Cod, $14.95
___ Hidden British Columbia, $18.95
___ Hidden Cancún & the Yucatán, $16.95
___ Hidden Carolinas, $17.95
___ Hidden Coast of California, $18.95
___ Hidden Colorado, $15.95
___ Hidden Disneyland, $13.95
___ Hidden Florida, $18.95
___ Hidden Florida Keys & Everglades, $13.95
___ Hidden Georgia, $16.95
___ Hidden Guatemala, $16.95
___ Hidden Hawaii, $18.95
___ Hidden Idaho, $14.95
___ Hidden Kauai, $13.95
___ Hidden Los Angeles, $14.95
___ Hidden Maui, $13.95
___ Hidden Miami, $14.95
___ Hidden Montana, $15.95
___ Hidden New England, $18.95
___ Hidden New Mexico, $15.95
___ Hidden New Orleans, $14.95
___ Hidden Oahu, $13.95
___ Hidden Oregon, $15.95
___ Hidden Pacific Northwest, $18.95
___ Hidden San Diego, $14.95
___ Hidden Salt Lake City, $14.95
___ Hidden San Francisco & Northern California, $18.95
___ Hidden Seattle, $13.95
___ Hidden Southern California, $18.95
___ Hidden Southwest, $19.95
___ Hidden Tahiti, $17.95
___ Hidden Tennessee, $16.95
___ Hidden Utah, $16.95
___ Hidden Walt Disney World, $13.95
___ Hidden Washington, $15.95
___ Hidden Wine Country, $13.95
___ Hidden Wyoming, $15.95

PARADISE FAMILY GUIDES

___ Paradise Family Guides: Kaua'i, $16.95
___ Paradise Family Guides: Maui, $16.95
___ Paradise Family Guides: Big Island of Hawai'i, $16.95

Mark the book(s) you're ordering and enter the total cost here ⇨

California residents add 8.25% sales tax here ⇨

Shipping, check box for your preferred method and enter cost here ⇨

❑ BOOK RATE   FREE! FREE! FREE!
❑ PRIORITY MAIL/UPS GROUND   cost of postage
❑ UPS OVERNIGHT OR 2-DAY AIR cost of postage

Billing, enter total amount due here and check method of payment ⇨

❑ CHECK   ❑ MONEY ORDER
❑ VISA/MASTERCARD _____EXP. DATE_____

NAME _____PHONE_____
ADDRESS _____
CITY _____ STATE _____ ZIP _____

MONEY-BACK GUARANTEE ON DIRECT ORDERS PLACED THROUGH ULYSSES PRESS.

ABOUT THE AUTHOR

RICHARD HARRIS has written or co-written 35 other guidebooks including Ulysses' *Hidden Colorado, Hidden Baja, Hidden Cancún and the Yucatán, Hidden Belize, Hidden Picture Perfect Escapes Santa Fe, Hidden Highways Arizona, Weekend Adventure Getaways: Yosemite Tahoe* and the bestselling *Hidden Southwest*. He has also served as contributing editor on guides to Mexico, New Mexico, and other ports of call for John Muir Publications, Insight Guides, Fodor's, Birnbaum and Access guides. He is a past president of PEN New Mexico and currently president of the New Mexico Book Association. When not traveling, Richard writes and lives in Santa Fe, New Mexico.